THE Taste of Home
RECIPE BOOK

Editor: Julie Schnittka
Food Editor: Mary Beth Jung
Assistant Food Editor: Coleen Martin
Art Director: Ellen Lloyd
Cover Photography: Tina Manley
Food Photography: Mike Huibregtse, Larry Chambers (page 71) and Murphy Frye (page 99)
Design Director: Jim Sibilski
Art Associates: Vicky Wilimitis, Judy Larson, Sue Myers, Julie Wagner

©1994, Reiman Publications, L.P.
5400 S. 60th St., Greendale WI 53129
International Standard Book Number: 0-89821-178-6
Library of Congress Catalog Card Number: 94-61368
All rights reserved.
Printed in U.S.A.

Pictured above. Clockwise from the top: Fluffy Cranberry Cheese Pie (recipe on page 77), Hot Fruit Compote (recipe on page 73), Cranberry Chicken (recipe on page 57) and Cranberry Pineapple Salad (recipe on page 93).

Pictured on the cover. Clockwise from bottom right: Hawaiian Kabobs, Peppered Rib Eye Steaks, Sour Cream Apple Pie and Crunchy Spinach Salad (all recipes on page 17).

FROM BOTTOM TO TOP, THIS COOKBOOK COVERS IT ALL!

HOW does a food magazine—in 1 short year—become the *most popular* in the country? You and your family are about to discover the delicious details!

This first edition of *The Taste of Home Recipe Book* is the single source for *over 350* mouth-watering dishes published by *Taste of Home* magazine during its historic first year…a year that saw the down-home cooking magazine grow from zero subscribers to well over a million.

On the colorful photo-filled pages that follow, you'll find all the things that make *Taste of Home* truly different from other food magazines:

● Favorite complete meals from *Taste of Home's* field editors (there are *1,000* of them in all, representing every state plus every province in Canada). Esther Shank of Harrisonburg, Virginia is one of these home cooks who each issue share their very best recipes—the convenient kind that call only for ingredients you already have on hand. Turn to page 7 and you'll find the recipes for her Oven Barbecued Chicken, Mexican Corn Bread, Favorite Broccoli Salad and Deluxe Chocolate Marshmallow Bars. Esther calls this meal her "Sunday standby"!

● "My Mom's Best Meal"—like Breaded Pork Chops, Chunky Applesauce, Cheese Potatoes and Chocolate Mayonnaise Cake from Deborah Amrine of Grand Haven, Michigan (recipes on page 27). It's the girlhood meal from long ago Deborah fondly recalls requesting for her birthday…year after year.

● Complete meals that can be prepared in just *30 minutes or less*. Next time you're fishing for quick and easy entrees, try Baked Lemon Haddock, Harvard Beets, Orange and Onion Salad and Chocolate Mint Delight (recipes on page 38). They're favorites of Jean Ann Perkins' clan in Newburyport, Maryland.

● And a bounty of budget meals—like Tuna Burgers and Summer Apple Salad from Kim Stoller of Smithville, Ohio (recipes on page 30)—that prove you don't have to sacrifice flavor to be frugal. Total cost of Kim's meal per plate: *84¢*!

There's more. In *The Taste of Home Recipe Book*, country cooks also share dozens of dishes that are perfect if you're cooking for a crowd—while others pass along their best recipes that serve just one or two. Plus, this big book brings you plenty of other delicious ideas for appetizers, main dishes, side dishes and desserts, along with soups and salads, breads…even breakfast and brunch!

With each recipe complete on a page, this cookbook is practical and easy to use besides. So why not start now? There's a whole year's worth of the best cooking in the country ahead of you!

CONTENTS

Our Editors' Favorite Meals

1,000 great country cooks help edit *Taste of Home* magazine.
On the following pages, you'll "meet"
six of our field editors who share their favorite meals.

*Editor Esther Shank shares recipes for her
favorite Sunday supper. Pictured clockwise from the top:
Deluxe Chocolate Marshmallow Bars,
Favorite Broccoli Salad, Mexican Corn Bread
and Oven Barbecued Chicken.*

By Esther Shank, Harrisonburg, Virginia

MY HUSBAND, Rawley, and I grew up on dairy farms and operated one of our own for 20 years, where we raised our three daughters. So, for most of my life I've cooked big meals for a hungry family, farmhands and others who often sat at our table—and have enjoyed doing it!

The chicken dish is my Sunday dinner standby. It goes into the oven before we leave for church, and its appetizing aroma welcomes us back home!

I think you and your family will find that the chicken is moist and flavorful, with a nice tang from vinegar and mustard in the easy, homemade barbecue sauce.

Zippy with peppers and cheese, the corn bread gets its pleasant, moist texture from the buttermilk.

I use a crunchy, colorful Favorite Broccoli Salad to add a garden-fresh accompaniment to my meal. While I've tried similar salads, this recipe has a winning combination of vegetables, bacon and hard-cooked eggs.

And the chewy layered bars are always a hit at potlucks, church events and parties.

Mexican Corn Bread

This tasty corn bread is easy to mix up. I serve it often with a meal or hearty bowl of soup as an alternative to rolls. Cheddar cheese makes it especially flavorful, and the diced peppers add nice color.

> 1 cup yellow cornmeal
> 1/3 cup all-purpose flour
> 2 tablespoons sugar
> 2 teaspoons baking powder
> 1 teaspoon salt
> 1/2 teaspoon baking soda
> 2 eggs, beaten
> 1 cup buttermilk
> 1/2 cup vegetable oil
> 1/2 cup shredded cheddar cheese
> 1 can (8-3/4 ounces) cream-style corn
> 1/3 cup chopped onion
> 2 tablespoons chopped green pepper

In a mixing bowl, combine first six ingredients. Combine remaining ingredients; add to dry ingredients and stir only until moistened. Pour into a greased 9-in. square baking pan or 10-in. heavy skillet. Bake at 350° for 30-35 minutes, or until bread is golden brown and tests done. **Yield:** 8-10 servings.

Oven Barbecued Chicken

Chicken and Sunday dinner go together in my mind. During my 20 years of married life on a dairy farm, I'd often brown the chicken and mix up the sauce while my husband milked, then pop it in the oven when we left for church.

> Cooking oil
> 3 to 4 pounds chicken pieces
> 1/3 cup chopped onion
> 3 tablespoons butter *or* margarine
> 3/4 cup ketchup
> 1/2 cup water
> 1/3 cup vinegar
> 3 tablespoons brown sugar
> 1 tablespoon Worcestershire sauce
> 2 teaspoons prepared mustard
> 1/4 teaspoon salt
> 1/8 teaspoon pepper

Heat a small amount of oil in a large skillet; fry chicken until browned. Drain; place chicken in a 13-in. x 9-in. x 2-in. baking dish. In a saucepan, saute onion in butter until tender; stir in remaining ingredients. Simmer, uncovered, for 15 minutes. Pour over chicken. Bake at 350° about 1 hour or until chicken is done, basting occasionally. **Yield:** 6-8 servings.

Favorite Broccoli Salad

"Fresh tasting...so colorful...delicious dressing" are some of the compliments I get whenever I serve this broccoli salad with a meal or take it to a church dinner. Although I use many other good salad recipes, I'm especially fond of this one.

> 1 bunch broccoli, separated into florets
> 1 head cauliflower, separated into florets
> 8 bacon strips, cooked and crumbled
> 1 cup chopped seeded tomatoes
> 1/3 cup chopped onion
> 2 hard-cooked eggs, sliced
> 1 cup mayonnaise *or* salad dressing
> 1/3 cup sugar
> 2 tablespoons vinegar

In a large salad bowl, combine broccoli, cauliflower, bacon, tomatoes, onion and eggs; set aside. In another bowl, combine mayonnaise, sugar and vinegar; mix until smooth. Just before serving, pour dressing over salad and toss. **Yield:** 6-8 servings.

Deluxe Chocolate Marshmallow Bars

I'd have to say that I've been asked to share this chocolaty layered bar recipe more than any other in my collection. It's a long-time favorite of our three daughters. I can't count how many times we've all made these!

> 3/4 cup butter *or* margarine, softened
> 1-1/2 cups sugar
> 3 eggs
> 1 teaspoon vanilla extract
> 1-1/3 cups all-purpose flour
> 3 tablespoons baking cocoa
> 1/2 teaspoon baking powder
> 1/2 teaspoon salt
> 1/2 cup chopped nuts, optional
> 4 cups miniature marshmallows

TOPPING:
> 1-1/3 cups (8 ounces) chocolate chips
> 1 cup peanut butter
> 3 tablespoons butter *or* margarine
> 2 cups crisp rice cereal

In a mixing bowl, cream butter and sugar. Add eggs and vanilla; beat until fluffy. Combine flour, baking powder, salt and cocoa; add to creamed mixture. Stir in nuts if desired. Spread in a greased jelly roll pan. Bake at 350° for 15-18 minutes. Sprinkle marshmallows evenly over cake; return to oven for 2-3 minutes. Using a knife dipped in water, spread the melted marshmallows evenly over cake. Cool. For topping, combine chocolate chips, peanut butter and butter in a small saucepan. Cook over low heat, stirring constantly, until melted and well blended. Remove from heat; stir in cereal. Spread over bars. Chill. **Yield:** about 3 dozen.

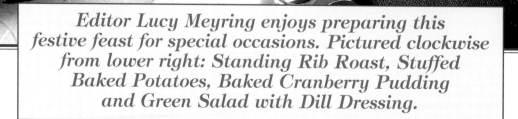

Editor Lucy Meyring enjoys preparing this festive feast for special occasions. Pictured clockwise from lower right: Standing Rib Roast, Stuffed Baked Potatoes, Baked Cranberry Pudding and Green Salad with Dill Dressing.

By Lucy Meyring, Walden, Colorado

SPECIAL OCCASIONS call for my special Standing Rib Roast with all the trimmings, like creamy Stuffed Baked Potatoes. For festive color and crunch, I serve Green Salad with Dill Dressing. And old-fashioned Baked Cranberry Pudding takes time to prepare, but it's worth it! This simple, yet elegant, feast is husband Danny's absolute favorite.

Green Salad with Dill Dressing

The creamy dressing turns an ordinary green salad into a real taste treat.

✓ This tasty dish uses less sugar, salt and fat. Recipe includes *Diabetic Exchanges.*

- 1 head Boston lettuce, torn
- 1/2 bunch romaine, torn
- 4 green onions, sliced
- 3 radishes, sliced
- 1 large green pepper, cut into strips
- 1 large tomato, diced
- 1 carrot, shredded
- 1 small cucumber, sliced

DILL DRESSING:
- 2 tablespoons red wine vinegar
- 1 teaspoon Dijon mustard
- 1/4 cup vegetable oil
- 3 tablespoons olive oil
- 2 tablespoons sour cream
- 2 teaspoons dill weed
- 1/4 teaspoon salt, optional

In a large bowl, combine the first eight ingredients. Refrigerate. For dressing, whisk the vinegar and mustard in a small bowl. Whisk in remaining ingredients. Refrigerate for at least 30 minutes. Stir well before serving with the salad. **Yield:** 8 servings (about 3/4 cup dressing). **Diabetic Exchanges:** One serving with 1 tablespoon dressing (prepared with light sour cream and without added salt) equals 1-1/2 fat, 1 vegetable; also, 101 calories, 20 mg sodium, 0 cholesterol, 7 gm carbohydrate, 3 gm protein, 9 gm fat.

Standing Rib Roast

Treat your family to tender slices of specially seasoned rib roast.

- 1 tablespoon lemon pepper
- 1 tablespoon paprika
- 1-1/2 teaspoons garlic salt
- 1 teaspoon dried rosemary, crushed
- 1/2 teaspoon cayenne pepper
- 1 standing beef rib roast (6 to 7 pounds)
- 2 cups boiling water
- 1 teaspoon instant beef bouillon granules

Combine lemon pepper, paprika, garlic salt, rosemary and cayenne pepper; rub over roast. Place roast with fat side up in a large roasting pan. Insert a meat thermometer. Bake, uncovered, at 325° until roast reaches desired doneness. Allow 23-25 minutes *per pound* for rare (140° on thermometer), 27-30 minutes for medium (160°) and 32-35 minutes for well-done (170°). Remove to serving platter and keep warm. Let stand 15 minutes before carving. Pour meat juices from roasting pan into a glass measuring cup; skim off fat. Add boiling water and bouillon to roasting pan and stir to remove drippings. Stir in meat juices. Serve with the roast. **Yield:** 10-12 servings.

Stuffed Baked Potatoes

These potatoes are an extra-nice side dish without a lot of extra effort.

- 8 baking potatoes (about 3 pounds)
- Vegetable oil, optional
- 1/3 cup butter *or* margarine, softened
- 1/4 cup chopped fresh chives *or* 2 tablespoons dried chives
- 1 teaspoon salt
- 1/4 teaspoon pepper
- 1/3 to 1/2 cup evaporated milk
- Paprika

Rub the potato skins with oil if desired; prick with a fork. Bake at 400° for 1 hour or until tender. Allow potatoes to cool to the touch. Slice a small portion off the top of each potato. Carefully scoop out pulp, leaving a thin shell. In a large bowl, mash the pulp with butter, chives, salt, pepper and enough milk to obtain desired consistency. Carefully stuff shells; sprinkle with paprika. Place on an ungreased baking sheet. Bake at 325° for 30 minutes or until heated through. (Potatoes may be stuffed ahead and refrigerated or frozen. Allow additional time for reheating.) **Yield:** 8 servings.

Baked Cranberry Pudding

Serve this warm topped with whipped cream for a cranberry lover's delight!

- 1 cup packed brown sugar
- 2 eggs, *separated*
- 1/2 cup whipping cream
- 2 teaspoons vanilla extract
- 1 teaspoon ground cinnamon
- 1/2 teaspoon ground nutmeg
- 1-1/2 cups all-purpose flour
- 3 tablespoons grated orange peel
- 1 teaspoon baking powder
- 1/2 teaspoon cream of tartar, *divided*
- 1/8 teaspoon salt
- 3 cups coarsely chopped cranberries
- 1/4 cup butter *or* margarine, melted

TOPPING:
- 1-1/2 cups sugar
- 1/2 cup orange juice
- 2-1/2 cups whole cranberries
- Sweetened whipped cream, optional

In a bowl, combine brown sugar and egg yolks. Add whipping cream, vanilla, cinnamon and nutmeg; set aside. In a large bowl, combine flour, orange peel, baking powder, 1/4 teaspoon cream of tartar and salt. Stir in chopped cranberries and completely coat them. Add brown sugar mixture and butter; mix well. (Batter will be very stiff.) Beat egg whites until foamy. Add remaining cream of tartar; beat until soft peaks form. Fold into batter. Pour into a greased 9-in. springform pan. Bake at 350° for 45-50 minutes or until a toothpick inserted near center comes out clean. Meanwhile, for topping, bring sugar and orange juice to a boil in a saucepan. Cook for 3 minutes or until sugar dissolves. Reduce heat; add cranberries and simmer 6-8 minutes or until berries begin to burst. Remove from heat and cover. When pudding tests done, place springform pan on a jelly roll pan. Spoon warm cranberry sauce evenly over top. Return to the oven for 10 minutes. Cool for 10 minutes before removing sides of springform pan. Cool at least 1 hour or overnight. Before serving, reheat at 350° for 10 minutes. Serve with whipped cream if desired. **Yield:** 8-10 servings.

Editor Sharon Mensing has a tasty menu that's great for easy-on-the-hostess entertaining. Pictured clockwise from lower left: Grilled Ham Steak, Party Potatoes, Hidden Pear Salad and Whole Wheat Refrigerator Rolls.

By Sharon Mensing, Greenfield, Iowa

HUSBAND KEITH and I raise hogs, cattle, corn and soybeans in partnership with Keith's brother and his family. As you might imagine, our meal schedule can be as changeable as our Iowa weather. That's why recipes that can be prepared ahead of time really appeal to me.

Grilling is a great way to cook ham —the seared pattern gives it an appealing look, and the zippy mustard sauce adds a delicious flavor.

Party Potatoes can be made a day ahead and stored in the refrigerator. I'll often prepare a batch and divide it into two casseroles—one for guests and one to freeze for later.

Likewise, I mix up my Whole Wheat Refrigerator Rolls the day before I plan to serve them. The dough rises overnight in the refrigerator, and I make up the rolls in the morning.

My Hidden Pear Salad became a family favorite even before Keith and I were married—I made it for him and his family while we were dating.

I love to entertain, and when we do have guests, I often serve this meal.

Party Potatoes

These creamy, tasty potatoes can be made the day before and stored in the refrigerator until you're ready to pop them in the oven (I often do that). The garlic powder and chives add zip, and the shredded cheese adds color.

4 cups mashed potatoes (about 8 to 10 large) *or* 4 cups prepared instant potatoes

1 cup (8 ounces) sour cream
1 package (8 ounces) cream cheese, softened
1 teaspoon dried chives *or* 1 tablespoon snipped fresh chives
1/4 teaspoon garlic powder
1/4 cup dry bread crumbs
1 tablespoon butter *or* margarine, melted
1/2 cup shredded cheddar cheese

In a large bowl, combine potatoes, sour cream, cream cheese, chives and garlic powder. Turn into a greased 2-qt. casserole. Combine bread crumbs with butter; sprinkle over potatoes. Bake at 350° for 50-60 minutes. Top with cheese and serve immediately. Dish can be assembled a day ahead and baked just before serving. **Yield: 10-12 servings.**

Grilled Ham Steak

I love to grill this ham steak all year-round. It's an impressive meat dish to make for company or family. So quick to prepare, the ham tastes great with the smoky flavor from the grill and the tangy sweetness of the sauce. It's irresistible!

1/4 cup apricot *or* plum preserves
1 tablespoon prepared mustard
1 teaspoon lemon juice
1/8 teaspoon ground cinnamon
1 ham steak (1 inch thick and about 2 pounds)

In a small saucepan, combine the preserves, mustard, lemon juice and cinnamon. Cook and stir over low heat until thoroughly combined, about 2-3 minutes. Score fat edges of ham. Grill over medium coals for 8-10 minutes per side, brushing with glaze during the last few minutes of grilling. **Yield: 6 servings.**

Hidden Pear Salad

Light and fluffy, this colorful salad is a very flavorful family favorite. When I made it for my husband's family before we were married, we all joked about not being able to find any pears, so the name stuck.

1 can (16 ounces) pears, liquid drained and reserved
1 package (3 ounces) lime-flavored gelatin
1 package (3 ounces) cream cheese, softened
1/4 teaspoon lemon juice

1 envelope whipped topping mix
Lettuce leaves

In a saucepan, bring pear liquid to a boil. Stir in gelatin until dissolved. Remove from the heat and cool at room temperature until syrupy. Meanwhile, puree pears in a blender. In a mixing bowl, beat cream cheese and lemon juice until fluffy and smooth. Add pureed pears and mix well. Prepare whipped topping according to package directions; fold into pear mixture. Fold in cooled gelatin. Pour into an oiled 4-1/2-cup mold. Chill overnight. Just before serving, unmold salad onto a lettuce-lined platter. **Yield: 6-8 servings.**

Whole Wheat Refrigerator Rolls

This roll recipe is easy and versatile. I like to mix up the dough beforehand and let it rise in the refrigerator. The rolls brown nicely and are wonderful served warm.

2 packages (1/4 ounce *each*) active dry yeast
2 cups warm water (110° to 115°)
1/2 cup sugar
2 teaspoons salt
4-1/2 to 5 cups all-purpose flour, *divided*
1 egg
1/4 cup vegetable oil
2 cups whole wheat flour

In a mixing bowl, dissolve yeast in water. Let stand 5 minutes. Blend in sugar, salt and 3 cups all-purpose flour at low speed until moistened; beat 2 minutes at medium speed. Beat in egg and oil. By hand, gradually stir in whole wheat flour and enough remaining all-purpose flour to make a soft dough. Turn out onto a lightly floured surface. Knead until smooth and elastic, about 6-8 minutes. Place in a greased bowl, turning once to grease top. Cover and let rise until doubled or cover and refrigerate overnight. Punch dough down and form into dinner-size rolls. Place on greased baking sheets for plain rolls or knots, or in greased muffin tins for cloverleaf rolls. Cover and let rise until doubled, about 1 hour for dough prepared the same day or 1-2 hours for refrigerated dough. Bake at 375° for 10-12 minutes or until light golden brown. Serve warm. If desired, dough may be kept up to 4 days in the refrigerator. Punch down daily. **Yield: 2 dozen.**

Editor Norma Poole prepares this spectacular spread for any gathering of friends and family. Pictured clockwise from the bottom: Herbed Rice Pilaf, Turkey with Corn Bread Dressing, Lemon Orange Cake and Creamy Sweet Potatoes.

By Norma Poole, Auburndale, Florida

WHEN family gathers for Thanksgiving, my favorite menu is flavored with Southern tradition and the tang of citrus.

My crumbled homemade corn bread, along with the sage and poultry seasoning, gives the dressing its down-home good taste.

To the sweet potatoes Mom always served, I've added orange juice to make my own "Florida special" Creamy Sweet Potatoes. It's another dish the family has come to *expect* at Thanksgiving!

My Herbed Rice Pilaf is really very basic and easy to fix. The celery adds a pleasant crunch, and dashes of soy sauce and Worcestershire sauce add a little zip.

Did you expect pie for dessert? My Lemon Orange Cake may be a departure from most folks' idea of a Thanksgiving dessert, but we love this special sweet treat.

Turkey with Corn Bread Dressing

Nothing gets family hanging around the kitchen like the aroma of a turkey stuffed with savory dressing roasting in the oven. Drizzled with hot gravy, it tastes even better than it smells!

        2 cups chopped celery
        1 cup chopped onion
    1/2 cup butter *or* margarine
        6 cups cubed day-old corn bread
        2 cups fresh bread crumbs
        1 tablespoon dried sage
        1 tablespoon poultry seasoning
        2 eggs, lightly beaten
        1 cup chicken broth
        1 turkey (10 to 12 pounds)
Melted butter *or* margarine

In a skillet, saute celery and onion in butter until tender. Place in a large bowl with corn bread, crumbs, sage and poultry seasoning. Combine eggs and chicken broth; add to corn bread mixture, stirring gently to mix. Rinse and dry turkey. Just before baking, stuff the body cavity and inside of the neck with dressing. Skewer or fasten openings. Tie the drumsticks together. Place on a rack in a roasting pan. Brush with melted butter. Bake at 325° for 3-1/2 to 4 hours. When turkey begins to brown, cover lightly with a tent of aluminum foil. When turkey is done, allow to stand for 20 minutes. Remove all dressing to a serving bowl. **Yield:** 8-10 servings. **Editor's Note:** Dressing may be prepared as above and baked in a greased 2-qt. casserole dish. Cover and bake at 400° for 20 minutes. Uncover and bake 10 minutes longer or until lightly browned. Dressing yields 8 cups.

Herbed Rice Pilaf

The zesty flavor of onion is great with the crunch of celery in this light dish, but sometimes I'll add chopped shrimp, chicken or beef to make it into a one-dish meal.

✓ **This tasty dish uses less sugar, salt and fat. Recipe includes** *Diabetic Exchanges*.

        2 cups uncooked long grain rice
        1 cup chopped celery
    1/2 cup chopped onion
    1/4 cup butter *or* margarine
        4 cups chicken broth
        1 teaspoon Worcestershire sauce
        1 teaspoon soy sauce
        1 teaspoon dried oregano
        1 teaspoon dried thyme

In a skillet, saute rice, celery and onion in butter until the rice is lightly browned and the vegetables are tender. Spoon into a greased 2-qt. casserole. Combine all remaining ingredients; pour over rice mixture. Cover and bake at 325° for 50 minutes or until the rice is done. **Yield:** 8 servings. **Diabetic Exchanges:** One serving (prepared with margarine) equals 1 starch, 1 vegetable, 1/2 fat; also, 124 calories, 65 mg sodium, 0 cholesterol, 21 gm carbohydrate, 2 gm protein, 3 gm fat.

Lemon Orange Cake

I love to bake this lovely three-layer cake instead of a more traditional pie for Thanksgiving. It has that tangy Florida citrus flavor and isn't any more difficult to make than a two-layer cake.

        1 cup butter *or* margarine, softened
    1/4 cup shortening
        2 cups sugar
        5 eggs
        3 cups all-purpose flour
        1 teaspoon baking powder
    1/2 teaspoon baking soda
    1/2 teaspoon salt
        1 cup buttermilk
        1 teaspoon vanilla extract
    1/2 teaspoon lemon extract
FROSTING:
    1/2 cup butter *or* margarine, softened
        3 tablespoons orange juice
        3 tablespoons lemon juice
        1 to 2 tablespoons grated orange peel
        1 to 2 tablespoons grated lemon peel
        1 teaspoon lemon extract
    5-1/2 to 6 cups confectioners' sugar

In a mixing bowl, cream butter, shortening and sugar until light and fluffy. Add eggs, one at a time, beating well after each addition. Combine dry ingredients; add to creamed mixture alternately with buttermilk, beginning and ending with dry ingredients. Stir in extracts. Pour into three greased and floured 9-in. cake pans. Bake at 350° for 25-30 minutes or until cakes test done. Cool for 10 minutes in pans before removing to wire racks to cool completely. For frosting, beat butter in a mixing bowl until fluffy; add the next five ingredients and mix well. Gradually add confectioners' sugar; beat until frosting has desired spreading consistency. Spread between layers and over the top and sides of cake. **Yield:** 10-12 servings.

Creamy Sweet Potatoes

I took my mother's delicious sweet potato casserole recipe and gave it a new twist by adding the tempting taste of orange—a fruit very abundant in our state. The flavors are wonderful together and make this dish a family favorite.

        5 pounds sweet potatoes, peeled and cooked
        4 eggs, lightly beaten
    1/2 cup orange juice
    1/2 cup butter *or* margarine, softened
    1/2 cup sugar
        1 teaspoon vanilla extract
    1/2 teaspoon ground nutmeg
Dash salt
Miniature marshmallows

In large bowl, mash sweet potatoes. Add eggs, orange juice, butter, sugar, vanilla, nutmeg and salt; mix well. Transfer to a greased 3-qt. baking dish. Bake at 350° for 35-40 minutes or until set. Top with marshmallows; return to oven until they just begin to puff and melt, about 5-10 minutes. **Yield:** 10-12 servings.

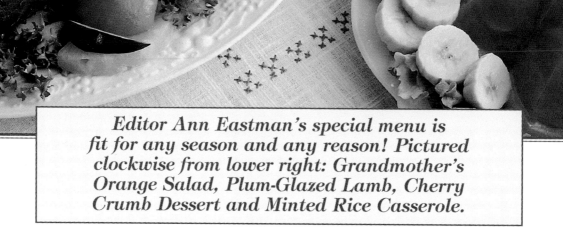

Editor Ann Eastman's special menu is fit for any season and any reason! Pictured clockwise from lower right: Grandmother's Orange Salad, Plum-Glazed Lamb, Cherry Crumb Dessert and Minted Rice Casserole.

By Ann Eastman, Greenville, California

MY HUSBAND, Ken, and I love our life on a mile-high perch in the Sierra Nevada Mountains near Greenville, California. We have 6 beautiful, forested acres with a creek running along one edge.

When we first retired here, we decided to remodel the old "barn house", especially the kitchen which was deplorable. We gutted it and started from scratch and now have the most workable, efficient and cozy kitchen I could have ever dreamed of!

With our daughter, Diane, married with a family of her own, I mostly cook for just the two of us. But I love preparing special meals for family and friends.

One of my favorite meals (and theirs, too, I'm told) is especially appropriate for springtime—Plum-Glazed Lamb. It's a wonderful Easter dinner or makes an elegant meal for company.

To complement the flavorful lamb, I serve Minted Rice Casserole (crunchy with almonds), garden vegetables and Grandmother's Orange Salad. Easy-to-fix Cherry Crumb Dessert, served warm with whipped cream or ice cream, provides the fruitful finale.

Grandmother's Orange Salad

This gelatin salad is slightly sweet and tangy, too. It adds beautiful color to any meal and appeals to appetites of all ages! When the weather starts turning warm, this cool, fruity salad is just right.

  1 can (11 ounces) mandarin
    oranges
  1 can (8 ounces) crushed
    pineapple
Water
  1 package (6 ounces)
    orange-flavored gelatin
  1 pint orange sherbet, softened
  2 bananas, sliced

Drain oranges and pineapple, reserving juices. Set oranges and pineapple aside. Add water to juices to measure 2 cups. Place in a saucepan and bring to a boil; pour over gelatin in a large bowl. Stir until gelatin is dissolved. Stir in sherbet until smooth. Chill until partially set (watch carefully). Fold in oranges, pineapple and bananas. Pour into an oiled 6-cup mold. Chill until firm. **Yield: 8-10 servings.**

Plum-Glazed Lamb

Fruity and flavorful, this wonderful glaze is simple to prepare, and its hint of garlic really complements the lamb. The recipe makes enough glaze to baste the lamb during roasting and leaves plenty to pass when serving.

  1 leg of lamb (4 to 5 pounds)
Salt and pepper to taste
  2 cans (16-1/2 ounces *each*)
    purple plums, pitted
  2 garlic cloves
  1/4 cup lemon juice
  2 tablespoons soy sauce
  2 teaspoons Worcestershire
    sauce
  1 teaspoon dried basil

In a shallow baking pan, place lamb, fat side up, on rack. Season with salt and pepper. Roast at 325° for 2-1/2 to 3 hours or until meat thermometer reads 160° (medium) or meat reaches desired doneness. Meanwhile, drain plums, reserving 1/2 cup syrup. In a food processor or blender, place plums, reserved syrup, garlic, lemon juice, soy sauce, Worcestershire sauce and basil. Cover and process until smooth. Using half of the plum sauce, baste lamb every 15 minutes during the last hour of roasting. Simmer remaining sauce for 5 minutes and serve with meat. **Yield: 10-12 servings.**

Minted Rice Casserole

The mild, minty flavor and almond crunch make this a nice side dish for a meal with lamb. People will likely be impressed when you prepare this different and palate-pleasing rice casserole.

  2 cups water
  2 teaspoons salt
  1 cup uncooked long grain rice
  1/4 cup butter *or* margarine
Dash garlic salt
  1 can (14-1/2 ounces) chicken
    broth
  1/2 teaspoon dried mint leaves
  1/4 cup slivered almonds, toasted

In a saucepan, bring water and salt to a boil. Remove from the heat; add rice. Cover and let stand for 3 minutes. Drain. Rinse rice with cold water; drain well. In a skillet, melt butter. Add rice and cook over medium heat, stirring frequently, until butter is almost absorbed, about 5 minutes. Turn into a 1-qt. casserole; sprinkle with garlic salt. Pour chicken broth over rice. Cover and bake at 325° for 35-40 minutes or until most of liquid is absorbed. Add mint and fluff with a fork. Sprinkle almonds over top. Bake, uncovered, 5-10 minutes more. **Yield: 6 servings.**

Cherry Crumb Dessert

This dessert is a sweet treat, especially when garnished with a dollop of whipped cream or a scoop of ice cream! The crust and crumb topping have a wonderful nutty flavor, and the smooth fruit filling looks beautiful when served.

  1/2 cup butter *or* margarine,
    chilled
  1 package (18-1/2 ounces)
    yellow cake mix
  1 can (21 ounces) cherry *or*
    blueberry pie filling
  1/2 cup chopped walnuts
Whipped cream *or* ice cream,
  optional

In a mixing bowl, cut butter into cake mix as for pastry dough. Set aside 1 cup. Pat remaining crumbs onto the bottom and 1/2 in. up the sides of a greased 13-in. x 9-in. x 2-in. baking pan. Spread pie filling over crust. Combine the walnuts with reserved crumbs; sprinkle over top. Bake at 350° for 30-35 minutes. Serve warm, with whipped cream or ice cream if desired. **Yield: 12-16 servings.**

Editor Sharon Bickett's family agrees her savory summer fare is hard to top. Pictured clockwise from bottom right: Hawaiian Kabobs, Peppered Rib Eye Steaks, Sour Cream Apple Pie and Crunchy Spinach Salad.

By Sharon Bickett
Chester, South Carolina

HUSBAND AL AND I are very fortunate to live on a beautiful farm atop a long, sloping ridge. So grilling and eating outdoors give us a chance to enjoy the breathtaking panorama of fields and woods surrounding our place.

My summertime meals need to be quick and easy to prepare, while still being satisfying and refreshing for our busy family. Peppered Rib Eye Steaks and Hawaiian Kabobs fill the bill deliciously!

The steaks start out with a quick herb rubdown known as a "dry marinade". Applied 1 hour before grilling, the delicious herb flavors and zesty cayenne are absorbed into the meat.

A perfect flavor companion to these spicy steaks, the Hawaiian Kabobs have the pleasant, sweet-tart taste of pineapple.

My family loves the crunch of bacon and water chestnuts as well as the tangy dressing on my Spinach Salad.

And the Sour Cream Apple Pie's creamy filling, tender apples and buttery topping give it a rich, homey taste we all love.

Peppered Rib Eye Steaks

I love to cook—especially on the grill. This recipe is one of my favorites! The seasoning rub makes a wonderful marinade, and nothing beats the taste of these flavorful grilled steaks!

4 beef rib eye steaks
  (1-1/2 inches thick)
1 tablespoon olive oil
1 tablespoon garlic powder

1 tablespoon paprika
2 teaspoons dried thyme
2 teaspoons dried oregano
1-1/2 teaspoons pepper
1 teaspoon salt
1 teaspoon lemon pepper
1 teaspoon cayenne pepper
Orange slices, optional
Parsley sprigs, optional

Brush steaks lightly with olive oil. In a small bowl, combine all seasonings. Sprinkle seasonings over steaks and press into both sides. Cover and chill for 1 hour. Grill steaks, turning once, over medium-hot coals 14-18 minutes for rare; 18-22 minutes for medium; 24-28 minutes for well-done. Place on a warm serving platter; cut across the grain into thick slices. Garnish with orange slices and parsley if desired. **Yield:** 8 servings.

Crunchy Spinach Salad

A fresh salad is the perfect complement to any summer meal. This salad, with its tangy dressing and crisp, crunchy ingredients, has become one of our very favorites.

2 quarts fresh torn spinach
1 can (16 ounces) bean
  sprouts, drained *or* 2 cups
  fresh bean sprouts
1 can (8 ounces) sliced water
  chestnuts, drained
4 hard-cooked eggs, chopped
6 bacon strips, cooked and
  crumbled
1 small onion, thinly sliced
DRESSING:
1/2 cup packed brown sugar
1/2 cup vegetable oil
1/3 cup vinegar
1/3 cup ketchup
1 tablespoon Worcestershire
  sauce

In a large bowl, combine spinach, bean sprouts, water chestnuts, eggs, bacon and onion. In a bottle or jar, combine all dressing ingredients. Cover and shake well to mix. Just before serving, pour dressing over salad and toss. **Yield:** 8 servings.

Hawaiian Kabobs

Fun and different, these kabobs are a treat exclusively from the grill! The pineapple gives ordinary summer vegetables a fresh, tropical taste. This colorful side dish is always a hit with family or at a get-together.

1 can (20 ounces) unsweetened
  pineapple chunks
2 large green peppers, cut into
  1-inch pieces

1 large onion, quartered, optional
12 to 16 medium fresh mushrooms
16 to 18 cherry tomatoes
1/2 cup soy sauce
1/4 cup olive oil
1 tablespoon brown sugar
2 teaspoons ground ginger
1 teaspoon garlic powder
1 teaspoon dry mustard
1/4 teaspoon pepper
Cooked rice, optional

Drain pineapple, reserving 1/2 cup juice. Place pineapple chunks and vegetables in a large bowl; set aside. In a saucepan, combine reserved pineapple juice with soy sauce, olive oil, brown sugar and seasonings; bring to a boil. Reduce heat and simmer, uncovered, for 5 minutes. Pour over vegetable mixture; cover and refrigerate for at least 1 hour, stirring occasionally. Remove pineapple and vegetables from marinade and reserve marinade. Alternate pineapple, green pepper, onion if desired, mushrooms and tomatoes on skewers. Grill kabobs for 20 minutes or until soft, turning and basting with marinade frequently. Serve over rice if desired. **Yield:** 8 servings.

Sour Cream Apple Pie

A cool, creamy version of the original, this delicious dessert is the perfect finish to a satisfying summer meal. Its crumbly topping and smooth apple filling are crowd-pleasers! Be prepared to serve seconds.

2 eggs
1 cup (8 ounces) sour cream
1 cup sugar
6 tablespoons all-purpose flour,
  divided
1 teaspoon vanilla extract
1/4 teaspoon salt
3 cups chopped peeled baking
  apples
1 unbaked pie shell (9 inches)
3 tablespoons butter *or*
  margarine, softened
1/4 cup packed brown sugar

In a large bowl, beat eggs. Add sour cream. Stir in sugar, 2 tablespoons flour, vanilla and salt; mix well. Stir in apples. Pour into pie shell. Bake at 375° for 15 minutes. Meanwhile, combine butter, brown sugar and remaining flour. Sprinkle over top of pie. Return to oven for 20-25 minutes or until filling is set. Cool completely on a wire rack. Serve or cover and refrigerate. **Yield:** 8 servings.

'MY MOM'S BEST MEAL'

*In this chapter, six cooks share one of
their Mom's most treasured meals. They're
likely to become your family's favorites, too!*

*Pictured clockwise from the top:
Pumpkin Raisin Cake, Garlic-Stuffed Pork Roast,
Black-Eyed Peas with Bacon and Cabbage Casserole.*

Delightful Dishes for New Year's Day

"ALL 10 of my sisters and brothers agree that our mom's best meal was this one that she always cooked on New Year's Day," relates Ruby Williams of Bogalusa, Louisiana.

"With such a large family, Mom cooked simple, nourishing meals for the most part. No matter what she prepared, it was always delicious. We were brought up to appreciate family and friends, and Mom made sure we were generous with our hospitality. So when we rang in the New Year with family and friends, this is the meal she would prepare.

"Mom never followed recipes. And I was always amazed how she knew how much of everything she needed to make meals taste 'just right'. After years of watching her cook from scratch, I finally decided to record the recipes for this special-occasion meal.

"The flavorful pork roast, creamy cabbage casserole, black-eyed peas and pumpkin raisin cake are one meal we all remember well.

"It wasn't easy to pick one of Mom's meals as her best…but this delicious spread started the New Year off right."

"Of course, now when I make this meal for my family, I also add the special secret 'ingredient' Mom added to every recipe…love."

Cabbage Casserole

Even those folks who don't care for the taste of cabbage will enjoy it made this way. This tangy, creamy, comforting side dish goes exceptionally well with pork roast.

- 1 large head cabbage, shredded (about 12 cups)
- 1 onion, chopped
- 6 tablespoons butter *or* margarine, *divided*
- 1 can (10-3/4 ounces) condensed cream of mushroom soup, undiluted
- 8 ounces process American cheese, cubed

Salt and pepper to taste
- 1/4 cup dry bread crumbs

Cook cabbage in boiling salted water until tender; drain thoroughly. In a large skillet, saute onion in 5 tablespoons butter until tender. Add soup and mix well. Add cheese; heat and stir until melted. Remove from the heat. Stir in cabbage, salt and pepper. Transfer to an ungreased 2-qt. baking dish. In a small skillet, melt remaining butter. Cook and stir crumbs in butter until lightly browned; sprinkle over casserole. Bake, uncovered, at 350° for 20-30 minutes or until heated through. **Yield:** 6-8 servings.

SIMPLE SOLUTION. Keep cabbage odor to a minimum when cooking by putting a celery rib or several lemon wedges in the kettle.

Garlic-Stuffed Pork Roast

Mom cooked for 11 children, so her menus usually featured basic, simple foods. But on New Year's Day, she always treated us to this special pork roast. All of us kids agree this was our mom's best meal!

- 1 pork loin roast, backbone loosened (about 5 pounds)
- 1/2 medium green pepper, finely chopped
- 1/2 cup thinly sliced green onions
- 1/2 cup chopped celery
- 8 garlic cloves, minced
- 1 teaspoon salt
- 1/4 teaspoon cayenne pepper

With a sharp knife, cut a deep pocket between each rib on meaty side of roast. Combine green pepper, green onions, celery and garlic; stuff deeply into pockets. Season roast with salt and cayenne pepper. Insert meat thermometer. Place roast, rib side down, in a shallow roasting pan. Bake, uncovered, at 325° for 2-3 hours or until thermometer reads 170°. Let stand for 15 minutes before carving. **Yield:** 6-8 servings.

Black-Eyed Peas With Bacon

A real Southern favorite, black-eyed peas are traditionally served on New Year's Day to bring good luck. My mother's recipe with bacon, garlic and thyme makes ordinary black-eyed peas extra special.

- 1 pound black-eyed peas, rinsed and sorted
- 1/2 pound bacon, cooked and crumbled
- 1 large onion, chopped
- 1 garlic clove, minced
- 1 tablespoon butter *or* margarine
- 1/2 teaspoon dried thyme

Salt to taste
Additional crumbled bacon, optional

Place peas, bacon and enough water to cover in a large kettle; bring to a boil. Boil for 2 minutes. Remove from the heat; cover and let stand for 1 hour. *Do not drain.* In a skillet, saute onion and garlic in butter until tender. Add to pea mixture with thyme and salt. Return to the heat; simmer, covered, for 30 minutes or until peas are soft. Top with crumbled bacon if desired. **Yield:** 6-8 servings.

Pumpkin Raisin Cake

This nutty, golden cake is one of my mom's best because it's a wonderfully different use for pumpkin. After just one taste, I'm sure it will become a favorite with your family, too.

- 2 cups all-purpose flour
- 2 cups sugar
- 2 teaspoons pumpkin pie spice
- 2 teaspoons baking powder
- 1 teaspoon baking soda
- 1/2 teaspoon salt
- 4 eggs
- 1 can (16 ounces) pumpkin
- 3/4 cup vegetable oil
- 2 cups bran cereal (not flakes)
- 1 cup chopped pecans
- 1 cup raisins

Confectioners' sugar, optional

Combine flour, sugar, pumpkin pie spice, baking powder, baking soda and salt; set aside. In a large bowl, beat eggs. Add pumpkin and oil; stir in cereal just until moistened. Add dry ingredients and stir just until combined. Fold in pecans and raisins. Pour into a greased 10-in. tube pan. Bake at 350° for 60-65 minutes or until cake tests done. Cool in pan for 10 minutes before removing to a wire rack to cool completely. Dust with confectioners' sugar before serving if desired. **Yield:** 12-16 servings.

BETTER BACON. When a recipe calls for crumbled bacon, dice it before frying for more even cooking.

Pictured clockwise from the top: Hot Milk Cake, Sauerkraut Casserole, Glazed Sweet Potatoes and Old-Fashioned Baked Ham.

SUNDAY DINNER WAS FARMHOUSE FAVORITE

"WHILE I was growing up on our family farm, Mom would always prepare down-home, simple country meals that were packed with natural, delicious flavors. The meals were always tasty and satisfying," says Rosemary Pryor of Pasadena, Maryland.

"As far as I'm concerned, my mom is the best cook ever! She'd hardly use a recipe—she'd add a dash of this and a dab of that and end up with a delectable work of art...such as this traditional Sunday dinner. Of all my mom's delightful meals, this was certainly her best.

"The 150-year-old farmhouse where I grew up is gone now. But wonderful memories of the time spent at our huge kitchen table—always meticulously set—remain fresh in my mind. Sunday dinners always meant good company, good food and just plain good times.

"How I remember the aroma of her glazed ham baking...her sweet potatoes cooking... and her sauerkraut brewing. And, oh, her Hot Milk Cake! That was the perfect ending to a perfectly wonderful meal.

"Through her down-home hearty cooking, Mom still continues to make delicious memories for me and my family."

Old-Fashioned Baked Ham

I can still see the table meticulously set for a traditional country meal at our 150-year-old family farm, and I vividly recall the aroma of mouth-watering ham baking. Nothing can top that tasty memory! Whenever I make a ham, I think of my mom—who was, in my opinion, the best cook ever.

> 1 can (8 ounces) pineapple slices
> 1 canned ham (5 pounds)
> 1/2 cup packed brown sugar
> 1/4 teaspoon ground cloves
> 1 teaspoon dry mustard
> 1 tablespoon vinegar
> Maraschino cherries

Drain pineapple, reserving 2 tablespoons of the juice; set aside. Place ham in a baking pan; bake at 350° for 30 minutes. Combine brown sugar, cloves, mustard and vinegar in a small bowl; stir in reserved pineapple juice. Score ham; place pineapple slices and cherries on top of ham; spoon glaze over fruit and ham. Bake for another 40-45 minutes, basting occasionally. **Yield:** 8-10 servings.

> **HAM IT UP!** You'll appreciate any leftovers from a meal of baked ham. Slice and package leftovers in meal-size servings in aluminum foil, then label and freeze them to use when you need dinner in a hurry. And put diced pieces of ham in freezer bags for use in future casseroles.

Hot Milk Cake

This simple, old-fashioned cake tastes so good it will surprise you! This dessert was always the perfect ending to one of Mom's delicious meals. She always used "a dash of this and a dab of that" to come up with what we thought was "the best"!

> 4 eggs
> 2 cups sugar
> 2-1/4 cups all-purpose flour
> 2-1/4 teaspoons baking powder
> 1 teaspoon vanilla extract
> 1-1/4 cups milk
> 10 tablespoons butter *or* margarine

In a mixing bowl, beat eggs at high speed until thick, about 5 minutes. Gradually add sugar, beating until mixture is light and fluffy. Combine flour and baking powder; add to batter with vanilla and beat at low speed until smooth. In a saucepan, heat milk and butter just until the butter melts, stirring occasionally. Add to batter, beating until combined. Pour into a greased 13-in. x 9-in. x 2-in. baking pan. Bake at 350° for 30-35 minutes or until cake tests done. Cool on a wire rack. **Yield:** 12-16 servings.

Sauerkraut Casserole

Mom brewed her own sauerkraut and, of course, the cabbage was from our big farm garden! Blending the kraut with spicy sausage and apples was Mom's favorite way to fix it, and I still love this country dish.

> 1 pound mild Italian sausage links, cut into 1-inch slices
> 1 large onion, chopped
> 2 apples, peeled and quartered
> 1 can (27 ounces) sauerkraut, undrained
> 1 cup water
> 1/2 cup packed brown sugar
> 2 teaspoons caraway seed
> Snipped parsley, optional

In a skillet, cook sausage and onion until sausage is brown and onion is tender; drain. Stir in apples, sauerkraut, water, brown sugar and caraway seed. Transfer to a 2-1/2-qt. baking dish. Cover and bake at 350° for 1 hour. Garnish with parsley if desired. **Yield:** 6-8 servings.

Glazed Sweet Potatoes

Fresh sweet potatoes Mom grew disappeared fast at our family table when she served them with this easy, flavorful glaze. She still makes them this way, and now they've become favorites with her grandchildren as well!

> 2 pounds medium sweet potatoes *or* 2 cans (18 ounces *each*) sweet potatoes, drained
> 1/4 cup butter *or* margarine
> 1/4 cup maple-flavored syrup
> 1/4 cup packed brown sugar
> 1/4 teaspoon ground cinnamon

If using fresh sweet potatoes, place in a kettle; cover with water and cook, covered, for 25-35 minutes or just until tender. Drain; cool slightly. Peel and cut into chunks. Place cooked or canned sweet potatoes in a 2-qt. baking dish. In a small saucepan, combine butter, syrup, brown sugar and cinnamon; cook and stir until mixture boils. Pour over potatoes. Bake at 350° for 30-40 minutes or until heated through. **Yield:** 8 servings.

> **COLORED KETTLE?** If your kettles become discolored when boiling fresh sweet potatoes, try rubbing the inside of the kettle with cooking oil or margarine before adding the water and potatoes. Clean up will be easy!

Pictured clockwise from the bottom:
Chicken Macaroni Casserole, Garden Potato Salad,
Picnic Baked Beans and Peanut Butter Pie.

GRANDMA'S MEAL IS FAMILY TRADITION

"YEARS AGO, my grandmother invited family and friends over on her birthday and served this delicious chicken casserole and hearty baked beans," remembers Julianne Johnson of Grove City, Minnesota.

"My mom did the same, adding her own special potato salad to the menu. With the addition of Mom's wonderful peanut butter pie, this meal's become a family tradition I now serve on our family birthdays."

Julianne recalls how her mom, who still loves to cook, made her tempting potato salad for summer picnics as well. "The homemade dressing and radishes make it extra-special," she says. "It's always one of the first dishes to disappear!"

Also original is the rich and creamy peanut butter pie. "We loved a similar pie served at a local Mennonite restaurant, but they wouldn't share the recipe with Mom. She was determined to come up with her own version, and did. People still rave over this delicious, simple dessert."

Chicken Macaroni Casserole

My favorite main dish recipe from Mom, this casserole is considered "birthday food" because we often requested it for our birthdays. But it's so hearty and flavorful, that it's become a real family-pleaser anytime!

- 2 tablespoons butter *or* margarine
- 1/4 cup all-purpose flour
- 2 cups light cream
- 1-1/2 to 2 cups chicken broth, *divided*
- 3/4 pound process American cheese, cubed
- 2 boxes (7 ounces *each*) elbow macaroni, cooked and drained
- 3 cups cubed cooked chicken
- 1 jar (2 ounces) diced pimientos, drained
- 1 teaspoon salt
- 1/2 teaspoon pepper
- Snipped fresh parsley, optional

In a large saucepan, melt butter. Stir in flour until combined. Add cream and 1-1/2 cups of the broth all at once; stir until smooth. Cook and stir until thickened and bubbly; cook and stir 2 minutes more. Remove from the heat; add the cheese and stir until melted. Stir in macaroni, chicken, pimientos, salt and pepper. Add additional broth if needed. Pour into a 3-qt. baking dish. Bake, uncovered, at 350° for 40 minutes or until heated through. Sprinkle with parsley if desired. **Yield:** 6-8 servings.

> **EASY EQUIVALENT.** A 3-pound chicken will yield about 2-1/2 to 3 cups of cut-up cooked chicken.

Garden Potato Salad

The tasty dressing on this potato salad makes it homemade special! A great combination of flavors is a real treat and gives a traditional recipe a new twist. It's perfect for almost any occasion.

- 6 large potatoes (about 3 pounds), cooked, peeled and cubed
- 4 hard-cooked eggs, sliced
- 2 celery ribs, diced
- 6 green onions with tops, sliced
- 6 radishes, sliced
- 1 teaspoon salt
- 1/2 teaspoon pepper
- DRESSING:
- 3 eggs, beaten
- 1/4 cup vinegar
- 1/4 cup sugar
- 1/2 teaspoon dry mustard
- 1/2 teaspoon salt
- 1 cup mayonnaise *or* salad dressing

In a large bowl, combine potatoes, eggs, celery, green onions, radishes, salt and pepper; set aside. For dressing, combine eggs, vinegar, sugar, dry mustard and salt in a saucepan. Cook and stir over medium heat until thickened. Cool. Stir in mayonnaise; mix well. Pour over potato mixture; toss to coat. Refrigerate for several hours. **Yield:** 8 servings.

Picnic Baked Beans

I loved it when my mom made these classic baked beans...now I love to make them for my family. They have great old-fashioned flavor and are a real crowd-pleaser. I like to make them for potlucks, picnics or as part of everyday family dinners.

- 3 cups dry navy beans (about 1-1/2 pounds)
- 4 quarts cold water, *divided*
- 1 medium onion, chopped
- 1 cup ketchup
- 1 cup packed brown sugar
- 2 tablespoons molasses
- 1 tablespoon salt
- 2 teaspoons dry mustard
- 1/4 pound bacon, cooked and crumbled

Rinse beans; place in a Dutch oven with 2 qts. water. Bring to a boil; reduce heat and simmer for 3 minutes. Remove from the heat and let stand for 1 hour. Drain and rinse. Return beans to Dutch oven with remaining water; bring to a boil. Reduce heat; simmer for 1 hour or until beans are tender. Drain, reserving cooking liquid. In the Dutch oven or a 3-qt. baking dish, combine beans, 1 cup cooking liquid, onion, ketchup, brown sugar, molasses, salt, mustard and bacon; mix well. Cover and bake at 300° for 2 to 2-1/2 hours or until beans are as thick as desired. Stir occasionally and add more of the reserved cooking liquid if needed. **Yield:** 16 servings.

Peanut Butter Pie

This smooth, creamy pie with a big peanut butter taste reminds me of Mom. It's sure to be a hit around your house, too. I especially like to make this dessert in the summer because it's simple to prepare and the kitchen stays cool.

- 2 packages (3 ounces *each*) cook and serve vanilla *or* chocolate pudding
- 4 cups milk
- 1/2 cup creamy peanut butter
- 3/4 cup confectioners' sugar
- 1 pastry shell (9 inches), baked
- Whipped cream

In a saucepan, cook pudding and milk over medium heat until thickened and bubbly. Remove from the heat and cool slightly. Meanwhile, in a bowl, cut peanut butter into confectioners' sugar until small crumbs form. (Peanut butter consistency may vary; add additional confectioners' sugar if necessary.) Set aside about 2 tablespoons of crumbs; sprinkle remaining mixture into pie shell. Pour pudding over crumbs. Chill until set. Top with whipped cream; sprinkle reserved crumbs on top. **Yield:** 6-8 servings.

Pictured clockwise from the bottom left:
Old-Fashioned Pot Roast, Peach Bavarian,
Garlic-Buttered Green Beans and Parsley Potatoes.

PLEASING POT ROAST IS PERFECT ANYTIME!

"MY MOM loved cooking," recalls country cook Adeline Piscitelli of Sayreville, New Jersey.

"Mom made delicious meals for our family, and she was always cooking for a wedding reception or other party. My sister and I liked to help her, and I learned a lot about cooking from working with Mom.

"This delicious pot roast meal is one Mom made often when I was growing up. Her flavorful Garlic-Buttered Green Beans, filling Parsley Potatoes and refreshing Peach Bavarian fruit mold were the perfect additions to the meal.

"Years later, I served these same dishes in the family restaurant my husband and I ran. Our customers raved about the tasty beef, potatoes and beans. I was always pleased to bring a taste of my home to their table.

"I'm retired from the restaurant business now, but I still like to do some catering. This pot roast meal is often requested…it's a comforting meal with a look and aroma that just says 'home cooking'!"

Old-Fashioned Pot Roast

I got this recipe from my mom, a great cook. My sister, dad and I loved it when she made her pot roast. Later, I served this dish in our restaurant for many years. It's a recipe that just says "home cooking".

  1 boneless beef chuck roast
    (about 3 pounds)
  6 tablespoons all-purpose flour,
    divided
  6 tablespoons butter *or*
    margarine, *divided*
  3 cups hot water
  2 teaspoons beef bouillon
    granules
  1 medium onion, quartered
  1 celery rib, cut into pieces
  1 teaspoon salt
1/2 teaspoon pepper
  4 carrots, cut into
    2-inch pieces

Sprinkle the roast with 1 tablespoon flour. In a Dutch oven, brown the roast on all sides in half of the butter. Add the water, bouillon, onion, celery, salt and pepper; bring to a boil. Reduce heat; cover and simmer for 1 hour. Add carrots; cover and simmer 45-60 minutes longer or until meat is tender. Remove meat and carrots to a serving platter and keep warm. Strain cooking juices; set aside. In the same Dutch oven, melt remaining butter. Stir in remaining flour; cook and stir until bubbly. Add 2 cups of the cooking juices and blend until smooth. Cook and stir until thickened; add additional cooking juices until gravy has desired consistency. **Yield:** 6-8 servings.

Parsley Potatoes

This simple recipe is anything but plain. The fresh flavor of parsley is perfect with hot buttered potatoes—it adds a little extra zip. I used this recipe when I did all the cooking at our restaurant, and customers loved it.

  2 pounds potatoes, peeled and
    cut into 2-inch pieces
1/2 cup butter *or* margarine,
    melted
1/4 cup minced fresh parsley
Salt and pepper to taste

In a saucepan, cook potatoes in water to cover until tender; drain. Combine butter and parsley; pour over the potatoes and toss to coat. Season with salt and pepper. **Yield:** 6-8 servings.

DO YOUR POTATOES tend to discolor slightly when boiling them? Keep them white by adding a teaspoon of vinegar to the water.

Garlic-Buttered Green Beans

These dressed-up beans are simple to make but look and taste special. They're a perfect side dish for nearly any meal so I make them often.

  1 pound fresh *or* frozen green
    beans
1/2 cup sliced fresh mushrooms
  6 tablespoons butter *or*
    margarine
  2 to 3 teaspoons onion powder
  1 to 1-1/2 teaspoons garlic
    powder
Salt and pepper to taste

Cook green beans in water to cover until crisp-tender. Meanwhile, in a skillet, saute mushrooms in butter until tender. Add onion powder and garlic powder. Drain beans; add to skillet and toss. Season with salt and pepper. **Yield:** 6 servings.

Peach Bavarian

Fruit molds are my specialty, and I enjoy making and serving them. This one, with its refreshing peach taste, makes a colorful salad or dessert. And its impressive appearance is perfect for company.

  1 can (16 ounces) sliced
    peaches
  2 packages (3 ounces *each*)
    peach- *or* apricot-flavored
    gelatin
1/2 cup sugar
  2 cups boiling water
  1 teaspoon almond extract
  1 carton (8 ounces) frozen
    whipped topping, thawed
Additional sliced peaches, optional

Drain peaches, reserving 2/3 cup juice. Chop peaches into small pieces; set aside. In a bowl, dissolve gelatin and sugar in boiling water. Stir in reserved syrup. Chill until slightly thickened. Stir extract into whipped topping; gently fold into gelatin mixture. Fold in peaches. Pour into an oiled 6-cup mold. Chill overnight. Unmold; garnish with additional peaches if desired. **Yield:** 8-10 servings.

Pictured clockwise from the top:
Chocolate Mayonnaise Cake, Chunky Applesauce,
Breaded Pork Chops and Cheese Potatoes.

BIRTHDAY MEAL WAS WORTH THE WAIT

"MY MOM is such a wonderful lady," relates Deborah Amrine of Grand Haven, Michigan.

"While growing up, she had a knack for making my brother, my two sisters and me feel so special, especially on our birthdays. That's when we would choose our favorite meal and she would prepare it for us.

"We could hardly wait for each other's birthdays so that we could sample one of our mom's many memorable meals. I never looked forward to birthdays so much!

"Of course, my family would tease me because year after year, I'd always request the exact same meal...Mom's mouth-watering Breaded Pork Chops, creamy Cheese Potatoes, slightly-sweet Chunky Applesauce and irresistible Chocolate Mayonnaise Cake."

The hearty, flavorful meal pictured at left still reminds Deborah of growing up in Columbus, Ohio, she says.

"We kids were always underfoot as Mom cooked, using recipes she got from her mother. The pork chops sizzling in the pan made the house smell so good!

"Whenever my husband, our three boys and I visit Mom, I still request this meal. Not surprising, the boys now think this is one of *their* mom's best meals!"

Chunky Applesauce

There's just something extra special about homemade applesauce...and this version is no exception. The simple recipe is tart and not too sweet. It makes the perfect side dish, especially with pork chops or a pork roast.

- **8 cups chopped peeled tart cooking apples (about 3-1/2 pounds)**
- **1/2 cup packed brown sugar**
- **2 teaspoons vanilla extract**
- **1 teaspoon ground cinnamon**

Place apples, brown sugar, vanilla and cinnamon in a large saucepan or Dutch oven. Cover and cook over medium-low heat for 30-40 minutes or until apples are tender. Remove from the heat; mash apples (a potato masher works well) until sauce is desired consistency. Serve warm or cold. **Yield:** 6 servings (about 3-1/2 cups).

A-PEEL-ING IDEA. Apples are easier to peel if you first cut them into quarters.

Breaded Pork Chops

These traditional pork chops have a wonderful home-cooked flavor like the ones Mom used to make when I was young...and like she still does when I come to visit. The breading makes them crispy outside and tender and juicy inside. Why not treat your family to them tonight?

- **1/2 cup milk**
- **1 egg, lightly beaten**
- **6 pork chops (1 inch thick)**
- **1-1/2 cups crushed saltines**
- **1/4 cup cooking oil**

In a shallow pan, combine milk and egg. Dip each pork chop in the mixture, then coat with cracker crumbs, patting to make a thick coating. Heat oil in a large skillet. Cook pork chops, uncovered, for about 8-10 minutes per side or until browned and no pink remains inside. **Yield:** 6 servings.

TATER TIP. Don't buy potatoes that are soft or have excessive cuts, cracks, bruises or discoloration. And avoid green potatoes—they've been exposed to light and are actually "sunburned," which turns the flavor bitter. You can peel or pare the green away, but if the potato is more than half green, throw it out.

Cheese Potatoes

Don't let the simple name and basic ingredients fool you—this recipe has anything but ordinary taste. The hearty potatoes have a wonderful cheesy flavor and melt in your mouth. You'll love them because they're easy to prepare and impressive to serve.

- **3 tablespoons butter *or* margarine**
- **6 large potatoes, peeled and thinly sliced**
- **1 teaspoon salt**
- **1/4 teaspoon pepper**
- **1 cup milk**
- **2 cups (8 ounces) shredded cheddar cheese**
- **Chopped fresh parsley**

Melt butter in a large nonstick skillet. Cook potatoes until almost tender and lightly browned. Sprinkle with salt and pepper. Pour milk over all; cook gently until milk is absorbed. Sprinkle with cheese and allow to melt. Stir; sprinkle with parsley and serve immediately. **Yield:** 6 servings.

Chocolate Mayonnaise Cake

Mom always made this special cake for my birthday meal. It's very moist and has a nice, light chocolate taste. And the flavorful frosting is the perfect topping.

- **2 cups all-purpose flour**
- **1 cup sugar**
- **3 tablespoons baking cocoa**
- **2 teaspoons baking soda**
- **1 cup water**
- **1 cup mayonnaise**
- **1 teaspoon vanilla extract**
- **BROWN SUGAR FROSTING:**
- **1/4 cup butter *or* margarine**
- **1/2 cup packed brown sugar**
- **2 tablespoons milk**
- **1-3/4 cups sifted confectioners' sugar**

In a large mixing bowl, combine flour, sugar, cocoa and baking soda. Add water, mayonnaise and vanilla; beat at medium speed until thoroughly combined. Pour into a greased 9-in. square or 11-in. x 7-in. x 2-in. baking pan. Bake at 350° for 30-35 minutes or until cake tests done. Cool completely. For frosting, melt butter in a saucepan. Stir in brown sugar; cook and stir until bubbly. Remove from the heat and stir in milk. Gradually add confectioners' sugar; beat by hand until frosting is of spreading consistency. Immediately frost cake. **Yield:** 9-12 servings.

*Pictured clockwise from the top: Lemon Bars,
Homemade Bread, Carrot Raisin Salad
and Chicken and Rice Dinner.*

HUSBAND COOKS UP TASTY MEMORIES

"AS the youngest of six children, I learned pretty quickly to not be bashful at supper time," recalls Peter Baumert of Jameson, Missouri.

"And I have to confess that I would often rush through the blessing so that I could be the first in the family to get a taste of Mom's home-cooked meals. It smelled so good, I could hardly wait!

"When Mom would *finally* pass the food, my brothers and I ate quickly so we'd be sure to get seconds. Of course, Mom always made plenty. But we weren't taking any chances, especially when she served our favorite meal…Chicken and Rice Dinner, Carrot Raisin Salad, Homemade Bread and, for dessert, Lemon Bars."

The delicious meal pictured at left reminds Peter of spring and summer on the family's 160-acre homestead in Nebraska, where his parents still live and still prepare such wonderful meals.

"When I left home as a bachelor, Mom sent along that chicken recipe, knowing it was my favorite. For years, it was my only recipe card," says Peter.

He passed on that treasured card to wife Denise, who checked with his mom for the recipes to round out the menu, which she now fixes often.

Carrot Raisin Salad

This colorful traditional salad is one of my mother-in-law's favorites…and one of mine, too. It's fun to eat because of its crunchy texture, and the raisins give it a slightly sweet flavor. Plus, it's easy to prepare, so it's perfect for any meal.

✓ This tasty dish uses less sugar, salt and fat. Recipe includes *Diabetic Exchanges*.

    4 cups shredded carrots (about 4 to 5 large)
    3/4 to 1-1/2 cups raisins

    1/4 cup salad dressing
    2 tablespoons sugar
    2 to 3 tablespoons milk

Place carrots and raisins in a bowl. In another bowl, mix together salad dressing, sugar and enough milk to reach a salad dressing consistency. Pour over carrot mixture and toss to coat. **Yield:** 8 servings. **Diabetic Exchanges:** One serving (prepared with skim milk and 1 cup raisins) equals 1 fruit, 1 vegetable, 1/2 fat; also, 110 calories, 80 mg sodium, 2 mg cholesterol, 24 gm carbohydrate, 1 gm protein, 2 gm fat.

Lemon Bars

Memorable family meals were complete when these tangy bars were served, my husband remembers from his childhood. That's still true today for our family. Their sweetness rounds out the meal, but the lemony flavor keeps them light. Don't expect many leftovers once family and friends taste these bars! I often make a double batch to keep on hand.

CRUST:
    1 cup all-purpose flour
    1/3 cup butter *or* margarine, softened
    1/4 cup confectioners' sugar
TOPPING:
    1 cup sugar
    2 eggs
    2 tablespoons all-purpose flour
    2 tablespoons lemon juice
    1/2 teaspoon lemon extract
    1/2 teaspoon baking powder
    1/4 teaspoon salt
Confectioners' sugar

Combine crust ingredients and pat into an 8-in. square baking pan. Bake at 375° for 15 minutes. Meanwhile, for topping, combine sugar, eggs, flour, lemon juice, extract, baking powder and salt in a mixing bowl. Mix until frothy; pour over crust. Bake at 375° for 18-22 minutes or until light golden brown. Dust with confectioners' sugar. **Yield:** 9 servings.

Chicken and Rice Dinner

My family lines up for seconds of this hearty main dish from my mother-in-law, Mary Lou Baumert—a great cook! In this easy tasty recipe, the chicken bakes to a beautiful golden brown, and the moist rice is packed with flavor. The taste is unbeatable.

    1 broiler/fryer chicken (2 to 3 pounds), cut up
    1/4 to 1/3 cup all-purpose flour
    2 tablespoons cooking oil
    2-1/3 cups water
    1-1/2 cups uncooked long grain rice
    1 cup milk
    1 teaspoon poultry seasoning
    1 teaspoon salt
    1/2 teaspoon pepper
Chopped fresh parsley

Dredge chicken pieces in flour. In a skillet, heat oil on medium and brown chicken on all sides. Meanwhile, combine water, rice, milk, poultry seasoning, salt and pepper. Pour into a greased 13-in. x 9-in. x 2-in. baking pan. Top with chicken. Cover tightly with foil and bake at 350° for 55 minutes or until rice and chicken are tender. Sprinkle with parsley before serving. **Yield:** 4-6 servings.

> **POULTRY POINTER.** After working with raw poultry, always be sure to thoroughly wash your hands, the utensils used and the surface with hot soapy water.

Homemade Bread

My husband recalls that on more than one occasion while he was growing up, he stayed home from school sick, napped on the couch and woke to the aroma of his mother's freshly baked bread. That's enough to make anyone feel better!

    2 cups warm water (105° to 115°)
    2 packages (1/4 ounce *each*) active dry yeast
    2/3 cup powdered milk
    2 tablespoons butter *or* margarine, melted
    2 tablespoons sugar
    1 tablespoon salt
    6 to 7 cups all-purpose flour

In a large bowl, stir together warm water and yeast. Let stand until dissolved. Stir in milk, butter, sugar, salt and enough flour to form a stiff dough. Turn out onto a floured surface and knead until smooth and elastic, about 10-12 minutes. Place in a greased bowl, turning once to grease top. Cover and let rise in a warm place until doubled, about 1 hour. Punch down and divide in half. Shape into two loaves and place in greased 8-in. x 4-in. x 2-in. pans. Cover and let rise until doubled, about 1 hour. Bake at 400° for 30 minutes or until golden brown. **Yield:** 2 loaves.

MEALS ON A BUDGET...
FROM FRUGAL COOKS

Feed Your Family...for 84¢ Per Plate!

FEED your family for pennies a person? Even at today's prices, it can be done!

In this chapter, some of the country's best cooks share their recipes for frugal but flavorful meals using ingredients purchased in local grocery stores.

The extra-economical meal featured here comes from Kim Stoller of Smithville, Ohio, who estimates the cost of just 84¢ a setting.

"These savory burgers are tasty inside and cook up golden brown and crispy on the outside," relates Kim. "They're also simple and quick to make."

Kim pairs her burgers with a great-tasting, colorful salad that contains a mixture of crunchy, fresh ingredients. "Apple salad really goes well with Tuna Burgers or any other sandwiches," Kim says.

Tuna Burgers

- **1 can (6 to 7 ounces) tuna, drained and flaked**
- **1/2 cup dry bread crumbs**
- **1/2 cup finely chopped celery**
- **1/3 cup mayonnaise**
- **1/4 cup finely chopped onion**
- **2 tablespoons chili sauce**
- **1 egg, beaten**
- **2 tablespoons butter *or* margarine**
- **4 hamburger buns, split and toasted**

Lettuce, optional
Sliced tomatoes, optional

In a bowl, combine tuna, bread crumbs, celery, mayonnaise, onion, chili sauce and egg. Shape into four patties. Melt butter in a skillet; cook patties for about 4-5 minutes per side or until lightly browned. Serve on buns with lettuce and tomatoes if desired. **Yield:** 4 servings.

Summer Apple Salad

- **3 medium tart red apples, cored and diced**
- **1 can (8 ounces) pineapple tidbits, drained**
- **1-1/2 cups sliced celery**
- **1 cup grape halves**
- **1 carrot, shredded**
- **1/2 cup coarsely chopped almonds**
- **3/4 cup sour cream**
- **1 tablespoon sugar**
- **1/2 teaspoon lemon juice**

In a large salad bowl, combine apples, pineapple, celery, grapes, carrot and almonds. In a small bowl, combine sour cream, sugar and lemon juice; mix well. Add to apple mixture and toss to coat. Chill. **Yield:** 12 servings.

Feed Your Family...for $1.14 Per Plate!

DARLENE Alexander of Nekoosa, Wisconsin estimates that the flavorful meal pictured below costs just $1.14 a person.

"With this hearty main-dish recipe, your bread is baked right in the casserole," Darlene points out. "My family loves this dish's slightly spicy flavor."

Along with Western Beef and Cornmeal Pie, Darlene serves Tangy Fruit Salad as a sweet and refreshing side dish or dessert.

"The complete meal covers all four food groups. Not only is this frugal meal delicious, it's fast as well.

"I got these recipes from friends years ago," she relates. "Besides being great for family meals, they're both perfect for church potlucks."

With the money you save, you can treat your family to a Western movie!

Tangy Fruit Salad

- 1 can (20 ounces) pineapple chunks, juice drained and reserved
- 1 package (3.4 ounces) instant vanilla pudding mix
- 1/4 cup dry orange-flavored instant breakfast drink
- 1 can (11 ounces) mandarin oranges, drained
- 1 can (16 ounces) fruit cocktail, drained
- 2 bananas, sliced
- 2 apples *or* pears, cut into chunks
- 1 cup sliced fresh strawberries, optional

In a small bowl, combine reserved pineapple juice, pudding mix and breakfast drink; set aside. In a large bowl, combine all the fruit. Fold juice mixture into fruit. Refrigerate before serving.
Yield: 6-8 servings.

Western Beef and Cornmeal Pie

FILLING:
- 1 pound ground beef
- 1 can (11 ounces) Mexican-style corn, drained
- 1 can (6 ounces) tomato paste
- 1 cup (4 ounces) shredded cheddar cheese
- 3/4 cup barbecue sauce
- 1/2 teaspoon salt
- 1/2 teaspoon chili powder

CRUST:
- 1 cup all-purpose flour
- 1/2 cup cornmeal
- 1/2 cup milk
- 1/4 cup butter *or* margarine, softened
- 1 egg
- 2 tablespoons sugar
- 1 teaspoon baking powder
- 1 teaspoon salt
- 1 cup (4 ounces) shredded cheddar cheese, *divided*

In a skillet, brown ground beef; drain. Stir in remaining filling ingredients; set aside. In a large bowl, combine all crust ingredients except 1/2 cup cheddar cheese; mix well. Spread on the bottom and up the sides of a greased 2-1/2-qt. baking dish or 10-in. ovenproof skillet. Pour filling into prepared crust. Sprinkle with remaining cheese. Bake, uncovered, at 400° for 25-30 minutes.
Yield: 6-8 servings.

Feed Your Family... for $1.34 Per Plate!

FOR THIS inexpensive and tasty meal, three great country cooks prove you don't have to sacrifice flavor to be frugal.

They estimate that the appealing dishes pictured above cost just $1.34 a setting.

Moist and delicious Teriyaki Chicken comes from Jean Clark of Albion, Maine. "These drumsticks get their great flavor and golden color from the tasty, easy-to-prepare marinade," she explains.

From Columbus, Mississippi, Judy Howle shares her family's favorite Scalloped Pineapple Casserole. "This sweet and satisfying side dish disappears quickly whenever I prepare it," Judy notes.

French Dressing from Mrs. Robert Lieske of Ripon, Wisconsin adds tangy flavor to an ordinary lettuce salad. The price of this meal includes the head of lettuce plus 2 tablespoons of dressing per person.

Add whatever garden-fresh vegetables you have on hand to the salad to complete an inexpensive meal that's sure to become a favorite in your family.

Teriyaki Chicken

3/4 cup soy sauce
1/4 cup vegetable oil
3 tablespoons brown sugar
2 tablespoons cooking sherry, optional
1/2 teaspoon ground ginger
1/2 teaspoon garlic powder
12 chicken drumsticks (about 2-1/2 pounds)

In a large glass dish, combine the soy sauce, oil, brown sugar, cooking sherry if desired, ginger and garlic powder; mix well. Add drumsticks; turn to coat. Cover and refrigerate for 1 hour or overnight, turning occasionally. Drain and discard marinade. Place chicken in a single layer on a foil-lined baking sheet. Bake at 375° for 35-45 minutes or until chicken is no longer pink. **Yield:** 6 servings.

Scalloped Pineapple Casserole

3/4 cup butter *or* margarine
1-1/4 cups sugar
3 eggs

1 can (20 ounces) crushed pineapple, well drained
1-1/2 teaspoons lemon juice
4 cups firmly packed cubed white bread (crusts removed)

In a mixing bowl, cream butter and sugar. Add eggs, one at a time, beating well after each addition. Stir in the pineapple and lemon juice. Gently fold in bread cubes. Spoon into a greased 2-qt. baking dish. Bake, uncovered, at 350° for 40-45 minutes or until top is lightly golden. Serve warm. **Yield:** 6 servings.

French Dressing

1 cup vegetable oil
2/3 cup ketchup
2/3 cup sugar
1/2 cup vinegar
2 teaspoons paprika
2 teaspoons salt
1 small onion, quartered

Combine all ingredients in a blender container. Cover and blend at medium-high until well mixed. Chill before serving. Store in a covered container in the refrigerator. **Yield:** 3 cups.

Feed Your Family...for 97¢ Per Plate!

NOTHING feeds a family more economically than a hearty casserole served with fresh-from-the-oven bread.

The meal featured here comes from two cooks who estimate the cost of just 97¢ a setting.

Savory Sausage 'n' Sauerkraut comes from Robert Walker of Glen Dale, West Virginia. "Not only is it economical, it's delicious. You're family will love the hearty, down-home flavor. I'm positive you'll serve it often," Robert says.

Carol Allen of McLeansboro, Illinois shares her recipe for Favorite Corn Bread. "A great addition to any meal, this corn bread uses basic ingredients and is simple to make," reports Carol.

This satisfying spread goes to show you don't have to forgo flavor when eating inexpensively.

Sausage 'n' Sauerkraut

- **2 pounds fresh Polish sausage**
- **1 can (16 ounces) sauerkraut, rinsed and drained**
- **1 can (16 ounces) tomatoes with liquid, cut up**
- **1 cup chopped celery**
- **1 large onion, chopped**
- **1 large green pepper, chopped**
- **3 tablespoons brown sugar**
- **1 bay leaf**
- **1 teaspoon dried oregano**
- **1/2 teaspoon salt**
- **1/4 teaspoon pepper**
- **Mashed potatoes, optional**

Cut the sausage into 1-in. slices; saute in a Dutch oven until fully cooked and browned. Drain. Add sauerkraut, tomatoes with liquid, celery, onion, green pepper, brown sugar and seasonings; mix well. Cover and simmer for 20-25 minutes or until vegetables are tender. Remove bay leaf. Serve over mashed potatoes if desired. **Yield:** 8 servings.

Favorite Corn Bread

- **1 cup all-purpose flour**
- **1 cup cornmeal**
- **1/4 cup sugar**
- **4 teaspoons baking powder**
- **3/4 teaspoon salt**
- **1 cup milk**
- **2 eggs**
- **1/4 cup shortening**

In a mixing bowl, combine flour, cornmeal, sugar, baking powder and salt. Add the milk, eggs and shortening; beat for 1 minute. Pour into a greased 9-in. square baking pan. Bake at 425° for 20-25 minutes or until bread is golden brown and tests done. **Yield:** 9 servings.

Feed Your Family...for 65¢ Per Plate!

THE EXTRA-ECONOMICAL meal here comes from Joyce McDowell of Winchester, Ohio, who estimates a cost of just *65¢ a person.*

"Nothing chases hunger away quicker than a tasty sandwich and steaming bowl of hot soup," explains Joyce, Extension home economist for Adams County, Ohio. And the unbeatable combination pictured above makes a satisfying and nutritious meal.

With help from sons Chad and Chris, Joyce and her husband, Gary, an agriculture teacher, raise registered Polled Hereford cattle and tobacco. So by the time Joyce gets home from a full day of work, they're ready to eat!

"These two dishes are perfect for our hectic lives because they're easy and quick to assemble," adds the busy farm woman and mom.

To round out this pleasing, penny-pinching supper, Joyce suggests you can add a favorite homemade dessert.

Broccoli Soup

3 cups *or* **2 cans (14-1/2 ounces each) chicken broth**
1 large bunch broccoli, chopped (about 5 cups)
1-1/2 cups chopped onion
3 bay leaves
6 tablespoons butter *or* **margarine**
7 tablespoons all-purpose flour
3 cups milk
Salt and pepper to taste

In a saucepan, bring chicken broth to a boil. Add broccoli, onion and bay leaves. Reduce heat and simmer until broccoli is tender; remove bay leaves. Meanwhile, in another saucepan, melt butter. Stir in flour to make a smooth paste. Gradually stir in milk. Cook over medium heat until mixture is hot and thickened, stirring occasionally. Add 1 cup of broccoli stock to milk mixture; stir until well blended. Gradually add remaining broccoli stock to milk mixture. Heat and stir until well-blended. Season with salt and pepper. **Yield:** 6 servings.

Curried Egg Salad

1/2 cup mayonnaise
1/2 teaspoon honey
1/2 teaspoon ground curry
Dash ground ginger
6 hard-cooked eggs, coarsely chopped
3 green onions, sliced
6 slices whole wheat bread
Sliced tomato, optional

In a bowl, blend mayonnaise, honey, curry and ginger. Stir in eggs and green onions. Divide among bread slices and spread to cover. Top with a tomato slice if desired. **Yield:** 6 servings.

Feed Your Family...for 68¢ Per Plate!

MARCIA SALISBURY's favorite frugal meal to serve her family is Red Beans and Rice and Corn Bread Squares. "I often add leftover ham or sausage to the basic recipe to add extra flavor," relates the Extension home economist for Waukesha County, Wisconsin.

Red Beans and Rice

1/2 pound dry kidney beans, rinsed
1/2 pound dry pinto beans, rinsed
4 cups water
4 cups chicken broth
2 garlic cloves, minced
2 bay leaves
1 can (14-1/2 ounces) tomatoes with liquid, chopped
1 jar (4 ounces) chopped pimientos, drained
1 large green pepper, chopped
1 large sweet red pepper, chopped
1 large onion, chopped
1 cup chopped celery
1 can (4 ounces) diced green chilies
1 teaspoon paprika
1 teaspoon salt
1 tablespoon vinegar
1/4 cup snipped fresh parsley
1/4 to 1/2 teaspoon crushed red pepper flakes
1/4 to 1/2 teaspoon ground cumin
1/4 to 1/2 teaspoon hot pepper sauce
Hot cooked rice

Place beans in a Dutch oven with water. Bring to a boil; simmer 2 minutes. Remove from the heat. Cover and let stand 1 hour. Drain and rinse beans. Return to Dutch oven with broth, garlic and bay leaves; bring to a boil. Reduce heat; cover and simmer for 1-1/4 hours. Stir in all remaining ingredients. Cover and simmer for 1 hour or until beans and vegetables are tender and gravy is thick. Remove bay leaves. Serve over rice. This dish keeps well. **Yield:** 12 servings.

Corn Bread Squares

1 cup all-purpose flour
1 cup yellow cornmeal
1/4 cup sugar
2 teaspoons baking powder
3/4 teaspoon salt
2 eggs, beaten
1 cup milk
1/4 cup vegetable oil

In a mixing bowl, combine flour, cornmeal, sugar, baking powder and salt. Add eggs, milk and oil. Beat just until moistened. Spoon into a greased 8-in. square baking pan. Bake at 400° for 20-25 minutes or until bread tests done. **Yield:** 9 servings.

MEALS IN MINUTES

HOMEMADE SAUCE MADE EASY

TAKING TIME in the kitchen to prepare an elaborate meal can be a pleasure for those of us who enjoy cooking—when there's time to do it.

Often, however, even the most accomplished cook has a hungry family anxiously waiting for her to "bring on the food"...and only minutes to make it.

In this chapter, cooks from across the country share quick favorite dishes that together make for meals you can take from start to serving in *half an hour*.

You'll find this first fast-but-flavorful meal pictured at right has a tangy Italian taste to it:

● Quick Italian Spaghetti has been a standby for Ruth Peterson of Jenison, Michigan for some 40 years now. "I can make it in a jiffy, and there's no other spaghetti recipe my husband's even interested in trying!" Ruth says.

● Celery Seed Bread comes from Norma Erne of Albuquerque, New Mexico, who reports, "This is my most requested recipe."

● Crunchy Vegetable Salad is a tasty and colorful side dish Linda Russell of Exeter, Ontario frequently puts on her table. "Kids love it!" she relates.

● Taffy Apple Dip quickly completes the meal. "My mother-in-law gave me this recipe," notes Sue Gronholz of Columbus, Wisconsin. "It's simple to make, and it tastes like the real thing!"

Crunchy Vegetable Salad

 2 cups cauliflowerets
 2 cups broccoli florets
 2 carrots, thinly sliced
 1 small zucchini, sliced
 1 small red onion, sliced
 1 to 1-1/2 cups Italian salad
   dressing

Combine vegetables in a large mixing bowl. Pour salad dressing over and toss to coat evenly. Refrigerate until serving time. **Yield:** 4-6 servings.

Celery Seed Bread

 6 tablespoons butter *or*
   margarine, softened
1/2 teaspoon celery seed
1/4 teaspoon paprika
1/4 teaspoon dried parsley flakes
 4 hot dog rolls, sliced

In a mixing bowl, combine butter, celery seed, paprika and parsley flakes, stirring well to blend. Spread on cut sides of each roll. Place on baking sheet; broil until golden brown. **Yield:** 4 servings.

SUPER SPAGHETTI! If you like your spaghetti sauce a little sweeter, try adding 1 tablespoon of grape jam to your favorite sauce.

Quick Italian Spaghetti

1/2 pound ground beef
3/4 cup thinly sliced green onions
 2 teaspoons sugar
 1 teaspoon Worcestershire
   sauce
1/2 teaspoon salt
1/8 teaspoon pepper
 3 cans (8 ounces *each*)
   tomato sauce
 1 can (2-1/4 ounces) sliced
   ripe olives, drained
Cooked spaghetti
Grated Parmesan *or* Romano
   cheese
Real bacon bits, optional

In a skillet, brown ground beef and onions. Add next five ingredients; cover and simmer for 10 minutes. Add olives; simmer 5 minutes longer. Spoon over spaghetti; sprinkle with cheese and bacon bits if desired. **Yield:** 4 servings.

Taffy Apple Dip

 1 package (8 ounces) cream
   cheese, softened
3/4 cup packed brown sugar
 1 tablespoon vanilla extract
1/2 cup chopped peanuts
 6 apples, cut into wedges

In a small bowl, beat cream cheese, brown sugar and vanilla until smooth. Spread mixture on a small serving plate; top with nuts. Serve with apple wedges. **Yield:** 6 servings.

A Plateful of Flavor

WHETHER you're running errands, working on a project or spending time with family, suppertime can suddenly creep up on you!

Not only can the down-home meal pictured at right be prepared in a snap, it's guaranteed to satisfy your hungry clan…in 30 minutes or less!

• Hamburger Spanish Rice is a favorite busy-day dish for Bernice Morris of Marshfield, Missouri. "Even though we're retired, I'm usually working on crafts right up to mealtime," reports Bernice. "So I often prepare this quick-and-easy main dish. My family loves the combination of ground beef, rice and seasonings and thinks the flavor is fantastic!"

• Wilted Lettuce Salad comes from Alberta McKay of Bartlesville, Oklahoma. "Don't let the name of this salad fool you," relates Alberta. "This version of Spinach Salad with Hot Bacon Dressing will perk up your family's taste buds."

• Quick Biscuits from Diane Hixon of Niceville, Florida make a satisfying accompaniment to the meal. "I never made biscuits until I tried this two-ingredient recipe," Diane explains. "Now my husband wants biscuits all the time!"

• Ambrosia Pudding is a speedy and special way to round out this menu. "Serving this cool and creamy dessert in a parfait glass really showcases the layers," notes Debbie Jones of California, Maryland.

Hamburger Spanish Rice

1 pound lean ground beef
1 medium onion, chopped
1/2 green pepper, chopped
1 cup uncooked instant rice
1 can (15 ounces) tomato sauce
3/4 cup hot water
1 teaspoon prepared mustard
1 teaspoon Worcestershire sauce
1 teaspoon salt
1 teaspoon sugar

In a skillet, brown beef, onion, green pepper and rice. Add remaining ingredients; mix well. Bring to a boil. Reduce heat; cover and simmer 20-25 minutes or until the rice is tender. **Yield:** 4-6 servings.

Wilted Lettuce Salad

8 cups torn leaf lettuce *or* spinach
1/4 cup sliced green onions
Pepper to taste
3 bacon strips, diced
1 tablespoon white wine vinegar
2 teaspoons lemon juice
1/2 teaspoon sugar
1/4 teaspoon salt
1 hard-cooked egg, chopped

Place lettuce or spinach and onions in a large salad bowl. Sprinkle with pepper; set aside. In a large skillet, cook bacon until crisp. Do not drain off drippings. Stir in vinegar, lemon juice, sugar and salt. Pour over lettuce and toss gently until well coated. Top with hard-cooked egg. Serve immediately. **Yield:** 6 servings.

RUST-PROOF. Wrap your washed lettuce in paper towel when storing it in the refrigerator to prevent "rust".

Quick Biscuits

2 cups self-rising flour
1 cup heavy cream

In a large bowl, combine the flour and cream. Turn out onto a floured board; knead for 5 minutes or until no longer sticky. On a floured surface, roll dough to a 1/2-in. thickness. Cut into 3-in. biscuits. Place on a greased baking sheet. Bake at 450° for 8-10 minutes. **Yield:** 9 biscuits. **Editor's Note:** If you don't have self-rising flour, add 1 tablespoon baking powder and 1 teaspoon salt to 2 cups all-purpose flour.

Ambrosia Pudding

1 package (3.4 ounces) instant vanilla pudding mix
2 cups cold milk
1/4 cup honey
2 teaspoons grated orange peel
1/4 teaspoon vanilla extract
1 cup whipping cream, whipped
1 banana, sliced
1 can (11 ounces) mandarin orange sections, drained
1/4 cup shredded coconut
1/4 cup sliced almonds

In a bowl, blend pudding and milk according to package directions. Add honey, orange peel and vanilla. Fold in the whipped cream. In individual dessert dishes, layer half of the pudding, banana slices, orange sections, coconut and almonds. Repeat the layers. Chill. **Yield:** 4-6 servings.

No More Fishing For Fast Foods

IF the hustle and bustle of everyday life keeps you out of the kitchen, a satisfying fast-to-fix meal like the one pictured at right is the perfect gift to give yourself and your family!

"I use this meal for my family and for guests, too," reports Jean Ann Perkins of Newburyport, Maryland. "It's a wonderful combination of colors and flavors—and is no fuss to prepare. So it's a perfect satisfying meal for your busy days...either during the week or on weekends.

"My husband just loves fish, and this delicious Baked Lemon Haddock is one of his favorites. And it's one of my best recipes because it can be made in a hurry. For a different kind of side dish, I like to serve Harvard Beets.

"Almonds give refreshing Orange and Onion Salad special flair. And Chocolate Mint Delight is a delectable dessert any time of year. Your family is guaranteed to love this meal!"

Baked Lemon Haddock

✓ This tasty dish uses less sugar, salt and fat. Recipe includes *Diabetic Exchanges*.

- 2 **pounds haddock fillets**
- 1 **cup seasoned dry bread crumbs**
- 1/4 **cup butter** *or* **margarine, melted**
- 2 **tablespoons dried parsley flakes**
- 2 **teaspoons grated lemon peel**
- 1/2 **teaspoon garlic powder**

Cut fish into serving-size pieces. Place in a greased 11-in. x 7-in. x 2-in. baking dish. Combine remaining ingredients; sprinkle over fish. Bake at 350° for 25 minutes or until fish flakes easily with a fork. **Yield:** 6 servings. **Diabetic Exchanges:** One serving (prepared with margarine) equals 3 lean meat, 1 starch; also, 239 calories, 650 mg sodium, 67 mg cholesterol, 15 gm carbohydrate, 25 gm protein, 9 gm fat.

Harvard Beets

- 1 **can (16 ounces) sliced beets**
- 1/4 **cup sugar**
- 1-1/2 **teaspoons cornstarch**
- 2 **tablespoons vinegar**
- 2 **tablespoons orange juice**
- 1 **tablespoon grated orange peel**

Drain beets, reserving 2 tablespoons juice; set beets and juice aside. In a saucepan, combine sugar and cornstarch. Add vinegar, orange juice and beet juice; bring to a boil. Reduce heat and simmer for 3-4 minutes or until thickened. Add beets and orange peel; heat through. **Yield:** 4-6 servings.

Orange and Onion Salad

- 1 **head Boston lettuce, separated into leaves**
- 1 **medium red onion, thinly sliced into rings**
- 1 **can (11 ounces) mandarin oranges, drained**

Sliced almonds
Bottled poppy seed dressing

Arrange lettuce leaves, onion and oranges on salad plates. Chill. Just before serving, sprinkle with almonds. Serve with poppy seed dressing. **Yield:** 4-6 servings.

Chocolate Mint Delight

- 1 **package (3.9 ounces) instant chocolate pudding mix**
- 2 **cups cold milk**
- 28 **miniature cream-filled chocolate cookies, crushed, *divided***
- 1/4 **cup crushed candy canes** *or* **peppermint candy**

Frozen chocolate-flavored whipped topping, thawed
Additional peppermint candy *or* **miniature candy canes**

Prepare pudding with milk according to package directions. Divide among individual dessert dishes. Reserve 2 tablespoons crushed cookies; sprinkle the remaining cookies over pudding. Top with crushed candy. Spoon whipped topping over candy. Sprinkle with reserved crushed cookies. Garnish with peppermints or miniature candy canes. **Yield:** 4-6 servings.

STOP SCRAMBLING FOR MORNING MEALS

THE BEST WAY to start out the day is with a hearty, scrumptious breakfast. But if you have a busy morning planned, you don't want to spend half of it in the kitchen.

A fast-to-fix breakfast meal—like the one pictured at right—is the answer to getting your gang off to a good start…in a hurry!

● Zucchini Scramble, shared by Betty Claycomb of Alverton, Pennsylvania, has a garden-fresh taste that's sure to please. "Whenever my family craves an egg dish, I often prepare this. It's a favorite because I can change it as other fresh vegetables become available. These scrambled eggs also make a tasty light lunch or dinner," Betty notes. "And it's easy to adjust the recipe for the number of servings needed."

● Pork Patties come from Lois Fetting of Nelson, Wisconsin. "What would breakfast be without the sizzling goodness of sausage?" Lois asks. With their down-home country flavor, these provide a taste-bud wake-up call with a variety of herbs and spices. And best of all, they're quick to put together.

● These deliciously moist Bran Muffins can bake while you're preparing your other menu items. Sent in by Amber Sampson of Somonauk, Illinois, these muffins are a nutritious and hearty addition to the meal. Serve them fresh-from-the-oven with butter or jam. Amber assures they're a great way to start the day and also make a tasty anytime snack!

Bran Muffins

✓ This tasty dish uses less sugar, salt and fat. Recipe includes *Diabetic Exchanges*.

- 1-1/4 cups all-purpose flour
- 1 tablespoon baking powder
- 1/3 cup sugar
- 1/2 teaspoon salt
- 1 cup 100% bran cereal
- 1 cup milk
- 1 egg
- 1/4 cup vegetable oil

Combine flour, baking powder, sugar and salt; set aside. In a mixing bowl, combine cereal and milk; let stand for 2 minutes. Add egg and oil; mix well. Add dry ingredients, stirring just until combined. Spoon into 12 greased muffin cups. Bake at 400° for 18-20 minutes or until golden brown. Serve warm. **Yield:** 1 dozen. **Diabetic Exchanges:** One serving (prepared with skim milk) equals 1-1/2 starch, 1/2 fat; also, 116 calories, 299 mg sodium, 18 mg cholesterol, 23 gm carbohydrate, 4 gm protein, 2 gm fat.

Pork Patties

- 1 pound lean ground pork
- 2 tablespoons water
- 1-1/2 teaspoons salt
- 1/2 teaspoon dried sage
- 1/4 teaspoon pepper
- 1/4 teaspoon ground nutmeg
- 1/4 teaspoon dried thyme
- Pinch ground ginger

In a bowl, combine all of the ingredients; mix well. Shape into six patties. Fry in a skillet until meat is browned and cooked throughout. **Yield:** 6 servings.

Zucchini Scramble

- 2 to 3 small zucchini (about 1 pound), sliced
- 1 medium onion, chopped
- 2 tablespoons butter *or* margarine
- Salt and pepper to taste
- 6 to 8 eggs, beaten
- 1/2 cup shredded cheddar cheese
- Tomato wedges, optional

In a skillet, saute zucchini and onion in butter until tender. Season with salt and pepper. Add the eggs; cook and stir until set. Sprinkle with cheese. Remove from the heat; cover until cheese melts. Serve with tomato wedges if desired. **Yield:** 4-6 servings.

HOT DOG! HERE'S AN EGG-CEL-LENT IDEA! Looking for a fun and interesting way to serve scrambled eggs? Try this idea: Cut up leftover wieners into bite-size pieces. Saute in butter or margarine with onion. Add two scrambled eggs for each wiener used. Salt and pepper to taste.

EASY ENTREE EVERYONE WILL LOVE

WHEN pre-holiday activities arrive on the coattails of the cooler air, even dedicated cooks can't always spend as much time as usual in the kitchen. That's when hearty, fast-to-fix meals—like the one pictured at right—come in handy!

● Reuben Sandwiches are shared by Kathy Jo Scott of Hemingford, Nebraska. "My mouth waters just thinking of these sandwiches," confesses Kathy Jo. "I adapted the recipe from one my mother found several years ago. Now my family requests them often. That's alright with me…these tasty sandwiches are also one of my favorites both because of their ease of preparation and fantastic flavor."

● Hot Potato Salad is a hearty side dish with old-fashioned flavor from Alpha Wilson of Roswell, New Mexico. "This potato salad is so appealing and flavorful, you're hungry bunch will think you slaved for hours over this super salad," relates Alpha.

● Fruited Pistachio Pudding comes from Sue Gronholz of Columbus, Wisconsin. "It's a quick dessert with broad appeal and so easy to make," Sue reports. "This tasty creamy pudding is not only perfect for everyday family meals, it's a quick and easy dessert that's great to serve unexpected guests," adds Sue.

Hot Potato Salad

> 6 bacon strips
> 1 medium onion, chopped
> 2 tablespoons all-purpose flour
> 2 tablespoons sugar
> 1-1/2 teaspoons salt
> 1/2 teaspoon celery seed
> 1/8 teaspoon pepper
> 3/4 cup water
> 1/2 cup vinegar
> 5 medium potatoes (about 2 pounds), peeled, cooked and sliced

In a skillet, cook bacon until crisp. Remove to paper towel to drain; crumble and set aside. In bacon drippings, saute the onion until tender. Remove from the heat. Combine flour, sugar, salt, celery seed and pepper; stir into onion mixture. Add water and vinegar. Return to the heat; cook, stirring constantly, until mixture comes to a boil. Boil for 1 minute. Place potatoes and bacon in a large bowl; pour sauce over and toss gently. Serve warm. **Yield:** 4-6 servings.

HOT POTATO TIP. To make your favorite potato salad in a hurry, cook the potatoes already diced and peeled.

Fruited Pistachio Pudding

> 1 package (3.4 ounces) instant pistachio-flavored pudding mix
> 1 carton (8 ounces) frozen whipped topping, thawed
> 2 tablespoons salad dressing or mayonnaise
> 1 can (16 ounces) fruit cocktail, undrained
> 1 can (8 ounces) crushed pineapple, undrained
> 2 bananas, sliced
> 1 cup miniature marshmallows

In a large bowl, combine pudding mix, whipped topping and salad dressing; mix well. Fold in remaining ingredients. Leave in bowl or spoon into individual serving dishes. Serve immediately or chill. **Yield:** 6-8 servings.

Reuben Sandwiches

> 12 ounces thinly sliced canned or fully cooked corned beef
> 8 slices light or dark rye bread
> 1 can (8 ounces) sauerkraut, drained
> 1/2 cup Thousand Island dressing
> 4 slices Swiss cheese
> Butter or margarine

Arrange corned beef on four slices of bread. Top each with a quarter of the sauerkraut, 2 tablespoons of dressing and a slice of cheese. Top with remaining bread slices. In a skillet over medium heat, melt 2-3 tablespoons butter. Toast sandwiches until bread is lightly browned on one side. Turn sandwiches and brown other side, adding more butter if necessary. Cook until cheese is melted and meat is heated through. **Yield:** 4 servings.

STIR-FRY MAKES SUPER SUPPER

EVEN folks who love to cook may want to spend less time in the kitchen when beautiful summer days beckon and busy outdoor activities get into full swing.

Fresh air builds appetites, and the nutritious, fast-to-fix meal at right is sure to satisfy everyone!

● Mardi Gras Beef, shared by Lucy Meyring of Walden, Colorado, tastes great right from the grill, which also speeds cleanup. The seasoning and vegetables give the beef a wonderful summertime twist.

● Broccoli Salad comes from Jane Hale of Desert Hot Springs, California. "Keep frozen broccoli in your freezer, and you'll always have the fixings for this quick, delicious salad when company drops in," Jane notes. "It's also a great make-ahead salad, so I often prepare this the night before to save even more time. Everyone will love it's crunchy, fresh flavor."

● Creamy Pineapple Pie is a light and refreshing dessert that's quick to make and impressive to serve, promises Sharon Bickett of Chester, South Carolina. "This is one of our favorite ways to complete any meal."

Mardi Gras Beef

1 medium onion, chopped
1 small green pepper, cut into strips
1 teaspoon dried thyme
2 teaspoons garlic powder, *divided*
2 tablespoons cooking oil
1 to 1-1/2 pounds sirloin steak (1 inch thick)
1 can (14-1/2 ounces) stewed tomatoes, juice drained and reserved
2 teaspoons cornstarch
Salt and pepper to taste

In a skillet, saute onion, green pepper, thyme and 1/2 teaspoon garlic powder in oil until vegetables are crisp-tender.

Meanwhile, sprinkle steak with remaining garlic powder. Grill or broil steak 5 in. from the heat for 6-8 minutes (for medium-rare), turning once, or until desired doneness is reached. Add tomatoes to skillet. Combine reserved tomato juice and cornstarch; add to vegetable mixture. Cook and stir until thickened. Season to taste with salt and pepper. Thinly slice meat; top with vegetables. **Yield:** 4 servings.

Broccoli Salad

1/4 cup mayonnaise
1/4 cup sweet pickle relish
1 teaspoon sugar
Salt and pepper to taste
1 cup chopped celery
1 cup sliced green onions with tops
2 packages (10 ounces *each*) frozen cut broccoli, thawed and drained

In a bowl, combine mayonnaise, relish, sugar, salt and pepper. Add celery and green onions; mix well. Add broccoli and toss gently to coat. Chill until serving. **Yield:** 6-8 servings.

REFRESHING CELERY. When celery loses its crispness, place the celery in a pan of water with raw potato slices for a few hours. When you remove the celery, it will be crisp.

Creamy Pineapple Pie

1 can (14 ounces) sweetened condensed milk
1 can (8 ounces) crushed pineapple, undrained
1/4 cup lemon juice
1 carton (8 ounces) frozen whipped topping, thawed
1 prepared graham cracker crust (9 inches)

In a bowl, mix milk, pineapple and lemon juice. Fold in whipped topping. Pour into the crust. Chill until ready to serve. **Yield:** 8 servings.

IT'S SAID that "good things come in small packages"…but finding interesting and nutritious recipes that work well for just one or two people can be a real challenge.

So in this chapter, cooks from across the country share some of the best recipes that they often reach for when cooking for one or two people.

Garlic Chicken on Rice

(PICTURED ON THIS PAGE)

"I like lighter fare than my husband and three children," explains Becky Bolte of Jewell, Kansas. *"So, I often make a single-serving dish for myself and something else for the rest of the family. This recipe may make a small portion, but it has big flavor!"*

- 1/4 cup chopped onion
- 2 garlic cloves, minced
- 1/4 cup lemon juice
- 2 tablespoons soy sauce
- 1 tablespoon honey
- 2 teaspoons ground ginger
- 1 chicken breast half, skinned, boned and cut into strips
- 1/2 cup chicken broth
- 1/2 cup uncooked instant rice
- 1 tablespoon chopped fresh parsley
- 1/2 teaspoon grated orange peel

In a small bowl, combine onion, garlic, lemon juice, soy sauce, honey and ginger. Add chicken; cover and refrigerate for at least 1 hour. In a small saucepan, bring chicken broth to a boil. Remove from the heat; stir in rice, parsley and orange peel. Cover and let stand for 5 minutes. Meanwhile, cook the chicken and marinade in a hot skillet until no longer pink. Serve over rice. **Yield:** 1 serving.

Tuna Macaroni Toss

"My husband's on a restricted diet so I often prepare two single-serving dishes—one for him and one for me," says Peggy Burdick of Burlington, Michigan. *"I received this recipe from my aunt many years ago, and it's still one of my favorites today. It makes a tasty lunch or supper."*

- 1/3 cup chopped onion
- 2 tablespoons butter *or* margarine
- 1 tablespoon all-purpose flour
- 3/4 cup milk
- 1 chicken bouillon cube
- 1/4 teaspoon salt, optional
- 1/8 teaspoon pepper
- 1 can (3-1/4 ounces) tuna, drained and flaked
- 1/2 cup frozen peas
- 2 teaspoons diced pimientos
- Cooked noodles
- Chopped fresh parsley

In a saucepan, saute onion in butter until tender. Stir in the flour, forming a smooth paste; cook and stir for 1 minute. Gradually stir in milk. Add bouillon, salt if desired and pepper; cook until thickened. Stir in tuna, peas and pimientos; heat through. Serve over noodles and garnish with parsley. **Yield:** 1 serving.

Creamy Basil Fettuccini

Ruth Bolduc of Conway, New Hampshire admits that purchasing one-serving prepared foods is a convenient option for singles. "But what I cook—including Creamy Basil Fettuccini— is far better than anything that I can buy!" she adds.

- 2 to 4 ounces fettuccini
- 1/2 to 1 teaspoon olive oil
- 1 garlic clove, minced
- 1/2 cup plain nonfat yogurt
- 2 tablespoons grated Parmesan cheese
- 1 tablespoon snipped fresh basil *or* 1 teaspoon dried basil
- Salt and pepper to taste

Cook fettuccini according to package directions. Drain and immediately toss with oil, garlic and yogurt. Add Parmesan cheese, basil, salt and pepper. Serve immediately. **Yield:** 1 serving.

Ham for One

"Growing up here in Royal City, Washington, my children didn't care for turkey," relates Margery Bryan. *"So I'd make these ham slices just for them…they were always a hit."*

- 1 small ham steak *or* slice of leftover baked ham
- 1 tablespoon brown sugar
- 2 tablespoons crushed pineapple with juice

Line a 9-in. pie pan with foil. Place ham in pan; sprinkle with brown sugar. Top with pineapple. Bake, uncovered, at 350° for 20-25 minutes or until heated through. **Yield:** 1 serving.

CHOICE CHICKEN. Pictured above: Garlic Chicken on Rice (recipe on this page).

• Split the cost of produce with other friends or family members who live alone so you can buy larger, more economical quantities. Blanch and freeze fresh vegetables in single-portion containers.
—*Ruth Bolduc*
Conway, New Hampshire

• Avoid bad eating habits when alone—like standing when eating—just because there's no one there to see you. Plan a wholesome menu instead of snacks, and eat slowly, *seated.*
—*Katie Koziolek*
Hartland, Minnesota

• A pretty setting with a colorful napkin from a past festive occasion or a cherished mug promotes happy memories and a pleasant state of mind when having a meal alone.
—*Florence Palmer, Paris, Illinois*

• Make a big pot of soup to freeze in single-serving containers to be heated later in the microwave. It's nice to go to the freezer and have a variety of soups on hand.
—*Bethel Walters*
Willow River, Minnesota

• Set a pretty table, eat by a window or invite a friend or neighbor over to share a meal. Fresh, colorful meals with an array of foods will not only do your body good, but your spirit as well.
—*Marion Platt*
Sequim, Washington

DELECTABLE DESSERTS. Pictured above, left to right: Mini Apple Crisp and Yogurt Parfait (recipes on this page).

Yogurt Parfait

(PICTURED ON THIS PAGE)

"I'm on a restricted diet, but my husband is not," states Dottye Wolf of Rolla, Missouri. *"I often make two different single-serving recipes. Yogurt Parfait is a delicious breakfast or luncheon treat, especially with wafers on the side."*

✓ This tasty dish uses less sugar, salt and fat. Recipe includes *Diabetic Exchanges.*

- 1 carton (6 ounces) flavored yogurt
- 1/4 cup granola
- 1/2 cup sliced fresh fruit (apple, strawberries, banana, etc.)

In a parfait glass or large glass mug, layer one-third of the yogurt, half of the granola and then half of the fruit. Repeat layers. Top with the remaining yogurt. **Yield:** 1 serving. **Diabetic Exchanges:**

One serving (prepared with low-fat sugar-free yogurt and low-fat granola) equals 1 skim milk, 1 fat, 1/2 starch, 1/2 fruit; also, 209 calories, 171 mg sodium, 3 mg cholesterol, 30 gm carbohydrate, 10 gm protein, 5 gm fat.

Mini Apple Crisp

(PICTURED ON THIS PAGE)

"With my family's hectic schedule, I cook for one quite frequently," relates Sherry Krenz from Woodworth, North Dakota. *"My Mini Apple Crisp is so easy to make. It works equally well as a nice single-serving dessert for me or as an afternoon snack."*

- 1 medium apple, peeled and sliced
- 1 tablespoon all-purpose flour
- 2 tablespoons brown sugar
- 1 tablespoon butter *or* margarine
- 2 tablespoons quick-cooking oats
- 1/8 teaspoon ground cinnamon

Cream, optional

Place apple slices in a small greased baking dish. In a small bowl, combine flour and brown sugar; cut in butter until mixture resembles coarse crumbs. Add oats and cinnamon. Sprinkle over apple slices. Bake, uncovered, at 350° for 35-40 minutes or until tender. Serve with cream if desired. **Yield:** 1 serving.

Lime Cream Dessert

"This Lime Cream Dessert recipe was shared by a good friend," reveals Peggy Burdick of Burlington, Michigan. *"I love the cool, tart and sweet combination. It's so refreshing."*

- 1 egg, beaten
- 1/4 cup sugar
- 1/4 cup butter *or* margarine
- 1/4 cup lime juice
- 1 teaspoon grated lime peel
- 2 drops green food coloring
- 2/3 cup whipped cream

In the top of a double boiler, combine the egg and sugar. Cut the butter into tablespoons; add to double boiler. Add lime juice and peel; cook and stir over boiling water for 8-10 minutes or until thick. Remove from the heat; add food coloring. Cool. Fold in the whipped cream. Chill for at least 1 hour. **Yield:** 1 serving.

PERFECTLY PORTIONED FOR TWO. Pictured above: Vegetable Meat Loaf (recipe on this page).

Festive Chicken

"This chicken recipe is a perfect example of how a tasty main course can be tailored to two," relates Dorothy Pritchett, Wills Point, Texas. *"The chicken breasts can be prepared two at a time so you don't have to worry about leftovers."*

- 4 bacon strips
- 2 chicken breasts halves, with skin and bones
- 1/2 cup soy sauce
- 1/4 cup sugar
- 2 garlic cloves, minced
- 1-1/2 teaspoons ground ginger
- 1/8 teaspoon paprika
- 2 to 3 drops hot pepper sauce

Wrap two bacon strips around each chicken breast; place in a shallow glass baking dish and set aside. In a small mixing bowl, combine soy sauce and sugar; add remaining ingredients. Pour over chicken, turning to coat evenly. Cover with plastic wrap and refrigerate for several hours or overnight. Drain and reserve marinade. Bake at 325° for 50-60 minutes or until chicken tests done, basting occasionally with marinade. **Yield:** 2 servings.

Vegetable Meat Loaf

(PICTURED ON THIS PAGE)

"I hate the thought of making too much and having leftovers for a week," explains Judi Brinegar from her Liberty, North Carolina home. *"This recipe makes just the right amount."*

- 1/2 pound ground beef
- 1 slice bread, torn into small pieces
- 1 egg, beaten
- 1/4 cup shredded carrot
- 2 tablespoons finely chopped onion
- 2 tablespoons finely chopped green pepper
- 2 tablespoons finely chopped celery
- 1/2 teaspoon salt
- Dash *each* pepper and garlic powder
- 5 tablespoons chili sauce *or* ketchup, *divided*
- 2 baked potatoes, optional
- Shredded cheddar cheese, optional

In a bowl, combine ground beef, bread, egg, carrot, onion, green pepper, celery, seasonings and 2 tablespoons chili sauce or ketchup. Form into a loaf in an ungreased 5-3/4-in. x 3-in. x 2-in. loaf pan. Spoon remaining chili sauce or ketchup over loaf. Bake, uncovered, at 350° for 45-50 minutes or until meat is no longer pink. Serve with baked potatoes topped with shredded cheddar cheese if desired. **Yield:** 2 servings.

Apple Chicken Salad

(PICTURED ON THIS PAGE)

"Now that my six children have 'left the nest', I enjoy creating single-serving recipes like this salad," says Anne Stevens of Lake Charles, Louisiana. *"This recipe is a favorite of mine because it's colorful and a little different."*

- 1 medium apple, cored and chopped
- 1 cup diced cooked chicken
- 2 to 4 tablespoons regular *or* light mayonnaise
- 2 tablespoons diced green pepper
- 1 teaspoon chopped pimientos
- Dash dried rosemary, crushed
- Dash lemon pepper

SINGLE SERVING. Pictured above: Apple Chicken Salad (recipe on this page).

Lettuce leaf
Alfalfa sprouts, optional

In a small bowl, combine first seven ingredients. Chill until ready to serve. Place lettuce leaf on a serving plate and top with the chilled chicken salad. Garnish with alfalfa sprouts if desired. **Yield:** 1 serving.

Autumn Pork Chop Dinner

(PICTURED ON THIS PAGE)

"This tempting recipe for a one-dish meal is small in size but big in taste," states Cecelia Wilson of Rockville, Connecticut. *"My husband and I love the golden pork chops, tasty green beans and tangy cabbage."*

    1 tablespoon cooking oil
    2 loin pork chops (1 inch thick)
    2 cups shredded cabbage
    2 tablespoons brown sugar
    1 tablespoon chopped fresh
      parsley
    2 medium potatoes, peeled and
      sliced 1/4 inch thick
    1 cup fresh or frozen green
      beans
    1 to 1-1/2 teaspoons lemon
      pepper
  3/4 cup apple juice
  1/4 cup seasoned bread crumbs
    1 tablespoon butter or
      margarine, melted

In a large skillet, heat the oil over high. Brown chops on both sides; remove and set aside. Toss cabbage with brown sugar and parsley; place in an 11-in. x 7-in. x 2-in. baking dish. Top with potatoes and beans. Arrange chops over vegetables. Sprinkle with lemon pepper. Pour apple juice over all. Cover and bake at 350° for 45 minutes or until the pork chops and vegetables are tender. Combine the bread crumbs and butter; sprinkle on top. Return to the oven for 15 minutes. **Yield:** 2 servings.

Buttery Peas and Zucchini

"These vegetables are an excellent side dish for any meal," says Dorothy Pritchett of Wills Point, Texas. *"The recipe makes just enough for two to enjoy."*

    1 package (10 ounces) frozen
      peas in butter sauce
    2 tablespoons water
    1 medium zucchini, cut into
      thin strips
    1 tablespoon diced pimientos

Cook peas according to package directions. Pour into a serving bowl; cover with plastic wrap and set aside. Mean-

while, in a skillet, simmer water and zucchini over medium heat until water is evaporated and zucchini is tender. Stir in peas and pimiento. **Yield:** 2 servings.

Chocolate Bread Pudding

(PICTURED ON THIS PAGE)

A favorite dessert of Mildred Sherrer in Bay City, Texas is Chocolate Bread Pudding. "This is a fun recipe because the chocolate makes it different from traditional bread pudding."

    2 squares (1 ounce each)
      semisweet chocolate
  1/2 cup light cream
    1 egg
  2/3 cup sugar
  1/2 cup milk
    1 teaspoon vanilla extract
  1/4 teaspoon salt
    4 slices day-old bread, crusts
      removed and cut into cubes
      (about 3 cups)
  Confectioners' sugar or whipped
    cream, optional

In a saucepan, melt chocolate over low heat. Remove from the heat and stir in cream until smooth; set aside. In a large bowl, beat egg. Add sugar, milk, vanilla and salt; mix well. Stir in chocolate mixture. Add bread cubes and toss to coat. Let stand for 15 minutes. Spoon into two greased 2-cup souffle dishes. Bake at

350° for 30-35 minutes or until a knife inserted near the center comes out clean. If desired, sprinkle with confectioners' sugar or top with a dollop of whipped cream. **Yield:** 2 servings.

Apple Citrus Salad

"During the week, we like quick suppers for just us two," says Sandy Baratka, Phillips, Wisconsin. *"This crunchy, sweet-tart salad is perfect with a main dish."*

  1/4 cup frozen lemonade
      concentrate, thawed
    3 tablespoons honey
    3 tablespoons vegetable oil
  1/2 teaspoon poppy seeds
    1 apple, cored and sliced
    1 orange, peeled and sectioned
  Shredded lettuce or cabbage
  1/4 cup roasted cashews

In a small bowl, whisk together lemonade concentrate, honey, oil and poppy seeds. Set aside. On individual salad plates, arrange apple slices and orange sections over a bed of shredded lettuce or cabbage. Just before serving, drizzle with dressing and top with cashews. **Yield:** 2 servings.

HEARTY HELPINGS. Pictured above, left to right: Chocolate Bread Pudding and Autumn Pork Chop Dinner (recipes on this page).

WHEN THE GANG'S ALL HERE

COOKING for a crowd doesn't mean you need to sacrifice quality or prepare the food in a frazzle. In this chapter, experienced cooks offer some sensible recipes.

Sloppy Joe Sandwiches

"This recipe comes from a renowned local cook who was the lunchroom cook when my husband went to grade school," reveals Karen Ann Bland of Gove, Kansas.

- **20 pounds lean ground beef**
- **3 cups chopped onions**
- **1/4 cup Worcestershire sauce**
- **1 pound brown sugar**
- **1 cup prepared mustard**
- **2 tablespoons chili powder**
- **1 gallon ketchup**
- **Salt and pepper to taste**
- **Hamburger buns**

Brown beef; drain fat. Add the next seven ingredients; simmer or cook in an electric roaster for 1 hour. Stir occasionally. Serve on buns. **Yield:** about 100 servings.

Big-Batch Bean Soup

"Big-Batch Bean Soup was a favorite among the men in the service," recalls Jene Cain of Northridge, California. *"I now make my own version of this soup for large groups at home."*

- **6 pounds dry white beans (about 3-1/2 quarts)**
- **7 gallons ham or chicken stock**
- **8 ham bones**
- **4-1/2 cups finely chopped onion (about 2 pounds)**
- **2-3/4 cups shredded carrots (about 1 pound)**
- **2 teaspoons pepper**
- **3 cups cold water**
- **2 cups all-purpose flour**

Rinse beans. Place in a large kettle with stock and ham bones; bring to a boil. Reduce heat; cover and simmer for 2-3 hours or until the beans are tender. Stir in onion, carrots and pepper; cover and simmer for 30 minutes. Combine cold water and flour until smooth; gradually stir into soup. Cook for 10 minutes. If too thick, add additional water. **Yield:** 100 servings (6-1/4 gallons).

Big Appetite Pancakes

Annabelle Seidl of Ruth, Michigan says her church used this recipe for its pancake and sausage breakfast with great success. *"We also serve homemade sweet rolls, scrambled eggs and fruit,"* she informs.

- **12 eggs**
- **3 quarts milk**
- **12 cups all-purpose flour**
- **3/4 cup sugar**
- **3/4 cup baking powder**
- **2 tablespoons salt**
- **1-1/2 cups vegetable oil**

Beat eggs; add milk. Add dry ingredients and oil; mix well. Spoon batter onto hot greased griddles and brown on both sides. **Yield:** 85 servings.

Cheesy Apple Crisp

When the *"gang's all here"*, Rita Wilken of Bloomfield, Nebraska likes to serve this dessert topped with whipped cream.

- **13 quarts apples (about 42 medium), peeled and sliced**
- **2 cups water**
- **1/4 cup plus 2 tablespoons lemon juice**
- **8 cups all-purpose flour**
- **8 cups sugar**
- **2 tablespoons cinnamon**
- **1 tablespoon salt**
- **4 cups butter or margarine**
- **8 cups shredded cheddar cheese**
- **Whipped cream or ice cream, optional**

Arrange apples in four greased 13-in. x 9-in. x 2-in. baking pans. Combine water and lemon juice; sprinkle over apples. Combine flour, sugar, cinnamon and salt; cut in butter until crumbly. Stir in cheese lightly. Spread over apples. Bake at 350° for 30-35 minutes, or until apples are tender and topping is crisp. Serve with whipped cream or ice cream if desired. **Yield:** 100 servings.

Spaghetti Salad

"I've been making meals for larger groups for years," says Ken Churches from San Andreas, California. *"Using bottled Italian dressing makes this noodle salad a breeze to prepare."*

- **15 pounds spaghetti (broken into 2-1/2 inch pieces), cooked and drained**
- **1 gallon bottled Italian dressing**
- **5 bottles (2.62 ounces each) Salad Supreme Seasoning**
- **3 bunches celery, diced**
- **12 medium green peppers, diced**
- **12 medium onions, diced**
- **6 pounds cheddar cheese, cut into 1/4-inch cubes**
- **12 pounds tomatoes, seeded and diced**

In a large container, mix all ingredients and chill overnight. **Yield:** 150 servings. **Editor's Note:** Schilling's Salad Supreme Seasoning is found in most stores in the spice section. Other brands may be substituted.

Glazed Meat Loaf

"The brown sugar glaze on this meat loaf is what makes it special at any big gathering," says Dorothy Hoffmann of Wheatland, North Dakota. *"We usually serve it with baked potatoes, coleslaw and buns and butter."*

- **10-1/2 cups milk or tomato juice**
- **10-1/2 cups rolled oats**
- **3-1/2 cups chopped onion**
- **1/4 cup plus 3 tablespoons salt**
- **1-1/2 tablespoons pepper**
- **14 eggs**
- **21 pounds ground beef**
- **GLAZE:**
- **1-1/4 cups ketchup**
- **3/4 cup packed brown sugar**
- **3/4 cup prepared mustard**

In a large container, combine milk or tomato juice, oats, onion, salt, pepper and eggs; mix well. Add the ground beef in chunks; first mix with a large spoon, then with clean hands, until well blended. Shape into loaves of desired size and place in shallow baking pans. Bake at 350° for 30 minutes. Combine all of the glaze ingredients and spread over tops of loaves; bake for about 1 hour more. (Two-pound loaves will need to bake for 1-1/2 hours.) **Yield:** 100 servings.

Eclair Dessert

"I cook for a youth camp 2 weeks each summer," informs Joyce Mummau, Mt. Airy, Maryland. *"This heavenly Eclair Dessert is a favorite among the kids."*

- **4 gallons prepared vanilla pudding**
- **4 cartons (16 ounces each) frozen whipped topping, thawed**
- **6 pounds graham crackers**
- **ICING:**
- **5 cups confectioners' sugar**
- **1/3 cup corn syrup**
- **1/4 cup butter or margarine, softened**
- **1/4 cup baking cocoa**
- **3 tablespoons vegetable oil**
- **1/4 to 1/2 cup milk**

In a large container, mix pudding and whipped topping; set aside. Place one-third of the graham crackers side by side in bottoms of about twelve 13-in. x 9-in. x 2-in. baking pans. Pour about 2 in. pudding mixture over crackers. Add another layer of crackers and pudding. Top with remaining crackers. Cover and refrigerate overnight. For icing, combine confectioners' sugar, corn syrup, butter, baking cocoa and oil in a mixing bowl. Beat until smooth, adding enough milk to achieve spreading consistency. Spread on top of crackers; chill until serving. **Yield:** about 140 servings.

Quick Fruit Salad

This refreshing fruit salad comes from former restaurant owner Ruth Andrewson of Leavenworth, Washington. "It's very easy to make and is delicious as well."

- 10 **cans (20 ounces *each*) pineapple chunks, drained**
- 10 **cans (21 ounces *each*) peach pie filling**
- 10 **cans (11 ounces *each*) mandarin oranges, drained**
- 10 **cups green grapes**
- 10 **cups sliced bananas**

Combine all ingredients except bananas. Chill until ready to serve. Just before serving, fold in bananas. **Yield:** about 100 servings.

Hot Potato Salad for 100

"When I was in the service, I decided to learn all I could about cooking from the cooks in the galley," states Jene Cain of Northridge, California. "It was quite an adventure. I still use those skills today."

- 7 **pounds bacon, chopped**
- 5 **cups all-purpose flour**
- 3-1/2 **quarts vinegar**
- 3-1/2 **quarts water**
- 6 **cups sugar**
- 1 **cup salt**
- 4 **teaspoons pepper**
- 3-1/2 **quarts chopped onion (about 4-1/2 pounds)**
- 1-1/2 **quarts chopped pickles**
- 7 **gallons hot sliced peeled cooked potatoes (about 45 pounds)**

In a large skillet, fry bacon until crisp; remove to paper towels to drain. Add flour to drippings; cook and stir until bubbly. In a large kettle, heat vinegar, water and sugar to boiling. Gradually add flour mixture; cook and stir until thickened. Add salt, pepper, onion and pickles; mix well. Place hot potatoes in serving pans. Divide sauce among pans and stir to coat. Sprinkle with bacon. **Yield:** 100 servings (7 gallons).

Ham Balls

"I've made these Ham Balls for church functions many times. Everyone just loves the thick tomato sauce laced with the sweet taste of brown sugar," relates DeEtta Rasmussen of Olmsted, Illinois.

- 10 **pounds ground fully cooked ham**
- 8 **pounds lean ground pork**
- 4 **pounds lean ground beef**
- 12 **eggs, beaten**
- 12 **cups graham cracker crumbs**
- 6 **cups milk**

SAUCE:
- 8 **cans (10-3/4 ounces *each*) condensed tomato soup, undiluted**
- 8 **cups packed brown sugar**
- 1 **cup vinegar**
- 3 **tablespoons dry mustard**

In a large bowl, combine ham, pork and beef; mix well. Add eggs; mix well. Blend in crumbs and milk. Form into 1-1/2-in. balls. Place in a single layer in 12 ungreased 13-in. x 9-in. x 2-in. baking pans or larger pans if available; set aside. In a bowl, combine sauce ingredients. Divide evenly among pans, covering the ham balls. Bake, uncovered, at 350° for 60 minutes or until hot and bubbly. **Yield:** 100 servings.

Cocoa for a Crowd

"For a large gathering during the winter, this cocoa really hits the spot," assures Pat Monson from her Stewartville, Minnesota home.

- 4 **cups sugar**
- 3 **cups baking cocoa**
- 1/2 **teaspoon salt**
- 1 **quart warm water**
- 2 **quarts boiling water**
- 4 **gallons hot milk**

In a large kettle, combine sugar, cocoa, salt and warm water; mix well. Add boiling water; boil for 10 minutes. Remove from the heat; stir in hot milk. **Yield:** 100 servings.

PLANNING FOR 100?

Here are suggested guidelines for amounts needed to feed a group of 100 people. (Serving sizes vary depending on the type of crowd and meal served.)

MEATS
Bacon	20 to 25 pounds
Beef Roast	50 pounds
Chicken	55 to 60 pounds
Fish	25 pounds
Ground Beef	20 to 25 pounds
Ham (with bone)	35 to 40 pounds
Pork Roast	35 pounds
Spare Ribs	75 pounds
Stewing Beef	25 pounds
Turkey	75 to 100 pounds
Wieners	20 pounds

VEGETABLES
Baked Beans	12 pounds
Carrots	25 to 30 pounds
Celery	10 to 12 bunches
Lettuce (for salad)	12 to 15 heads
Potatoes (for mashed)	35 pounds
Potatoes (for scalloped)	35 to 40 pounds
Squash	50 pounds
String Beans	20 to 25 pounds
Sweet Potatoes	25 pounds
Tomatoes	25 to 38 pounds

FRUIT
Canned Fruit (25 ounces each)	20 to 25 cans
Cranberry Sauce (1 pound each)	6 cans
For Salad:	
Apples	25 pounds
Melon Balls	30 melons
Oranges	4 dozen
Peaches	37 pounds
Strawberries	20 quarts

DESSERTS
Cake:	
(13- x 9-inch pan)	7 cakes
(15- x 10-inch pan)	4 cakes
Ice Cream	4-1/2 gallons
Pie (9-inch)	12 to 15 pies
Whipping Cream	2 quarts

BEVERAGES
Coffee	2 pounds
Cream	1/2 gallon
Sugar	1-1/2 pounds
Fruit Juice (6 ounces each)	18 cans of concentrate
Milk	6-1/2 gallons
Soda	16 to 20 liters

STAPLES
Bread (for sandwiches)	12 to 15 loaves
Bread (with meal)	6 loaves
Butter	3 pounds
Coleslaw	24 pounds
Gravy	1-1/2 gallons
Olives	1 gallon
Pickles	1 gallon
Potato Chips	5 pounds
Rolls	12 dozen
Salad Dressing	2 quarts
Sandwich Filling	16 to 18 cups

LOVE THOSE SNACKS!

IN THIS CHAPTER, families from across the country share their best recipes that they reach for when they have an attack of the "munchies". They're great for anytime nibbling!

Cheesy Sun Crisps

(PICTURED ON THIS PAGE)

Says Mary Detweiler of Farmington, Ohio, "These crisps have a great cheesy flavor perfect for snacking."

- 2 cups (8 ounces) shredded cheddar cheese
- 1/2 cup grated Parmesan cheese
- 1/2 cup butter *or* margarine, softened
- 3 tablespoons water
- 1 cup all-purpose flour
- 1/4 teaspoon salt
- 1 cup quick-cooking oats
- 2/3 cup roasted salted sunflower seeds

In a mixing bowl, combine cheddar and Parmesan cheeses, butter and water until well mixed. Combine flour and salt; add to cheese mixture. Stir in oats and sunflower seeds. Knead dough until it holds together. Shape into a 12-in. roll. Cover with plastic wrap; chill for 4 hours or overnight. Allow to stand at room temperature for 10 minutes before cutting into 1/8-in. slices. Place on greased foil-lined baking sheets. Bake at 400° for 8-10 minutes or until edges are golden. Slide crackers and foil off baking sheets to wire racks to cool. **Yield:** 8 dozen.

Cinnamon-Raisin Granola

(PICTURED ON THIS PAGE)

"This granola recipe makes a great late-night or after-school snack," explains Ida Grove, Iowa cook Tammy Neubauer. "I like that it's nutritious, too."

- 4 cups old-fashioned oats
- 1 cup shredded coconut
- 1/4 cup packed brown sugar
- 1/4 cup vegetable oil
- 1/4 cup honey
- 1 teaspoon ground cinnamon
- 1-1/2 teaspoons vanilla extract
- 1 cup raisins

In a large bowl, combine oats and coconut; set aside. In a saucepan, combine brown sugar, oil, honey and cinnamon; bring to a boil. Remove from the heat and stir in vanilla. Pour over oat mixture; stir to coat. Spread in a large shallow baking pan. Bake at 350° for 15-20 minutes, stirring occasionally. Cool. Add raisins. Store in an airtight container. **Yield:** 6 cups.

Fresh Vegetable Dip

(PICTURED ON THIS PAGE)

"This cool and creamy dip is a real family favorite for snacking," relates Denise Goedeken of Platte Center, Nebraska.

- 1-1/2 cups (12 ounces) sour cream
- 3/4 cup mayonnaise
- 1 tablespoon dried minced onion
- 1 teaspoon dried dill weed
- 1 teaspoon dried parsley flakes
- 1 teaspoon garlic salt
- Dash Worcestershire sauce
- Fresh vegetables

In a small bowl, combine sour cream, mayonnaise, onion, dill, parsley, garlic salt and Worcestershire sauce. Chill for at least 1 hour. Serve with fresh vegetables. **Yield:** 2 cups.

Tomato Vegetable Juice

(PICTURED ON PAGE 71)

"This tangy juice is refreshing on its own and also works great in any recipe calling for tomato juice," states Sue Wille of Alexandria, Minnesota.

✓ This tasty dish uses less sugar, salt and fat. Recipe includes *Diabetic Exchanges*.

- 10 pounds tomatoes, peeled and chopped (about 8 quarts)
- 3 garlic cloves, minced
- 2 large onions, chopped
- 2 carrots, cut into 1/2-inch slices
- 2 cups chopped celery
- 1/2 cup chopped green pepper
- 1/4 cup sugar
- 1 tablespoon salt, optional
- 1 teaspoon Worcestershire sauce
- 1/2 teaspoon pepper
- Lemon juice

Combine tomatoes, garlic, onions, carrots, celery and green pepper in a large Dutch oven or soup kettle. Bring to a boil; reduce heat and simmer for 20 minutes or until vegetables are soft. Cool. Press mixture through a food mill or fine sieve. Return juice to Dutch oven; add sugar, salt, Worcestershire sauce and pepper. Bring to a boil. Ladle hot juice into hot sterilized quart jars, leaving 1/4-in. headspace. Add 2 table-

SNACK ATTACK. Pictured above, clockwise from the top: Cinnamon-Raisin Granola, Fresh Vegetable Dip and Cheesy Sun Crisps (all recipes on this page).

spoons lemon juice to each jar. Adjust caps. Process for 40 minutes in a boiling-water bath. **Yield:** 7-8 quarts. **Diabetic Exchanges:** One 1/2-cup serving (prepared without salt) equals 2 vegetable; also, 46 calories, 15 mg sodium, 0 cholesterol, 10 gm carbohydrate, 2 gm protein, trace fat.

Spicy Mint Tea

"I love to wake up in the morning with this soothing, flavorful tea," relates Ione Banks of Jefferson, Oregon.

> **6 cups water**
> **2 cinnamon sticks**
> **4 whole cloves**
> **4 whole allspice**
> **2 cups fresh mint leaves**
> **Honey, optional**

Bring the water, cinnamon, cloves and allspice to a boil. Boil for 1 minute. Stir in mint leaves. Remove from heat and steep for 5 minutes. Strain into cups. Sweeten with honey if desired. **Yield:** 4 servings.

Marshmallow Delights

Says Niceville, Florida cook Diane Hixon, "When you bake these snacks, the marshmallow inside disappears and creates a gooey, yummy cinnamon roll."

> **1 tube (8 ounces) refrigerated crescent rolls**
> **1/4 cup sugar**
> **1 tablespoon ground cinnamon**
> **8 large marshmallows**
> **1/4 cup butter *or* margarine, melted**

Separate rolls into eight triangles. Combine sugar and cinnamon. Dip each marshmallow into butter, roll in cinnamon-sugar and place on a triangle. Pinch dough around marshmallow, sealing all edges. Dip tops of dough into remaining butter and cinnamon-sugar. Place with sugar side up in greased muffin cups. Bake at 375° for 13-15 minutes. Serve warm. **Yield:** 8 servings.

Breakfast Wassail

(PICTURED ON THIS PAGE)

"I got this recipe from a co-worker and made it one Christmas for a family gathering. Now whenever we get together, I'm the designated wassail-maker," explains Amy Holtsclaw of Carbondale, Illinois.

> **1 bottle (64 ounces) cranberry juice**
> **1 bottle (32 ounces) apple juice**
> **1 can (12 ounces) frozen pineapple juice concentrate, undiluted**

REFRESHING BEVERAGE BREAK. Pictured above: Breakfast Wassail (recipe on this page).

> **1 can (12 ounces) frozen lemonade concentrate, undiluted**
> **3 to 4 cinnamon sticks**
> **1 quart water, optional**

In a large saucepan or Dutch oven, combine juices, lemonade and cinnamon sticks. Bring to a boil. Reduce heat; cover and simmer for 1 hour. Add water if desired. Serve hot or cold. **Yield:** about 4 quarts.

Honey-Glazed Snack Mix

"For a nice change of pace from packaged snacks, try this golden, slightly sweet mix," suggests Cindy Kolberg of Syracuse, Indiana.

> **4 cups Rice *or* Corn Chex cereal**
> **1-1/2 cups miniature pretzels**
> **1 cup pecan halves**
> **1/3 cup butter *or* margarine**
> **1/4 cup honey**

In a large mixing bowl, combine cereal, pretzels and pecans; set aside. Melt butter in a small saucepan; stir in honey and blend well. Pour over cereal mixture and stir to coat evenly. Spread in a jelly roll pan. Bake at 350° for 12-15 minutes or until mixture is lightly glazed, stirring occasionally. Remove from oven and cool slightly. Spread on waxed paper to cool completely. **Yield:** about 6-1/2 cups.

Olive Sandwich Spread

"This recipe was given to me by my mother many years ago," says Dorothy Warren of Toulon, Illinois. "It's tasty and unique."

> **2 packages (3 ounces *each*) cream cheese, softened**
> **1/2 cup mayonnaise**
> **1/2 cup chopped green olives**
> **1/2 cup chopped pecans**
> **1 tablespoon olive juice**

In a small bowl, combine all the ingredients. Spread on crackers or bread. **Yield:** 1-1/2 cups.

Zippy Horseradish Dip

"Horseradish really adds zip to our favorite vegetable dip," explains Cathy Seus of Tulelake, California.

> **1-1/2 teaspoons prepared horseradish**
> **1/2 cup plain yogurt**
> **1/2 cup sour cream**
> **1 green onion, chopped**
> **1/4 cup chopped peeled cucumber**
> **1/4 teaspoon salt**
> **1/4 teaspoon pepper**
> **Assorted fresh vegetables**

In a small bowl, combine first seven ingredients. Chill. Serve with fresh vegetables. **Yield:** 1 cup.

SHRIMP-LY DELICIOUS! Pictured above: Cappuccino Shake, Shrimp Spread (recipes on this page).

Shrimp Spread

(PICTURED ON THIS PAGE)

"This colorful and tasty appetizer is always a crowd-pleaser," says Norene Wright of Manilla, Indiana.

✓ This tasty dish uses less sugar, salt and fat. Recipe includes *Diabetic Exchanges*.

- 1 package (8 ounces) light cream cheese, softened
- 1/2 cup light sour cream
- 1/4 cup light mayonnaise
- 1 cup seafood cocktail sauce
- 2 cups (8 ounces) shredded light mozzarella cheese
- 2 cans (4-1/4 ounces *each*) shrimp, rinsed and drained
- 3 green onions, sliced
- 3/4 cup finely chopped tomato

In a small mixing bowl, beat the cream cheese, sour cream and mayonnaise until smooth. Spread on a 12-in. round serving platter. Cover with seafood sauce. Sprinkle with cheese, shrimp, onions and tomato. Cover and chill. **Yield:** 8-10 servings. **Diabetic Exchanges:** One 2-tablespoon serving equals 1 fat; also, 38 calories, 112 mg sodium, 12 mg cholesterol, 2 gm carbohydrate, 2 gm protein, 2 gm fat.

Creamy Hot Beef Dip

"I got this zesty recipe from a neighbor several years ago," reports Susan Wolfe of Olathe, Kansas. *"Every time I make this dip, I think of my friend and the fun times our families had together."*

- 1 package (8 ounces) cream cheese, softened
- 1 cup (8 ounces) sour cream
- 3 ounces dried beef, rinsed and finely chopped
- 2 tablespoons chopped green pepper
- 1-1/2 tablespoons minced onion
- 1 teaspoon dried green pepper flakes, optional
- 1/2 teaspoon garlic powder

Pepper to taste
Raw vegetables *or* crackers

Combine first eight ingredients in a 1-qt. baking dish. Bake at 375°, uncovered, for 30 minutes or until hot and bubbly. Serve with raw vegetables or crackers. **Yield:** about 2 cups.

Individual Cheese Balls

"With their creamy, nutty flavor, these small cheese balls are great to serve company," says Mildred Sherrer of Bay City, Texas.

- 2 packages (8 ounces *each*) cream cheese, softened
- 1 cup (4 ounces) shredded cheddar cheese
- 1 to 2 tablespoons chopped onion
- 1 to 2 tablespoons chopped fresh parsley

- 1 to 2 teaspoons lemon juice
- 1 to 2 teaspoons Worcestershire sauce
- 1-1/2 to 2 cups ground walnuts

In a small bowl, combine the first six ingredients; mix well. Shape into 1-1/2-in. balls. Roll in nuts. Chill thoroughly. Serve with crackers. **Yield:** 20 servings.

Cappuccino Shake

(PICTURED ON THIS PAGE)

"I created this quick and easy shake for my mom," reports Paula Pelis of Rocky Point, New York. *"She was tickled pink!"*

✓ This tasty dish uses less sugar, salt and fat. Recipe includes *Diabetic Exchanges*.

- 1 cup skim milk
- 1-1/2 teaspoons instant coffee crystals
- 2 packets powdered artificial sweetener (to equal 4 teaspoons sugar)
- 2 drops brandy extract *or* rum extract

Dash ground cinnamon

In a blender, combine milk, coffee crystals, sweetener and extract. Blend until coffee is dissolved. Serve with a dash of cinnamon. For a hot drink, pour into a mug and heat in a microwave. **Yield:** 1 serving. **Diabetic Exchanges:** One serving equals 1 skim milk; also, 100 calories, 128 mg sodium, 4 mg cholesterol, 15 gm carbohydrate, 9 gm protein, trace fat.

Buttery Onion Pretzels

"If you love the taste of onion, you'll love these zesty pretzels," writes Betty Claycomb of Alverton, Pennsylvania.

- 1-1/4 cups butter *or* margarine
- 1 package (1-1/2 ounces) dry onion soup mix
- 1 bag (16 ounces) chunky pretzels, broken into pieces

In a skillet, melt butter. Stir in soup mix. Heat and stir until well mixed. Add pretzels; toss to coat. Spread pretzel mixture in a baking pan. Bake at 250° for 1-1/2 hours, stirring every 15 minutes. Cool. Store in an airtight container. **Yield:** 6 cups.

Sweet Graham Snacks

"These snacks really travel well," assures Artimece Schmidt of Farmington, New Mexico. *"I've shared this recipe with many people we've visited."*

- 10 to 12 graham crackers, broken into quarters
- 1 cup butter *or* margarine
- 1/2 cup sugar
- 1/3 cup ground nuts

Line a 15-in. x 10-in. x 1-in. baking pan with graham crackers. In a saucepan, bring butter and sugar to a boil; boil for 2 minutes. Remove from the heat; stir in nuts. Spoon over the graham crackers. Bake at 325° for 10 minutes. Immediately remove from pan onto foil. Cool. Break apart. **Yield:** 3-4 dozen.

Nutty O's

(PICTURED ON PAGE 84)

"Almonds add a nice nutty flavor to this tasty snack," states Karen Buchholz of Sitka, Alaska. *"Served in a decorative dish, it has a golden festive look."*

- 1 cup packed brown sugar
- 1 cup dark corn syrup
- 1/2 cup butter *or* margarine
- 12 cups Cheerios
- 2 cups pecan halves
- 1 cup whole almonds

In a large saucepan, heat brown sugar, corn syrup and butter until sugar is dissolved. Stir in cereal and nuts; mix well. Spread onto greased 15-in. x 10-in. x 1-in. baking pans. Bake at 325° for 15 minutes. Cool for 10 minutes; stir to loosen from pan. Cool completely. Store in an airtight container. **Yield:** 16 cups.

Pecan Logs

"This is a favorite snack for me and my great-grandson," reports Ruby Williams of Bogalusa, Louisiana. *"It has a hearty pecan taste without being too sweet."*

- 1 box (12 ounces) vanilla wafers, crushed
- 3-3/4 cups finely chopped pecans
- 1 can (12 ounces) sweetened condensed milk

In a mixing bowl, combine all ingredients; mix well. Divide mixture in half. Between sheets of waxed paper, roll out each half into a 9-in. x 2-in. log. Tightly wrap each log in foil. Chill well. Cut into 1/4-in. slices. Store leftovers in the refrigerator. **Yield:** 50 servings.

Sweet Gingered Chicken Wings

(PICTURED ON THIS PAGE)

"When I prepare this recipe for a party, it's one of the first dishes to disappear," reports Debbie Dougal of Roseville, California.

- 1 cup all-purpose flour
- 2 teaspoons salt
- 2 teaspoons paprika
- 1/4 teaspoon pepper

- 24 chicken wings

SAUCE:
- 1/4 cup honey
- 1/4 cup frozen orange juice concentrate, thawed
- 1/2 teaspoon ground ginger

Snipped fresh parsley, optional

In a bowl, combine flour, salt, paprika and pepper. Coat chicken wings in flour mixture; shake off excess. Place wings on a large greased baking sheet. Bake at 350° for 30 minutes. Remove from the oven and drain. Combine honey, orange juice concentrate and ginger; brush generously over chicken wings. Reduce heat to 325°. Bake for 30-40 minutes or until chicken tests done, basting occasionally with more sauce. Sprinkle with parsley before serving if desired. **Yield:** 2 dozen.

Tex-Mex Dip

(PICTURED ON PAGE 57)

"This creamy dip adds some zip to any occasion," relates Mary Anne McWhirter of Pearland, Texas. *"It's easy to make ahead—perfect for a potluck or other gathering."*

- 2 cans (9 ounces *each*) bean dip
- 3 avocados, peeled
- 2 tablespoons lemon juice
- 1/2 teaspoon salt
- 1/4 teaspoon pepper
- 1 cup (8 ounces) sour cream
- 1/2 cup mayonnaise

- 1 package (1-1/4 ounces) taco seasoning
- 2 cups (8 ounces) shredded cheddar cheese
- 1 cup sliced ripe olives
- 4 green onions with tops, sliced
- 1 large tomato, chopped and seeded

Tortilla chips

Spread bean dip on a 12-in. serving plate. In a small bowl, mash the avocados with lemon juice, salt and pepper; spread over bean dip. Combine sour cream, mayonnaise and taco seasoning; spread over the avocado layer. Sprinkle with cheese, olives, onions and tomato. Serve with tortilla chips. **Yield:** 8-10 servings.

Stuffed Celery Snacks

"The creamy filling with each bite of crisp celery makes for a light, but satisfying, snack," promises Patsy Faye Steenbock of Shoshoni, Wyoming.

- 1 package (8 ounces) cream cheese, softened
- 1/3 cup shredded carrot
- 1-1/2 teaspoons dried parsley flakes
- 1/4 teaspoon dried thyme
- 1/4 teaspoon onion salt

Celery stalks, cut into 3-inch lengths

In a small bowl, combine cream cheese, carrot and seasonings. Stuff into celery. Cover and chill for at least 1 hour. **Yield:** about 2 dozen.

WONDERFUL WINGS! Pictured above: Sweet Gingered Chicken Wings (recipe on this page).

BLT Bites

(PICTURED ON THIS PAGE)

"These quick hors d'oeuvres may be mini, but their bacon and tomato flavor is full-size," explains Kellie Remmen of Detroit Lakes, Minnesota.

- **16 to 20 cherry tomatoes**
- **1 pound bacon, cooked and crumbled**
- **1/2 cup mayonnaise *or* salad dressing**
- **1/3 cup chopped green onions**
- **3 tablespoons grated Parmesan cheese**
- **2 tablespoons snipped fresh parsley**

Cut a thin slice off of each tomato top. Scoop out and discard pulp. Invert the tomatoes on a paper towel to drain. In a small bowl, combine all remaining ingredients; mix well. Spoon into tomatoes. Refrigerate for several hours. **Yield:** 16-20 appetizer servings.

Three-Herb Popcorn

Flo Burtnett of Gage, Oklahoma says, "My family loves munching on popcorn. And with its combination of herbs, this snack is their No. 1 nighttime treat!"

- **6 quarts (24 cups) popped popcorn (about 1 cup kernels)**
- **Salt to taste**
- **1/2 cup butter *or* margarine**
- **1 teaspoon dried basil**
- **1 teaspoon dried chervil**
- **1/2 teaspoon dried thyme**
- **1 can (12 ounces) mixed nuts, optional**

Place popcorn in a large container or oven roasting pan. Salt to taste and set aside. Melt butter in a small saucepan. Remove from heat; stir in basil, chervil and thyme. Drizzle butter mixture over popcorn and toss lightly to coat evenly. Stir in the nuts if desired. **Yield:** about 20 cups.

Pizza Cups

"My girls frequently have friends over at night," writes Suzanne McKinley of Lyons, Georgia. *"So I make these quick and easy miniature pizzas often."*

- **1 pound hot *or* mild pork sausage**
- **1 jar (14 ounces) pizza sauce**
- **2 tablespoons ketchup**
- **1/4 teaspoon garlic powder**
- **2 cans (10 ounces *each*) refrigerated biscuits**
- **Shredded mozzarella cheese**
- **Grated Parmesan cheese**

In a skillet, cook sausage over medium heat; drain. Stir in pizza sauce, ketchup and garlic powder; set aside. Press biscuits into 20 well-greased muffin cups. Spoon 1 or 2 tablespoons of the meat sauce into each biscuit; top with mozzarella cheese and sprinkle with Parmesan cheese. Bake at 350° for 10-15 minutes or until golden brown. (Refrigerate or freeze any remaining meat sauce.) **Yield:** 20 pizzas.

Puffed Wheat Balls

(PICTURED ON PAGE 85)

"Whenever my grandma comes over, she makes her famous Puffed Wheat Balls by the dozen," notes Lucile Proctor of Panguitch, Utah.

- **12 cups puffed wheat cereal**
- **2 cups packed brown sugar**
- **1 cup corn syrup**
- **2 tablespoons butter *or* margarine**
- **1 cup evaporated milk**
- **1/3 cup sugar**

Place cereal in a large bowl; set aside. In a heavy saucepan, bring brown sugar and corn syrup to a boil. Add butter. Combine evaporated milk and sugar; add to boiling mixture and continue cooking until a soft ball forms when liquid is dropped into cold water (240° on a candy thermometer). Pour over cereal and stir to coat. Shape into 2-in. balls. **Yield:** 2-1/2 to 3 dozen.

Sweet Minglers

"This snack mix is perfect for a late-night treat or a pick-me-up anytime of the day," shares Mary Obeilin from Selinsgrove, Pennsylvania.

- **1 cup (6 ounces) semisweet chocolate chips**
- **1/4 cup creamy peanut butter**
- **6 cups Corn *or* Rice Chex cereal**
- **1 cup confectioners' sugar**

In a large microwave-safe bowl, melt chocolate chips on high for 1 minute. Stir; microwave 30 seconds longer or until the chips are melted. Stir in peanut butter. Gently stir in cereal until well coated; set aside. Place confectioners' sugar in a 2-gal. plastic storage bag. Add cereal mixture and shake until well coated. Store in an airtight container in the refrigerator. **Yield:** about 6 cups.

Cheddar Herb Snacks

"These quick herbed rolls really hit the spot when you're looking for a savory snack," promises Peggy Burdick of Burlington, Michigan.

- **6 to 8 hot dog buns**
- **1 cup (4 ounces) shredded cheddar cheese**

MINI-BITES WITH FULL-SIZE FLAVOR. Pictured above: BLT Bites (recipe on this page).

1/2 cup butter **or** margarine, softened
2 tablespoons minced fresh parsley
2 tablespoons minced chives
2 tablespoons chopped pimientos
1 tablespoon chopped green onion

Slice hot dog buns lengthwise. Mix remaining ingredients together; spread over the buns. Place on a baking sheet. Bake at 400° for 6-8 minutes or until cheese is melted. Cut each bun into 1-in. pieces. **Yield:** 12-16 servings.

Pineapple Smoothie

(PICTURED ON THIS PAGE)

"I got this recipe over 20 years ago," reports Margery Bryan of Royal City, Washington. "It's a family favorite."

✓ This tasty dish uses less sugar, salt and fat. Recipe includes *Diabetic Exchanges*.

1 can (20 ounces) unsweetened pineapple chunks
1 cup buttermilk
2 teaspoons vanilla extract
2 teaspoons liquid sweetener
Mint leaves, optional

Drain pineapple, reserving 1/2 cup juice. Freeze pineapple chunks. Place juice, buttermilk, vanilla, sweetener and frozen pineapple into a blender container. Blend until smooth. Pour into glasses and garnish with mint if desired. Serve immediately. **Yield:** 5 servings. **Diabetic Exchanges:** One serving equals 1/2 skim milk, 1/2 fruit; also, 74 calories, 52 mg sodium, 2 mg cholesterol, 16 gm carbohydrate, 2 gm protein, 1 gm fat.

Fruit Punch

(PICTURED ON THIS PAGE)

"We've been making this punch for our church youth group for years," explains Ruth Tacoma of Falmouth, Michigan. "It's always a hit!"

✓ This tasty dish uses less sugar, salt and fat. Recipe includes *Diabetic Exchanges*.

1 package (.35 ounce) sugar-free tropical punch-flavored soft drink mix
4-3/4 cups water
1 can (12 ounces) unsweetened frozen orange juice concentrate, thawed
4 quarts diet white soda

In a large pitcher, combine soft drink mix and water; mix well. Add orange juice concentrate; mix well. When ready to serve, pour into punch bowl and add the white soda. **Yield:** 20 servings (5 quarts). **Diabetic Exchanges:** One

CAN'T BEAT THESE TREATS. Pictured above, left to right: Fruit Punch, Pineapple Smoothie (both recipes on this page) and Sugarless Apple Cookies (recipe on page 78).

serving equals 1/2 fruit; also, 38 calories, 3 mg sodium, 0 cholesterol, 9 gm carbohydrate, trace protein, trace fat.

Spiced Pecans

"These pecans are a treat to munch on anytime," assures Miriam Herschberger of Holmesville, Ohio.

1 egg white
1 teaspoon cold water
1 pound (4 cups) pecan halves
1/2 cup sugar
1/4 teaspoon salt
1/2 teaspoon ground cinnamon

In a mixing bowl, beat egg white lightly. Add water; beat until frothy but not stiff. Add pecans; stir until well coated. Combine sugar, salt and cinnamon. Sprinkle over pecans; toss to mix. Spread in a 15-in. x 10-in. x 1-in. greased baking pan. Bake at 250° for 1 hour, stirring occasionally. **Yield:** about 4 cups.

Spicy Snack Mix

"This mix helps satisfy the 'hungries'," says Betty Sitzman of Wray, Colorado. "And you can make it more or less spicy to suit your tastes."

1/2 cup butter **or** margarine
1 tablespoon seasoned salt
1 tablespoon Worcestershire sauce

1/2 to 1 teaspoon garlic powder
1/2 to 1 teaspoon hot pepper sauce
5 cups Wheat Chex cereal
7 cups Rice Chex cereal
6 cups Cheerios cereal
1 can (12 ounces) mixed nuts

In a small saucepan, melt butter. Add seasoned salt, Worcestershire sauce, garlic powder and hot pepper sauce; set aside. In a large mixing bowl, combine cereals and nuts; mix well. Stir in butter mixture; stir until well blended. Spread into two 15-in. x 10-in. x 1-in. baking pans. Bake at 250° for 1 hour, stirring every 15 minutes. **Yield:** 20 cups.

Egg Salad/ Cheese Spread

"Your family will enjoy this different version of typical egg salad," says Denise Goedeken of Platte Center, Nebraska.

2 cups shredded process cheese
4 hard-cooked eggs, chopped
1/2 cup mayonnaise **or** salad dressing
1/4 cup sweet pickle relish
1 teaspoon prepared mustard
Salt and pepper to taste

Combine first five ingredients in a mixing bowl; season with salt and pepper. **Yield:** about 3 cups.

MAIN DISHES

COMING UP WITH new and interesting main dishes for everyday meals or special occasions can be a real challenge. But you'll never run out of ideas with these wonderful beef, poultry, pork and game recipes.

Skillet Pork Chops With Zucchini

"My husband and I live on a small farm with our two young sons," relates Diane Banaszak of West Bend, Wisconsin. "We're always blessed with plenty of zucchini from our garden, so I try lots of different zucchini recipes. This is one of my family's favorites."

✓ This tasty dish uses less sugar, salt and fat. Recipe includes *Diabetic Exchanges*.

        3 tablespoons all-purpose flour
        5 tablespoons grated Parmesan cheese, *divided*
    1-1/2 teaspoons salt
        1/2 teaspoon dill weed
        1/4 teaspoon pepper
        6 pork chops (about 3/4 inch thick)
        1 tablespoon cooking oil
        2 medium onions, sliced
        1/3 cup water
        3 medium zucchini (about 1 pound), sliced
        1/2 teaspoon paprika

In a large plastic bag, combine flour, 2 tablespoons Parmesan cheese, salt, dill weed and pepper. Place pork chops in bag and shake to coat; shake off excess flour and reserve. Heat oil in a large skillet over medium-high; brown pork chops on both sides. Reduce heat. Place onion slices on chops. Add water to skillet; cover and simmer for 15 minutes. Place zucchini slices over the onion. Mix remaining Parmesan cheese with reserved flour mixture; sprinkle over zucchini. Sprinkle paprika on top. Cover and simmer for 25 minutes or until pork chops are tender. **Yield:** 6 servings. **Diabetic Exchanges:** One serving equals 3 meat, 1-1/2 vegetable; also, 279 calories, 638 mg sodium, 78 mg cholesterol, 9 gm carbohydrate, 27 gm protein, 15 gm fat.

No-Fuss Lasagna

"I like this recipe because it can be prepared a day ahead and baked just before serving," explains Denise Goedeken of Platte Center, Nebraska. "Packaged spaghetti sauce and noodles that are not pre-boiled makes preparation especially quick."

    1-1/2 pounds lean ground beef
        1 can (12 ounces) tomato paste
        3 cups water
        2 packages (1-1/2 ounces *each*) spaghetti sauce mix
        1 tablespoon sugar
        4 teaspoons dried parsley flakes
        1/2 teaspoon salt
        1/2 teaspoon garlic powder
        1/4 teaspoon pepper
        2 eggs, beaten
        1 carton (16 ounces) dry cottage cheese
        2 cups (8 ounces) shredded cheddar cheese, *divided*
        2 cups (8 ounces) shredded mozzarella cheese, *divided*
        1 package (16 ounces) lasagna noodles, uncooked

In a large saucepan, brown ground beef; drain. Add tomato paste, water, spaghetti sauce mix, sugar, parsley, salt, garlic powder and pepper. Simmer, partially covered, for 20 minutes. Stir occasionally. In a bowl, combine eggs with cottage cheese, half of the cheddar cheese and half of the mozzarella. Set aside. Spoon one-third of the meat sauce into a 13-in. x 9-in. x 2-in. baking pan. Place half of the uncooked noodles over sauce. Top with one-third of meat sauce and press down. Spoon cottage cheese mixture over all. Cover with remaining noodles and meat sauce. Cover and refrigerate overnight. Bake, covered, at 350° for 1 hour. Uncover; sprinkle with remaining cheddar and mozzarella cheeses. Bake an additional 15 minutes. Let stand 10 minutes before cutting. **Yield:** 8 servings.

Baked Chicken Breasts Supreme

"Perfect for a busy day, this saucy main dish can be prepared a day ahead and baked before serving," says Marjorie Scott of Sardis, British Columbia. "My brothers don't want me to make anything else when they come to dinner! Leftovers are great for sandwiches or sliced with potato salad."

✓ This tasty dish uses less sugar, salt and fat. Recipe includes *Diabetic Exchanges*.

    1-1/2 cups plain yogurt *or* sour cream
        1/4 cup lemon juice
        1/2 teaspoon Worcestershire sauce
        1/2 teaspoon celery seed
        1/2 teaspoon Hungarian sweet paprika

        1 garlic clove, minced
        1/2 teaspoon salt, optional
        1/4 teaspoon pepper
        8 boneless skinless chicken breast halves
        2 cups fine dry bread crumbs

In a large bowl, combine first eight ingredients. Place chicken in mixture and turn to coat. Cover and marinate overnight in the refrigerator. Remove chicken from marinade; coat each piece with crumbs. Arrange on a shallow baking pan. Bake, uncovered, at 350° for 45 minutes or until juices run clear. **Yield:** 8 servings. **Diabetic Exchanges:** One serving equals 3-1/2 lean meat, 1 starch, 1/4 skim milk; also, 271 calories, 293 mg sodium, 76 mg cholesterol, 22 gm carbohydrate, 32 gm protein, 5 gm fat.

Liver with Peppers And Onions

"My two children were just toddlers when I first served them this liver dish," states Naomi Giddis of Grawn, Michigan. "They remain wary of liver prepared other ways, but they still like this stir-fry version."

        1/2 cup all-purpose flour
        1 teaspoon salt
        1/4 teaspoon pepper
        1 pound liver, cut into bite-size pieces
        4 tablespoons vegetable oil, *divided*
        1 large onion, thinly sliced into rings
        1 medium green pepper, cut into 1-inch pieces
        1 sweet red pepper, cut into 1-inch pieces
        1 cup beef broth
        2 tablespoons soy sauce
        1 tablespoon cornstarch
Cooked rice *or* noodles

In a bowl, combine flour, salt and pepper. Add liver; toss to coat. Heat 2 tablespoons oil in a large skillet. Add onion and peppers; cook until crisp-tender. Remove from pan; set aside. Add remaining oil to the skillet. Cook and stir liver for 5-7 minutes or until no pink remains. In a small bowl, combine beef broth, soy sauce and cornstarch; stir into liver. Cook and stir constantly until sauce thickens. Return vegetables to the skillet and cook until heated through. Serve over rice or noodles. **Yield:** 4-6 servings.

Sausage Gravy

"This savory sausage gravy is a specialty among country folks in our area," says Mrs. J.N. Stine of Roanoke, Virginia. *"It's best served over fresh, hot biscuits. It makes a real 'sticks to the ribs' dish that we always enjoy!"*

- 1 pound sage-flavored bulk pork sausage
- 2 tablespoons finely chopped onion
- 6 tablespoons all-purpose flour
- 1 quart milk
- 1/2 teaspoon poultry seasoning
- 1/2 teaspoon ground nutmeg
- 1/4 teaspoon salt
- Dash Worcestershire sauce
- Dash hot pepper sauce
- Biscuits

Crumble sausage into a large saucepan; cook over medium-low heat. Add onion; cook and stir until transparent. Drain, discarding all but 2 tablespoons of drippings. Stir in flour; cook over medium-low heat about 6 minutes or until mixture bubbles and turns golden. Stir in milk. Add seasonings; cook, stirring, until thickened. To serve, slice biscuits and spoon gravy over halves. **Yield:** 4-6 servings.

Artichoke Chicken

(PICTURED ON THIS PAGE)

"Rosemary, mushrooms and artichokes combined give chicken a wonderful, savory flavor," reports Ruth Stenson of Santa Ana, California. *"It's always a big hit with everyone—especially my family!"*

- 8 skinless boneless chicken breast halves
- 2 tablespoons butter *or* margarine
- 2 jars (6 ounces *each*) marinated artichoke hearts, drained
- 1 jar (4-1/2 ounces) whole mushrooms, drained
- 1/2 cup chopped onion
- 1/3 cup all-purpose flour
- 1-1/2 teaspoons dried rosemary
- 1 teaspoon salt
- 1/4 teaspoon pepper
- 2 cups chicken broth *or* 1 cup broth and 1 cup dry white wine
- Cooked noodles
- Chopped fresh parsley

In a skillet, brown chicken in butter. Remove chicken to an ungreased 13-in. x 9-in. x 2-in. baking dish; do not drain pan juices. Cut the artichokes into quarters. Arrange artichokes and mushrooms on top of chicken; set aside. Saute onion in pan juices; blend in flour, rosemary, salt and pepper. Add chicken broth; cook until thickened and bubbly. Remove from the heat and spoon over chicken. Cover and bake at 350° for 50-60 minutes or until chicken is tender.

CHOICE CHICKEN. Pictured above, top to bottom: Nutty Oven-Fried Chicken and Artichoke Chicken (both recipes on this page).

Place noodles on serving platter; top with chicken and sauce. Sprinkle with parsley. **Yield:** 8 servings.

Nutty Oven-Fried Chicken

(PICTURED ON THIS PAGE)

"The pecans that give this dish its unique nutty flavor are plentiful in the South. I love to make and serve this easy dish because the chicken comes out moist, tasty and crispy," says Diane Hixon of Niceville, Florida.

- 1 cup buttermilk biscuit mix
- 1/3 cup finely chopped pecans
- 2 teaspoons paprika
- 1/2 teaspoon salt
- 1/2 teaspoon poultry seasoning
- 1/2 teaspoon dried sage
- 1 broiler-fryer chicken (2 to 3 pounds), cut up
- 1/2 cup evaporated milk
- 1/3 cup butter *or* margarine, melted

In a shallow dish, combine biscuit mix, pecans and seasonings; mix well. Dip chicken pieces in milk; coat generously with pecan mixture. Place in a lightly greased 13-in. x 9-in. x 2-in. baking dish. Drizzle butter over chicken. Bake, uncovered, at 350° for 1 hour or until juices run clear. **Yield:** 6-8 servings.

PLEASANT PHEASANT. Pictured above: Pheasant and Wild Rice (recipe on this page).

Chicken Fajitas

"Fajitas are great for when you want to serve something tasty yet keep cooking to a minimum," reports Lindsay St. John of Plainfield, Indiana.

✓ This tasty dish uses less sugar, salt and fat. Recipe includes *Diabetic Exchanges*.

- 1/4 cup lime juice
- 1 garlic clove, minced
- 1 teaspoon chili powder
- 1/2 teaspoon ground cumin
- 2 whole skinless boneless chicken breasts, cut into strips
- 1 medium onion, cut into thin wedges
- 1/2 medium sweet red pepper, cut into strips
- 1/2 medium yellow pepper, cut into strips
- 1/2 medium green pepper, cut into strips
- 1/2 cup salsa
- 12 flour tortillas (8 inches)
- 1-1/2 cups (6 ounces) shredded cheddar *or* Monterey Jack cheese

In a small bowl, combine lime juice, garlic, chili powder and cumin. Add chicken; stir. Marinate for 15 minutes. In a nonstick skillet, cook onion, chicken and marinade for 3 minutes or until chicken is no longer pink. Add peppers; saute for 3-5 minutes or until crisp-tender. Stir in salsa. Divide mixture among tortillas; top with cheese. Roll up and serve. **Yield:** 6 servings. **Diabetic Exchanges:** One serving (prepared with cheddar cheese) equals 2 meat, 1 vegetable, 1 starch; also, 228 calories, 353 mg sodium, 39 mg cholesterol, 19 gm carbohydrate, 17 gm protein, 12 gm fat.

Pheasant and Wild Rice

(PICTURED ON THIS PAGE)

"Everyone in my family hunts," says Debbie McCoic of Hillsboro, Wisconsin. *"This recipe works well with pheasant, wild turkey…even chicken."*

- 1 can (10-3/4 ounces) condensed cream of mushroom soup, undiluted
- 2 soup cans water
- 3/4 cup chopped onion
- 2-1/2 teaspoons dried parsley flakes
- 2 teaspoons dried oregano
- 2 teaspoons garlic powder
- 2 teaspoons salt
- 1-1/2 teaspoons paprika
- 1 teaspoon pepper
- 6 bacon strips, cut up
- 1 oven cooking bag
- 2 cups uncooked wild rice
- 1/2 pound fresh mushrooms, sliced
- 1 large pheasant, halved, *or* 2 small pheasants (about 4 pounds)

In a saucepan, combine first nine ingredients; bring to a boil. Meanwhile, place bacon in an oven cooking bag. Sprinkle rice and mushrooms over bacon. Add pheasant. Pour soup mixture into bag. Seal and slit according to package directions. Bake at 325° for 2 to 2-1/2 hours. **Yield:** 6-8 servings.

Broccoli-Ham Hot Dish

Margaret Wagner Allen of Abingdon, Virginia states, "This recipe is a delicious and colorful way to use up leftover ham."

- 2 packages (10 ounces *each*) frozen cut broccoli
- 2 cups cooked rice
- 6 tablespoons butter *or* margarine
- 2 cups fresh bread crumbs (about 2-1/2 slices)
- 1 medium onion, chopped
- 3 tablespoons all-purpose flour
- 1 teaspoon salt
- 1/4 teaspoon pepper
- 3 cups milk
- 1-1/2 pounds fully cooked ham, cubed

Shredded cheddar *or* Swiss cheese

Cook broccoli according to package directions; drain. Spoon rice into a 13-in. x 9-in. x 2-in. baking pan. Place broccoli over rice. Melt butter in a large skillet. Sprinkle 2 tablespoons of melted butter over the bread crumbs and set aside. In remaining butter, saute onion until soft. Add flour, salt and pepper, stirring constantly until bubbly. Stir in milk and continue cooking until sauce thickens and bubbles. Cook and stir for 1 minute; add ham and heat through. Pour over rice and broccoli. Sprinkle the crumbs over all. Bake at 350° for 30 minutes or until heated through. Sprinkle with cheese; let stand 5 minutes before serving. **Yield:** 8 servings.

Basil Burgers

"Basil is one of my favorite herbs," explains Jennie Wilburn of Long Creek, Oregon. *"This aromatic herb gives great flavor to ordinary burgers."*

- 2 pounds lean ground beef
- 1/4 cup red wine *or* beef broth
- 1/4 cup Italian bread crumbs
- 1/4 cup minced red onion
- 1/4 to 1/2 cup fresh basil leaves, minced
- 1 to 2 teaspoons garlic salt

8 hamburger buns
Monterey Jack cheese slices,
  optional

In a large bowl, combine first six ingredients; mix well. Shape into eight patties. Grill over medium-hot coals until burgers reach desired doneness. Serve on hamburger buns; top with cheese slices if desired. **Yield:** 8 servings.

Cranberry Chicken

(PICTURED ON PAGE 3)

"I serve this chicken over rice with salad and rolls," explains Dorothy Bateman of Carver, Massachusetts. "The ruby-red sauce has a tart cinnamony flavor."

1/2 cup all-purpose flour
1/2 teaspoon salt
1/4 teaspoon pepper
  6 boneless skinless chicken
     breast halves
1/4 cup butter *or* margarine
  1 cup fresh *or* frozen cranberries
  1 cup water
1/2 cup packed brown sugar
  1 tablespoon red wine vinegar,
     optional
Dash ground nutmeg
Cooked rice

In a shallow dish, combine flour, salt and pepper; dredge chicken. In a skillet, melt butter over medium heat. Brown the chicken on both sides. Remove and keep warm. In the same skillet, add cranberries, water, brown sugar, vinegar if desired and nutmeg. Cook and stir until the cranberries burst, about 5 minutes. Return chicken to skillet. Cover and simmer for 20-30 minutes or until chicken is tender, basting occasionally with the sauce. Serve over rice. **Yield:** 4-6 servings.

Tomato Pizza

"I developed this recipe for a nice change from the usual meat-topped pizza," says Lois McAtee of Oceanside, California.

✓ This tasty dish uses less sugar, salt and fat. Recipe includes *Diabetic Exchanges*.

  6 medium firm tomatoes, thinly
     sliced
  1 large baked pizza crust (13 to
     16 inches)
  2 tablespoons olive oil
  1 teaspoon salt
  1 teaspoon pepper
  1 can (2-1/4 ounces) sliced ripe
     olives, drained, optional
1/2 cup diced green pepper
1/2 cup diced onion
  1 tablespoon chopped fresh
     basil
  1 cup (4 ounces) shredded
     mozzarella cheese

1 cup (4 ounces) shredded
  cheddar cheese

Place tomato slices in a circle on crust, overlapping slightly until crust is completely covered. Drizzle with olive oil. Season with salt and pepper. Cover with olives if desired, green pepper and onion. Sprinkle basil over all. Cover with mozzarella and cheddar cheeses. Bake at 400° for 15 minutes or until cheese is melted. Serve immediately. **Yield:** 8 servings. **Diabetic Exchanges:** One serving (prepared with low-fat mozzarella and without olives) equals 1 starch, 1 meat, 1 vegetable, 1 fat; also, 223 calories, 599 mg sodium, 22 mg cholesterol, 21 gm carbohydrate, 12 gm protein, 12 gm fat.

Beef Enchiladas

(PICTURED ON THIS PAGE)

Mary Anne McWhirter of Pearland, Texas shares, "These enchiladas have a flavorful combination of ingredients and a rich homemade sauce."

  1 pound ground beef
  1 cup cottage cheese
  1 can (4-1/4 ounces) chopped
     ripe olives, drained
  2 tablespoons minced fresh
     parsley

1/2 teaspoon garlic powder
1/2 teaspoon salt
1/4 teaspoon pepper
  8 flour tortillas (7 inches)
SAUCE:
  1 medium onion, chopped
1/2 medium green pepper,
     chopped
  1 tablespoon cooking oil
  1 can (15 ounces) tomato sauce
  1 can (4 ounces) chopped
     green chilies
  2 teaspoons chili powder
  1 teaspoon sugar
1/2 teaspoon garlic powder
  1 cup (4 ounces) shredded
     cheddar cheese

In a skillet, brown the ground beef. Drain. Combine with cottage cheese, olives, parsley, garlic powder, salt and pepper. Place about 1/3 cup filling on each tortilla; roll up. Place tortillas, seam side down, in an ungreased 13-in. x 9-in. x 2-in. baking dish. For sauce, saute the onion and green pepper in oil until tender. Add tomato sauce, green chilies, chili powder, sugar and garlic powder. Pour over tortillas. Cover and bake at 350° for 30 minutes. Sprinkle with cheese and return to the oven for 5 minutes or until cheese melts. **Yield:** 4 servings.

MMMM-MEXICAN MEAL! Pictured above, clockwise from top left: Sopaipillas (recipe on page 85), Tex-Mex Dip (recipe on page 51) and Beef Enchiladas (recipe on this page).

Catfish with Lemon/Butter Sauce

"I created this recipe for a catfish cooking contest by modifying a recipe for shrimp and spaghetti, which I also developed," shares Rita Futral of Ocean Springs, Mississippi.

- 3/4 cup butter
- 8 ounces fresh mushrooms, sliced
- 1 garlic clove, minced
- 1/2 cup chicken broth *or* dry white wine
- 2 tablespoons lemon juice
- 1/4 to 1/3 cup chopped fresh parsley
- 1 teaspoon salt
- 1/2 teaspoon pepper
- 1-1/2 pounds catfish fillets, cut into bite-size pieces
- 16 ounces spaghetti, cooked and drained
- 1/2 cup grated Parmesan cheese
- Lemon slices *or* wedges, optional
- Additional parsley, optional

In a large skillet, melt butter over medium heat. Cook mushrooms and garlic, stirring occasionally, for 5 minutes. Add broth or wine, lemon juice, parsley, salt and pepper; cook 3 minutes, stirring occasionally. Add catfish; simmer, uncovered, for 6-8 minutes or until fish flakes easily with a fork. (Butter sauce will be thin.) Serve over spaghetti. Sprinkle with Parmesan cheese. Garnish with lemon and parsley if desired. **Yield:** 6-8 servings.

Spicy Rice Casserole

"Here's a recipe that makes a terrific main dish served with corn bread and your favorite dessert," reports Debbie Jones of California, Maryland. *"Made ahead, the casserole is easy to reheat in the microwave for fast meals."*

- 1 pound mild bulk pork sausage
- 1 teaspoon ground cumin
- 1/2 teaspoon garlic powder
- 2 medium onions, chopped
- 2 medium green peppers, chopped
- 2 beef bouillon cubes
- 2 cups boiling water
- 1 to 2 jalapeno peppers, finely minced and seeded
- 1 package (6-1/4 ounces) quick-cooking long grain and wild rice mix

In a large skillet, cook sausage, cumin and garlic powder, stirring often. Drain. Add onions and green peppers; saute until crisp-tender. Dissolve bouillon in water; add to skillet. Stir in jalapenos, rice and rice seasoning packet; bring to a boil. Reduce heat and simmer, uncovered, 5-10 minutes or until the water is absorbed. **Yield:** 4-6 servings.

Horseradish-Glazed Ham

"Here in Tulelake, California, my husband and I grow horseradish," says Cathy Seus. *"It's no surprise that this ham recipe is one of our favorites!"*

- 1 fully cooked bone-in *or* boneless ham (5 to 6 pounds)
- Whole cloves
- 1 cup packed brown sugar
- 1/3 cup prepared horseradish
- 1/4 cup lemon juice

Score ham and stud with cloves. Bake according to package directions. Meanwhile, combine brown sugar, horseradish and lemon juice. Baste ham during the last 30 minutes of baking. **Yield:** about 20-24 servings.

Vegetable Beef Casserole

"This easy one-dish recipe has been a family favorite ever since it was handed down to me 35 years ago from my husband's aunt," states Evangeline Rew of Manassas, Virginia *"A simple salad goes nicely with this dish."*

- 3 medium unpeeled potatoes, sliced
- 3 carrots, sliced
- 3 celery ribs, sliced
- 2 cups fresh *or* frozen green beans
- 1 medium onion, chopped
- 1 pound lean ground beef
- 1 teaspoon dried thyme
- 1 teaspoon salt
- 1 teaspoon pepper
- 4 medium tomatoes, peeled, chopped and seeded
- 1 cup (4 ounces) shredded cheddar cheese

In a 3-qt. casserole, layer half of the potatoes, carrots, celery, green beans and onion. Crumble half of the uncooked beef over vegetables. Sprinkle with 1/2 teaspoon each of thyme, salt and pepper. Repeat layers. Top with tomatoes. Cover and bake at 400° for 15 minutes. Reduce heat to 350°; bake about 1 hour longer or until vegetables are tender and meat is done. Sprinkle with cheese; cover and let stand until cheese is melted. **Yield:** 6-8 servings.

FOR A CHANGE of pace sandwich, trim the crust off a slice of bread and roll the bread flat. Add meat, cheese and a favorite spread, roll up and secure with a pretzel stick or toothpick.

Special Ham and Cheese Sandwiches

"When I tire of ordinary meat and cheese sandwiches for lunch, I try creative alternatives," explains Mattie Cheek of Lawrenceburg, Kentucky. *"I love these ham and cheese sandwiches because they're so convenient and a little different."*

- 1 package (3 ounces) cream cheese, softened
- 1/2 cup shredded cheddar cheese
- 2 tablespoons pickle relish
- 2 teaspoons Dijon mustard
- 2 ounces ham, finely chopped
- 6 slices bread

In a small bowl, combine cream cheese, cheddar cheese, relish and mustard. Add ham. Divide mixture among three slices of bread; top with remaining bread to make sandwiches. **Yield:** 3 servings.

Sour Cream Apple Chicken

"I've found that apples and chicken go well together because they both have subtle flavors. I developed this recipe myself. I think it's not only a great-tasting main course, it also looks nice on the table," says Carolyn Popwell of Lacey, Washington.

- 4 boneless skinless chicken breast halves
- 1 tablespoon cooking oil
- 2 medium baking apples, peeled and thinly sliced
- 1/2 cup apple juice *or* cider
- 1/3 cup chopped onion
- 1 teaspoon dried basil
- 1/2 teaspoon salt
- 1 cup (8 ounces) sour cream
- 1 tablespoon all-purpose flour
- Cooked spinach noodles
- Paprika

In a large skillet, cook chicken in oil over medium heat until browned and no longer pink inside, about 6-8 minutes per side. Remove from skillet and keep warm. Add apples, juice, onion, basil and salt to the skillet; bring to a boil. Reduce heat; cover and simmer until apples are tender. Combine sour cream and flour; add to skillet. Stir and cook until sauce is warm (do not boil). Arrange noodles on a serving platter. Top with chicken. Spoon apple sauce over all. Sprinkle with paprika. **Yield:** 4 servings.

Asparagus Ham Rolls

(PICTURED ON THIS PAGE)

"I love this delicious recipe because it includes three of my favorite locally produced foods—ham, asparagus and cheese," informs Laurie Timm of Minneiska, Minnesota.

✓ This tasty dish uses less sugar, salt and fat. Recipe includes *Diabetic Exchanges*.

    2 tablespoons butter *or* margarine
    1/4 cup all-purpose flour
    2 cups milk
    1/2 cup shredded cheddar cheese
    1/4 teaspoon salt
    1/4 teaspoon white pepper
    24 fresh *or* frozen asparagus stalks
    8 thin slices fully cooked ham (about 1/2 pound)
    1/4 cup bread crumbs

In a saucepan, melt butter; stir in flour and cook until thick. Gradually stir in milk and cook until bubbly and thickened. Stir in cheese, salt and pepper. Remove from the heat. Place three asparagus stalks on each ham slice. Roll up; secure with toothpicks if necessary. Place in a 13-in. x 9-in. x 2-in. baking pan; cover with cheese sauce. Sprinkle with crumbs. Bake at 375° for 20 minutes. **Yield:** 8 servings. **Diabetic Exchanges:** One serving (prepared with margarine and skim milk) equals 1 meat, 1 vegetable, 1/2 starch; also, 125 calories, 492 mg sodium, 19 mg cholesterol, 11 gm carbohydrate, 11 gm protein, 7 gm fat.

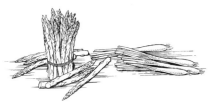

Barbecued Chicken

"We don't fry foods much anymore and prefer to barbecue, so I adapted my mother's recipe for barbecue sauce to suit our tastes," declares Linda Scott of Hahira, Georgia. *"Every summer, we have a neighborhood cookout. I take this chicken and watch it disappear!"*

    2 broiler-fryer chickens (2 to 3 pounds *each*), cut up
    SEASONING MIX:
    3 tablespoons salt *or* salt substitute
    2 tablespoons onion powder
    1 tablespoon paprika
    2 teaspoons garlic powder
    1-1/2 teaspoons chili powder
    1-1/2 teaspoons pepper

SUMMERTIME SPECIALTIES. Pictured above, clockwise from top: Rhubarb Upside-Down Cake (recipe on page 82), Asparagus Ham Rolls (recipe on this page) and Honey Fruit Dressing (recipe on page 96).

    1/4 teaspoon ground turmeric
    Pinch ground red pepper
    SAUCE:
    2 cups ketchup
    3 tablespoons brown sugar
    2 tablespoons dried minced onion
    2 tablespoons frozen orange juice concentrate, thawed
    1 tablespoon Seasoning Mix
    1/2 teaspoon liquid smoke

Pat chicken pieces dry so seasoning coats well; set aside. Combine seasoning mix ingredients; sprinkle generously over both sides of the chicken. Reserve 1 tablespoon mix for sauce and store leftovers in a covered container. Grill chicken, skin side down, uncovered, over medium coals for 20 minutes. Turn; grill 20-30 minutes more or until chicken is tender and no longer pink. Meanwhile, combine all sauce ingredients in a small bowl. During the last 10 minutes of grilling, brush chicken often with sauce. **Yield:** 12 servings.

1 green pepper, chopped
1 can (12 ounces) whole kernel corn, drained
1 can (10-3/4 ounces) condensed tomato soup, undiluted
1 can (8 ounces) tomato sauce
1/3 cup sliced stuffed olives
1 garlic clove, minced
1/2 teaspoon salt
8 ounces wide noodles, cooked and drained

In a large Dutch oven, brown the beef, sausage and onion. Drain off fat. Stir in 1 cup cheese, green pepper, corn, soup, tomato sauce, olives, garlic, salt and noodles. Place in a 13-in. x 9-in. x 2-in. baking pan. Sprinkle with remaining cheese. Cover and bake at 350° for 35 minutes. Uncover and bake 10 minutes longer. **Yield:** 8-10 servings.

Louisiana Chicken

"My family loves chicken and I do, too...there are so many different ways to prepare it!" exclaims Jill Werle of Saskatoon, Saskatchewan. "This recipe combines different ingredients for flavor that's hard to beat."

2 tablespoons all-purpose flour
1 large plastic roasting bag with tie
1 roasting chicken (3-1/2 to 5 pounds)
1 teaspoon salt
1 teaspoon cayenne pepper
3 medium onions, quartered
6 large potatoes, peeled and quartered
6 carrots, peeled and cut into 2-inch pieces
2 green peppers, quartered
2 garlic cloves
1 tablespoon dried parsley flakes
1-1/2 teaspoons dried mint *or* 1 tablespoon chopped fresh mint
2 cups chicken broth
1 tablespoon Worcestershire sauce
7 drops bitters, optional

Put flour in bag and shake. Place bag into a 13-in. x 9-in. x 2-in. pan or larger roasting pan. Distribute flour evenly on bottom of bag. Sprinkle chicken with salt and cayenne pepper; place in bag. Surround chicken with onions, potatoes, carrots and green peppers. Place one garlic clove inside the chicken and one with the vegetables. Sprinkle parsley and mint over vegetables and chicken. Combine chicken broth, Worcestershire sauce and bitters if desired. Pour under chicken inside of bag. Fasten the bag. Puncture the top of bag five or six times with a fork. Bake at 325° for 1-1/2 to 2-1/2 hours (25 to 30 minutes per pound of chicken). **Yield:** 6-8 servings.

WE'RE TALKING TURKEY. Pictured above, left to right: Turkey Stir-Fry (recipe on this page) and Turkey Wild Rice Soup (recipe on page 94).

Turkey Stir-Fry

(PICTURED ON THIS PAGE)

"My family loves the tender turkey strips, colorful vegetables and crunchy cashews in this recipe," says Julianne Johnson of Grove City, Minnesota. *"You don't always have to fix the whole bird to enjoy the wonderful taste of turkey."*

✓ **This tasty dish uses less sugar, salt and fat. Recipe includes** *Diabetic Exchanges.*

1-1/2 pounds raw boneless turkey, cut into strips
1 tablespoon cooking oil
1 small onion, chopped
1 carrot, julienned
1/2 medium green pepper, sliced
2 cups fresh mushrooms, sliced
1 cup chicken broth
3 tablespoons cornstarch
3 tablespoons soy sauce
1/2 teaspoon ground ginger
2 cups pea pods, trimmed
Cooked rice, optional
1/3 cup cashews, optional

In a large skillet or wok, stir-fry turkey in oil over medium-high heat until no longer pink, about 5-6 minutes. Remove turkey and keep warm. Stir-fry the onion, carrot, green pepper and mushrooms until crisp-tender, about 5 minutes. In a small bowl, combine chicken broth, cornstarch, soy sauce and ginger. Add to the skillet; cook and stir until thickened and bubbly. Return turkey to skillet with pea pods; cook and stir until heated through. If desired, serve over rice and top with cashews. **Yield:** 6 servings. **Diabetic Exchanges:** One serving (prepared with low-sodium chicken broth and soy sauce, and served without rice or cashews) equals 4 lean meat, 1 vegetable, 1/2 starch; also, 277 calories, 200 mg sodium, 84 mg cholesterol, 11 gm carbohydrate, 40 gm protein, 7 gm fat.

Reunion Casserole

"This noodle casserole is just like Mom used to make," recollects Bernice Morris of Marshfield, Missouri. *"Its down-home taste has appeal at family gatherings."*

1 pound ground beef
1/2 pound bulk hot sausage
1 cup chopped onion
2 cups (8 ounces) shredded cheddar cheese, *divided*

Cranberry Apple Relish

"Give this tart, rose-colored relish a try," urges Carla Hodenfield of Mandan, North Dakota. *"It's a special dish you can serve year-round."*

✓ This tasty dish uses less sugar, salt and fat. Recipe includes *Diabetic Exchanges*.

    2 cups ground fresh *or* frozen
      cranberries
  1/2 cup diced peeled apple
  1/4 cup raisins
  1/4 cup chopped walnuts,
      optional
    2 tablespoons liquid artificial
      sweetener
  1/2 teaspoon lemon juice

In a bowl, combine all ingredients. Refrigerate for at least 2 hours. **Yield:** 10 servings. **Diabetic Exchanges:** One 1/4-cup serving (prepared without walnuts) equals 1/2 fruit; also, 24 calories, 1 mg sodium, 0 cholesterol, 6 gm carbohydrate, trace protein, trace fat.

Catfish Cakes

"These cakes are crispy on the outside and moist and flavorful on the inside— a real treat! I like to serve them with hush puppies and coleslaw," informs Jan Campbell of Purvis, Mississippi.

1-1/2 pounds catfish fillets
    2 eggs, beaten
    1 large potato, peeled, cooked
      and mashed
    1 large onion, finely chopped
    1 to 2 tablespoons chopped
      fresh parsley
    2 to 3 drops hot pepper sauce
    1 garlic clove, minced
    1 teaspoon salt
  1/2 teaspoon pepper
  1/2 teaspoon dried basil
    2 cups finely crushed butter-
      flavored crackers
Cooking oil
Tartar sauce, optional

Poach or bake catfish fillets. Drain and refrigerate. Flake cooled fish into a large mixing bowl. Add eggs, potato, onion, parsley, hot pepper sauce, garlic, salt, pepper and basil; mix well. Shape into eight patties; coat with cracker crumbs. Heat a small amount of oil in a large skillet. Cook patties, a few at a time, until browned on both sides and heated through. Serve with tartar sauce if desired. **Yield:** 8 servings.

Tangy Meatballs

"These meatballs are a big hit wherever they go! In their tasty barbecue sauce, they're a great dish to pass," says Jane Barta of St. Thomas, North Dakota.

    2 eggs
    2 cups quick-cooking *or* old-
      fashioned oats
    1 can (12 ounces) evaporated
      milk
    1 cup chopped onion
    2 teaspoons salt
  1/2 teaspoon pepper
  1/2 teaspoon garlic powder
    3 pounds lean ground beef
SAUCE:
    2 cups ketchup
  1-1/2 cups packed brown sugar
  1/2 cup chopped onion
    1 to 2 teaspoons liquid smoke
  1/2 teaspoon garlic powder

In a large bowl, beat eggs. Add oats, milk, onion, salt, pepper and garlic powder. Add the ground beef; mix well. Shape into 1-1/2-in. balls. Place in two 13-in. x 9-in. x 2-in. baking pans. Bake, uncovered, at 375° for 30 minutes. Remove from the oven and drain. Place all of the meatballs in one of the pans. In a saucepan, bring all sauce ingredients to a boil. Pour over meatballs. Return to the oven and bake, uncovered, for 20 minutes or until meatballs are done. **Yield:** 4 dozen.

Chicken Tetrazzini

"My husband is not a casserole lover, but this creamy dish is one of his favorites! Nutmeg gives it a different taste," says Kelly Heusmann of Cincinnati, Ohio. *"As a busy mother with three young sons, I put this easy recipe to good use."*

    2 cups sliced mushrooms
  1/4 cup butter *or* margarine
  1/4 cup all-purpose flour
    2 cups chicken broth
  1/4 cup light cream
    1 tablespoon chopped fresh
      parsley
    1 teaspoon salt
  1/8 to 1/4 teaspoon ground nutmeg
  1/4 teaspoon pepper
    3 tablespoons dry white wine,
      optional
    3 cups cubed cooked chicken
    8 ounces spaghetti, cooked and
      drained
  3/4 cup shredded Parmesan
      cheese
Additional parsley

In a skillet, cook mushrooms in butter until tender. Stir in flour; gradually add the chicken broth. Cook, stirring constantly, until sauce comes to a boil. Remove from the heat; stir in cream, parsley, salt, nutmeg, pepper, and wine if desired. Fold in the chicken and spaghetti. Turn into a greased 12-in. x 8-in. x 2-in. baking dish; sprinkle with Parmesan cheese. Bake, uncovered, at 350° for 30 minutes or until heated through. Garnish with parsley. **Yield:** 8 servings.

Southern-Fried Baked Steak

"When my family gets together, they often ask me to prepare this dish. They love its down-home flavor," shares Howard Haug of Hewitt, Texas.

    2 pounds round steak, trimmed
    1 teaspoon salt
    1 teaspoon pepper
  1-1/2 cups all-purpose flour
  1/2 cup milk
    1 egg, lightly beaten
Cooking oil
    1 onion, chopped
    1 cup beef broth

Pound steak to tenderize; cut into serving-size pieces. Season with salt and pepper. Dust with flour. Combine milk and egg; dip meat into egg mixture and back into flour. In a skillet, brown meat on both sides in oil. Place onion in an ungreased 13-in. x 9-in. x 2-in. baking pan. Place meat over onion. Pour broth over all. Cover tightly and bake at 350° for 1-1/2 hours. Uncover; bake 20 minutes more. **Yield:** 6 servings.

Sausage-Stuffed Zucchini

"Growing up, I often helped Mom in the kitchen," comments Warren Knudtson of Las Vegas, Nevada. *"Now I love making lots of home-cooked meals."*

    4 medium zucchini (6 to 7
      inches)
  1/2 pound bulk mild Italian
      sausage
  1/4 cup chopped onion
    1 garlic clove, minced
    1 teaspoon dried oregano
  1/2 cup fresh *or* frozen corn
    1 medium tomato, seeded and
      diced
    1 cup (4 ounces) shredded
      cheddar cheese, *divided*

Cut each zucchini in half lengthwise. Place, cut side down, in a large skillet; add 1/2 in. of water. Bring to a boil; reduce heat and simmer until zucchini are crisp-tender, about 5 minutes. Remove zucchini and drain water. In the same skillet, cook sausage, onion and garlic until sausage is browned; drain fat. Add oregano, corn and tomato. Cook and stir until heated through. Remove from the heat and stir in 2/3 cup cheese; set aside. Scoop out and discard seeds from zucchini. Divide the sausage mixture among zucchini shells. Place in a greased 13-in. x 9-in. x 2-in. baking pan. Sprinkle with remaining cheese. Bake, uncovered, at 375° for 12-15 minutes or until heated through. **Yield:** 4-6 servings.

Baked Ziti

"This delicious pasta dish is easy to prepare," shares Christopher Gordon from his Springfield, Missouri home.

- 1 medium onion, chopped
- 2 garlic cloves, minced
- 2 tablespoons olive oil
- 1 can (28 ounces) tomatoes with liquid, cut up
- 1 teaspoon dried oregano
- 1 teaspoon dried basil
- 1/2 teaspoon salt
- 1/8 teaspoon pepper
- 8 ounces ziti, cooked and drained
- 2 cups (8 ounces) shredded mozzarella cheese
- 2 tablespoons grated Parmesan cheese

In a large skillet, saute onion and garlic in oil until tender. Add tomatoes, oregano, basil, salt and pepper. Cover; simmer for 20 minutes. Place ziti in an ungreased 11-in. x 7-in. x 2-in. baking dish. Cover with sauce. Bake, uncovered, at 350° for 20 minutes. Sprinkle with both cheeses. Bake 10 minutes longer or until cheese melts. **Yield:** 6-8 servings.

Hasenpfeffer

(PICTURED ON THIS PAGE)

Says Mary Calendine of Hiddenite, North Carolina. "The tender meat combined with the sour cream and seasonings makes this a wonderful dish."

- 1 large onion, sliced
- 3 cups vinegar
- 3 cups water
- 1 tablespoon pickling spice
- 2 teaspoons salt
- 1/2 teaspoon pepper
- 2 bay leaves
- 8 whole cloves
- 1 rabbit (2-1/2 pounds), skinned and cut into serving-size pieces
- 1/4 cup all-purpose flour
- 2 to 3 tablespoons butter *or* margarine
- 1 cup (8 ounces) sour cream

In a large nonmetallic bowl, combine onion, vinegar, water and seasonings. Add rabbit pieces; cover and refrigerate for 48 hours, turning occasionally. Remove meat; strain and reserve marinade. Dry meat well; coat lightly with flour. In a skillet, melt butter; brown meat well. Gradually add 2 to 2-1/2 cups of reserved marinade. Cover and bring to a boil. Reduce heat and simmer until tender, about 30 minutes. Remove meat to a warm platter. Add sour cream to pan juices; stir just until heated through. Spoon over the meat and serve immediately. **Yield:** 6 servings.

Halloween Pizza

"I like to perk up Halloween—or any occasion—by having the grandkids make these special pizzas," relates Flo Burtnett of Gage, Oklahoma.

- 1 frozen cheese pizza (12 inches)
- 1 medium sweet red pepper
- 1 small green pepper
- 1 can (5-3/4 ounces) pitted ripe olives, drained and halved

Place pizza on a baking sheet. Arrange olives in a circle around edge of pizza. Cut a nose, eyes and mouth out of red pepper. Cut a stem and eyebrows out of green pepper. Make a jack-o'-lantern face on pizza. Bake according to package directions. **Yield:** 6-8 servings.

Brown-Bag Burritos

"These burritos are great either cold or reheated in a microwave. So they're perfect for a brown-bag lunch," assures Rhonda Cliett of Barton, Texas.

- 1 pound lean ground beef
- 1 can (16 ounces) refried beans
- 2/3 cup enchilada sauce
- 1/4 cup water
- 3 tablespoons minced onion
- 1-1/2 tablespoons chili powder
- 1-1/2 teaspoons garlic powder
- 3/4 teaspoon salt
- 1/2 teaspoon dried oregano
- 15 to 20 flour tortillas (7 inches)
- 1-1/2 to 2-1/2 cups (6 to 10 ounces) shredded cheddar cheese

In a large skillet, brown ground beef; drain. Add next eight ingredients; bring to a boil. Reduce heat; cover and simmer for 20 minutes. Heat 3-4 tortillas in a microwave until warm, about 45 seconds. Spoon 3-4 tablespoons of beef mixture down side of each tortilla. Top with 2-3 tablespoons of cheese. Roll up. Wrap each burrito in paper towel, then in foil. Repeat with remaining ingredients. Refrigerate. Eat burritos cold, or remove foil and heat paper towel-wrapped burrito in a microwave on high for about 1 minute. **Yield:** 15-20 burritos.

Basic Chicken Medley

"Everyone who's tried this dish has raved about it," Susan Jansen of Smyrna, Georgia comments.

✓ This tasty dish uses less sugar, salt and fat. Recipe includes *Diabetic Exchanges*.

- 1 tablespoon olive oil
- 3 garlic cloves, minced
- 2 whole boneless skinless chicken breasts (about 1-1/4 pounds), cut into 1-inch chunks
- 1 medium zucchini, cut into chunks
- 2 medium tomatoes, cut into chunks
- 1 tablespoon dried basil
- 2 tablespoons vinegar
- 1/4 teaspoon pepper

Cooked rice *or* pasta

ARE YOU GAME FOR GAME? Pictured above: Hasenpfeffer (recipe on this page).

Heat oil in a skillet; saute garlic. Add chicken and cook until no longer pink; remove and keep warm. Combine zucchini, tomatoes, basil, vinegar and pepper; toss to coat vegetables well. Add to skillet; stir-fry 3-5 minutes. Return chicken to skillet and heat through. Serve immediately over rice or pasta. **Yield:** 4 servings. **Diabetic Exchanges:** One serving equals 3 lean meat, 1 vegetable; also, 205 calories, 70 mg sodium, 73 mg cholesterol, 8 gm carbohydrate, 28 gm protein, 7 gm fat.

Spicy Tomato Steak

Says Anne Landers of Louisville, Kentucky, "After eating a similar dish on vacation in New Mexico, I came home and tried to duplicate it from memory. The results were delicious!"

✓ This tasty dish uses less sugar, salt and fat. Recipe includes *Diabetic Exchanges*.

- 2 tablespoons vinegar
- 1 teaspoon salt
- 1 teaspoon pepper
- 1 pound round steak, trimmed and cut into 1/4-inch strips
- 1/4 cup all-purpose flour
- 2 tablespoons olive oil
- 3 medium tomatoes, peeled, cut into wedges and seeded
- 2 medium potatoes, peeled and thinly sliced
- 2 cans (4 ounces *each*) chopped green chilies
- 1 garlic clove, minced
- 1 teaspoon dried basil

In a mixing bowl, combine vinegar, salt and pepper; toss with beef. Cover and marinate for 30 minutes; drain. Place flour in a bowl; add beef and toss to coat. In a skillet, cook beef in oil over medium heat for 15-20 minutes or until tender. Add remaining ingredients. Cover and simmer for 20-30 minutes or until the potatoes are tender, stirring occasionally. **Yield:** 6 servings. **Diabetic Exchanges:** One serving equals 2 lean meat, 1 starch, 1/2 fat; also, 195 calories, 757 mg sodium, 24 mg cholesterol, 16 gm carbohydrate, 16 gm protein, 8 gm fat.

Lemon Herbed Salmon

(PICTURED ON THIS PAGE)

"We sometimes send our delicious Washington salmon to Michigan for my sister to use in this family-favorite," reveals Perlene Hoekema of Lynden, Washington.

- 2-1/2 cups fresh bread crumbs
- 4 garlic cloves, minced
- 1/2 cup chopped fresh parsley
- 6 tablespoons grated Parmesan cheese
- 1/4 cup chopped fresh thyme *or* 1 tablespoon dried thyme

FLAKY & FLAVORFUL. Pictured above: Lemon Herbed Salmon (recipe on this page).

- 2 teaspoons grated lemon peel
- 1/2 teaspoon salt
- 6 tablespoons butter *or* margarine, melted, *divided*
- 1 salmon fillet (3 to 4 pounds)

In a bowl, combine bread crumbs, garlic, parsley, Parmesan cheese, thyme, lemon peel and salt; mix well. Add 4 tablespoons butter and toss lightly to coat; set aside. Pat salmon dry. Place skin side down in a greased baking dish. Brush with remaining butter; cover with crumb mixture. Bake at 350° for 20-25 minutes or until salmon flakes easily with a fork. **Yield:** 8 servings.

Garlic Pork Roast

"Your family will love this version of pork roast," assures Dorothy Pritchett, Wills Point, Texas. "It's so tender and delicious!"

- 1 boned rolled pork loin roast (4 to 5 pounds)
- 4 garlic cloves, peeled and cut into thin slivers

Salt and pepper to taste
- 1 cup cooking wine *or* broth

Horseradish, optional

Using the point of a paring knife, make slits all around the roast. Insert garlic into slits. Rub roast with salt and sprinkle with pepper. Place in a roasting pan and insert a meat thermometer. Bake at 325° for 30-40 minutes *per pound* or until thermometer registers 160°-170°. Remove from the pan and let stand. Meanwhile, place pan on stovetop over high heat. Skim off fat. Add wine or broth; cook until gravy is reduced by half and coats the back of a spoon. Slice meat; serve with gravy, and horseradish if desired. **Yield:** 12-15 servings.

Mock Pasta Alfredo

"If you've been yearning for creamy pasta, indulge yourself with this," says Ruby Williams of Bogalusa, Louisiana.

✓ This tasty dish uses less sugar, salt and fat. Recipe includes *Diabetic Exchanges*.

- 1-1/2 cups 1% cottage cheese
- 1/2 cup skim milk
- 2 garlic cloves, minced
- 2 tablespoons all-purpose flour
- 1 tablespoon lemon juice
- 1 teaspoon dried basil
- 1/2 teaspoon dry mustard
- 1/2 teaspoon pepper
- 1/4 teaspoon salt, optional
- 8 ounces corkscrew noodles, cooked and drained
- 1 to 2 tomatoes, seeded and chopped

In a blender or food processor, process cottage cheese, milk and garlic until smooth. Add flour, lemon juice, basil, mustard, pepper and salt if desired; process until well blended. Pour into a saucepan. Cook over medium heat until thickened. Do not boil. Serve over noodles; sprinkle with chopped tomatoes. **Yield:** 4 servings. **Diabetic Exchanges:** One serving (prepared without added salt) equals 2-1/2 starch, 2 lean meat, 1 vegetable; also, 316 calories, 368 mg sodium, 8 mg cholesterol, 53 gm carbohydrate, 20 gm protein, 2 gm fat.

POTLUCK PLEASERS. Pictured above, clockwise from the top: Kodiak Casserole, Three Cheese Chicken Bake (recipes on this page) and White Texas Sheet Cake (recipe on page 83).

Kodiak Casserole

(PICTURED ON THIS PAGE)

Kathy Crow of Cordova, Alaska explains, "Because it packs a little kick and has a nice tasty mix of ingredients, this is a perfect potluck dish."

- 2 pounds ground beef
- 4 cups diced onions
- 2 garlic cloves, minced
- 3 medium green peppers, diced
- 4 cups diced celery
- 1 jar (5-3/4 ounces) stuffed green olives, undrained
- 1 can (4 ounces) mushroom stems and pieces, undrained
- 1 can (10-3/4 ounces) condensed tomato soup, undiluted
- 1 jar (8 ounces) picante sauce
- 1 bottle (18 ounces) barbecue sauce
- 2 tablespoons Worcestershire sauce
- 3 to 4 cups medium egg noodles, cooked and drained
- 1 cup (4 ounces) shredded cheddar cheese

In a Dutch oven, brown ground beef with onions and garlic; drain. Add remaining ingredients except cheese; mix well. Cover and bake at 350° for 1 hour or until hot and bubbly. Sprinkle with the cheese just before serving. **Yield:** 16-20 servings.

Phyllo Chicken

Joyce Mummau of Mt. Airy, Maryland says, "I found this recipe years ago. Phyllo is fun to work with, and its flakiness turns an entree into something special."

- 1/2 cup butter *or* margarine, melted, *divided*
- 12 sheets phyllo pastry dough
- 3 cups diced cooked chicken
- 1/2 pound bacon, cooked and crumbled
- 1 package (10 ounces) frozen chopped broccoli, thawed and drained
- 2 cups (8 ounces) shredded cheddar *or* Swiss cheese
- 6 eggs
- 1 cup light cream *or* evaporated milk
- 1/2 cup milk
- 1 teaspoon salt
- 1/2 teaspoon pepper

Brush sides and bottom of a 13-in. x 9-in. x 2-in. baking dish with some of the melted butter. Place one sheet of phyllo in bottom of dish; brush with butter. Repeat with five more sheets of phyllo. (Keep remaining phyllo dough covered with waxed paper to avoid drying out.) In a bowl, combine chicken, bacon, broccoli

Three Cheese Chicken Bake

(PICTURED ON THIS PAGE)

"This is a hearty, comforting casserole that's always a crowd-pleaser. The combination of flavors and interesting colors ensures I end up with an empty dish," informs Vicky Raatz of Waterloo, Wisconsin.

- 1/2 cup chopped onion
- 1/2 cup chopped green pepper
- 3 tablespoons butter *or* margarine
- 1 can (10-3/4 ounces) condensed cream of chicken soup, undiluted
- 1 can (8 ounces) sliced mushrooms, drained
- 1 jar (2 ounces) chopped pimientos, drained
- 1/2 teaspoon dried basil
- 1 package (8 ounces) noodles, cooked and drained
- 3 cups diced cooked chicken
- 2 cups Ricotta *or* cottage cheese
- 2 cups (8 ounces) shredded cheddar cheese
- 1/2 cup grated Parmesan cheese
- 1/4 cup buttered bread crumbs

In a skillet, saute onion and green pepper in butter until tender. Remove from the heat. Stir in the soup, mushrooms, pimientos and basil; set aside. In a large bowl, combine noodles, chicken and cheeses; add mushroom sauce and mix well. Transfer to a greased 13-in. x 9-in. x 2-in. baking dish. Bake, uncovered, at 350° for 40-45 minutes or until bubbly. Sprinkle with crumbs. Bake 15 minutes longer. **Yield:** 12-15 servings.

and cheese; spread evenly over phyllo in baking dish. In another bowl, whisk together eggs, cream, milk, salt and pepper; pour over chicken mixture. Cover filling with one sheet of phyllo; brush with butter. Repeat with remaining phyllo dough. Brush top with remaining butter. Bake, uncovered, at 375° for 35-40 minutes or until a knife inserted near the center comes out clean. **Yield:** 10-12 servings.

Chunky Fruit and Nut Relish

Relates Donna Brockett of Kingfisher, Oklahoma, "The medley of fruits and nuts in this colorful relish is delicious served with ham or poultry."

- **2 packages (12 ounces *each*) fresh *or* frozen cranberries**
- **1-1/2 cups sugar**
- **1 cup orange juice**
- **1 can (16 ounces) sliced peaches, drained and cut up**
- **1 can (8 ounces) pineapple tidbits, drained**
- **1 cup chopped pecans**
- **1/2 cup golden raisins**

In a large saucepan, bring cranberries, sugar and orange juice to a boil, stirring occasionally. Reduce heat and simmer, uncovered, for 8-10 minutes or until the berries burst. Remove from the heat; stir in peaches, pineapple, pecans and raisins. Cool. Cover and refrigerate at least 3 hours. **Yield:** about 6 cups.

Spicy Breaded Chicken

"This is one of our favorite ways to make chicken. The coating really stays on, and the pan is easy to clean," promises Polly Coumos of Mogadore, Ohio. *"We like to pack this chicken chilled for picnics."*

✓ **This tasty dish uses less sugar, salt and fat. Recipe includes *Diabetic Exchanges*.**

- **1/2 cup dry bread crumbs**
- **1 tablespoon nonfat dry milk powder**
- **1-1/2 teaspoons chili powder**
- **1/4 teaspoon garlic powder**
- **1/4 teaspoon dry mustard**
- **1/4 cup skim milk**
- **1 broiler-fryer chicken (3 pounds), cut into pieces and skinned**

In a plastic bag, mix bread crumbs, milk powder, chili powder, garlic powder and dry mustard; set aside. Place milk in a shallow pan. Dip chicken pieces into milk, then place in bag and shake to coat. Place chicken, bone side down, in a 13-in. x 9-in. x 2-in. baking pan coated with vegetable cooking spray. Bake, uncovered, at 375° for 50-55 minutes or until

juices run clear. **Yield:** 6 servings. **Diabetic Exchanges:** One serving equals 4 lean meat, 1/2 starch; also, 233 calories, 154 mg sodium, 93 mg cholesterol, 8 gm carbohydrate, 31 gm protein, 8 gm fat.

Greek Grilled Catfish

"My husband came up with this recipe, and our whole family likes the unique flavorful taste," says Rita Futral of Ocean Springs, Mississippi.

✓ **This tasty dish uses less sugar, salt and fat. Recipe includes *Diabetic Exchanges*.**

- **6 catfish fillets (8 ounces *each*)**
- **Greek seasoning to taste**
- **4 ounces feta cheese, crumbled**
- **1 tablespoon dried mint**
- **2 tablespoons olive oil**
- **Fresh mint leaves *or* parsley, optional**
- **Cherry tomatoes, optional**

Sprinkle both sides of fillets with Greek seasoning. Sprinkle each fillet with 1 rounded tablespoon feta cheese and 1/2 teaspoon mint. Drizzle 1 teaspoon olive oil over each. Roll up fillets and secure with toothpicks. Grill over medium coals for 20-25 minutes or until fish flakes easily with a fork. Or, place fillets in a greased baking dish and bake at 350° for 30-35 minutes or until fish flakes easily with a fork. Garnish with mint leaves or parsley and cherry tomatoes if desired. **Yield:** 6 servings. **Diabetic Exchanges:** One serving equals 4-1/2 lean meat, 1 fat; also, 288 calories, 319 mg sodium, 115 mg cholesterol, 1 gm carbohydrate, 34 gm protein, 16 gm fat.

New-World Stuffed Cabbage

(PICTURED ON THIS PAGE)

"One taste and you'll see why stuffed cabbage has been prepared by different cultures over hundreds of years," informs Katherine Stefanovich of Desert Hot Springs, California.

- **1 medium head cabbage**
- **1 can (16 ounces) sauerkraut, *divided***
- **3 bacon strips, diced**
- **1 cup finely chopped onion**
- **2 garlic cloves, minced**
- **1/4 cup all-purpose flour**
- **1 tablespoon Hungarian paprika**
- **1/4 teaspoon cayenne pepper**
- **1 can (16 ounces) crushed tomatoes**
- **2 cups beef broth**
- **1/2 cup long grain rice, cooked**
- **1 pound ground turkey**
- **2 tablespoons chopped fresh parsley**

CABBAGE. Pictured above: New-World Stuffed Cabbage (recipe on this page).

- **1 teaspoon salt**
- **1/2 teaspoon pepper**
- **1 egg, beaten**

Remove core from head of cabbage. Place in a large saucepan and cover with water. Bring to a boil; boil until outer leaves loosen from head. Lift out cabbage; remove softened leaves. Return to boiling water to soften more leaves. Repeat until all leaves are removed. Remove tough center stalk from each leaf. Set aside 12 large leaves for rolls; reserve the balance to use as the recipe directs. Spoon half of the sauerkraut into the bottom of a Dutch oven; set aside. In a heavy saucepan, fry bacon until crisp. Remove to paper towels. In drippings, saute onion and garlic until tender. Remove half to a bowl to cool. To remaining onion mixture, add flour, paprika and cayenne pepper. Cook and stir for 1-2 minutes. Stir in tomatoes and broth; bring to a boil. Remove from the heat and set aside. To cooled onion mixture, add rice, turkey, parsley, salt, pepper, egg and bacon; mix well. Place about 3-4 tablespoons on each cabbage leaf. Roll up, tucking in sides. Place rolls, seam side down, on sauerkraut in Dutch oven. Cover with remaining sauerkraut. Chop remaining cabbage leaves; place over sauerkraut. Pour tomato mixture over all, adding water to cover if necessary. Cover and bake at 325° for about 2 hours. **Yield:** 4-6 servings.

CHANGE-OF-PACE STEAK. Pictured above: Swiss Elk Steak (recipe on this page).

Swiss Elk Steak

(PICTURED ON THIS PAGE)

"You'll find this elk cooks up nice and tender," states Carma Ochse of Bremerton, Washington.

- **2 pounds elk steak**
- **All-purpose flour**
- **2 tablespoons butter *or* margarine**
- **1 can (15 ounces) tomato sauce**
- **1/2 cup red wine *or* beef broth**
- **2 tablespoons Worcestershire sauce**
- **1/2 cup diced onion**
- **1/2 cup diced green pepper**
- **1 can (2-1/4 ounces) sliced ripe olives, drained**
- **1 cup sliced fresh mushrooms**
- **1/2 teaspoon salt**
- **1/2 teaspoon pepper**
- **4 slices Swiss cheese, optional**
- **Cooked noodles**

Dredge elk steak lightly in flour; shake off excess. Melt butter in a large skillet; brown steak on both sides. Place in a shallow baking pan. Combine the next nine ingredients; pour over steak. Cover and bake at 350° for 1-1/2 hours or until cooked to desired tenderness. If desired, place cheese over steak before serving. Serve over noodles. **Yield:** 4 servings.

Chicken Cheese Lasagna

"Three cheeses and chicken blended with delicious spinach make this recipe a real crowd-pleaser," says Mary Ann Kosmas of Minneapolis, Minnesota.

- **1 medium onion, chopped**
- **1 garlic clove, minced**
- **1/2 cup butter *or* margarine**
- **1/2 cup all-purpose flour**
- **1 teaspoon salt**
- **2 cups chicken broth**
- **1-1/2 cups milk**
- **4 cups (16 ounces) shredded mozzarella cheese, *divided***
- **1 cup grated Parmesan cheese, *divided***
- **1 teaspoon dried basil**
- **1 teaspoon dried oregano**
- **1/2 teaspoon white pepper**
- **2 cups (15 to 16 ounces) ricotta cheese**
- **1 tablespoon minced fresh parsley**
- **9 lasagna noodles (8 ounces), cooked and drained**
- **2 packages (10 ounces *each*) frozen spinach, thawed and well drained**
- **2 cups cubed cooked chicken**

In a saucepan, saute onion and garlic in butter until tender. Stir in flour and salt; cook until bubbly. Gradually stir in broth and milk. Bring to a boil, stirring constantly. Boil 1 minute. Stir in 2 cups mozzarella, 1/2 cup Parmesan cheese, basil, oregano and pepper; set aside. In a bowl, combine ricotta cheese, parsley and remaining mozzarella; set aside. Spread one-quarter of the cheese sauce into a greased 13-in. x 9-in. x 2-in. baking dish; cover with one-third of the noodles. Top with half of ricotta mixture, half of spinach and half of chicken. Cover with one-quarter of cheese sauce and one-third of noodles. Repeat layers of ricotta mixture, spinach, chicken and one-quarter cheese sauce. Cover with remaining noodles and cheese sauce. Sprinkle remaining Parmesan cheese over all. Bake at 350°, uncovered, for 35-40 minutes. Let stand 15 minutes. **Yield:** 12 servings.

Herbed Stuffed Green Peppers

"This main dish has a wonderful fresh garden taste," comments Bea Taus of Fremont, California.

✓ This tasty dish uses less sugar, salt and fat. Recipe includes *Diabetic Exchanges*.

- **6 green peppers, tops and seeds removed**
- **1 pound ground turkey**
- **1 can (28 ounces) tomatoes with liquid, chopped**
- **1 medium onion, chopped**
- **2 celery stalks, chopped**
- **2 garlic cloves, minced**
- **1 teaspoon dried oregano**
- **1/2 teaspoon dried thyme**
- **1/2 teaspoon dried rosemary**
- **1/2 teaspoon dried basil**
- **1/2 teaspoon rubbed sage**
- **1/8 teaspoon pepper**
- **1-1/2 cups cooked rice**
- **1/3 cup shredded low-fat mozzarella cheese**

In a large kettle, blanch peppers in boiling water 3 minutes. Drain and rinse in cold water. Set aside. In a large skillet with a nonstick finish, brown the turkey. Remove and set aside. In the same skillet, combine tomato liquid, onion, celery, garlic and herbs. Simmer until vegetables are tender and the mixture has begun to thicken. Stir in tomatoes, turkey and rice. Stuff into peppers and place in a baking pan. Bake at 350° for 30 minutes. Top each pepper with about 1 tablespoon cheese. Return to oven for 3 minutes or until the cheese has melted. **Yield:** 6 servings. **Diabetic Exchanges:** One serving (rice prepared without salt) equals 2 meat, 2 vegetable, 1 starch; also, 267 calories, 483 mg sodium, 51 mg cholesterol, 29 gm carbohydrates, 21 gm protein, 10 gm fat.

Lime Broiled Catfish

(PICTURED ON THIS PAGE)

"In this recipe, lime juice adds a great fresh flavor to the mild taste of catfish," explains Nick Nicholson of Clarksdale, Mississippi.

✓ This tasty dish uses less sugar, salt and fat. Recipe includes *Diabetic Exchanges*.

1 tablespoon butter *or* margarine
2 tablespoons lime juice
1/2 teaspoon salt, optional
1/4 teaspoon pepper
1/4 teaspoon garlic powder
2 catfish fillets (6 ounces *each*)
Lime slices *or* wedges, optional
Fresh parsley, optional

Melt butter in a saucepan. Stir in lime juice, salt if desired, pepper and garlic powder; mix well. Remove from the heat and set aside. Place fillets in a shallow baking dish. Brush each fillet generously with lime-butter sauce. Broil for 5-8 minutes or until fish flakes easily with a fork. Remove to a warm serving dish; spoon pan juices over each fillet. Garnish with lime and parsley if desired. **Yield:** 2 servings. **Diabetic Exchanges:** One serving (prepared with margarine and without added salt) equals 4 lean meat, 1 fat; also, 254 calories, 156 mg sodium, 98 mg cholesterol, 2 gm carbohydrate, 31 gm protein, 14 gm fat.

Cashew Chicken

"This chicken stir-fry is my family's favorite! The cashews add crunch, and the tasty sauce adds richness to garden-fresh carrots and broccoli," conveys Ena Quiggle of Goodhue, Minnesota.

1 tablespoon sesame oil
1/4 cup rice vinegar
1/4 cup cooking sherry
1 teaspoon garlic powder
1-1/2 pounds skinless boneless chicken, cubed
3 tablespoons cooking oil
3 cups broccoli florets
1 cup thinly sliced carrots
2 teaspoons cornstarch
1/3 cup soy sauce
1/3 cup hoisin sauce
1 tablespoon ground ginger
1 cup roasted salted cashews
Cooked rice

In a large bowl, combine first four ingredients; add chicken and toss to coat. Cover and refrigerate for 2 hours. Remove chicken from marinade and reserve marinade. Heat oil in a wok or large skillet. Stir-fry chicken for 2-3 minutes or until it is no longer pink. With a slotted spoon, remove chicken and set aside. In the same skillet, stir-fry broccoli and carrots for 3 minutes or just until crisp-tender. Combine cornstarch, soy sauce, hoisin sauce, ginger and reserved marinade; stir into vegetables. Cook and stir until slightly thickened and heated through. Stir in cashews and chicken; heat through. Serve over rice. **Yield:** 6 servings.

Hungarian Stuffed Cabbage

States Katherine Stefanovich of Desert Hot Springs, California, *"This cabbage recipe is packed with hearty ingredients, like beef, rice and...cabbage!"*

1 medium head cabbage
1 can (28 ounces) sauerkraut, *divided*
1/2 pound ground beef
1/2 pound ground pork
1/2 cup long grain rice, cooked
1 teaspoon salt
1/2 teaspoon pepper
1 egg
3 bacon strips, diced
1 cup chopped onion
2 garlic cloves, minced
1 tablespoon Hungarian paprika
1/4 teaspoon cayenne pepper
1 can (16 ounces) tomatoes with liquid, cut up
1 tablespoon caraway seeds
2 cups water
2 tablespoons all-purpose flour
1 cup (8 ounces) sour cream

Remove core from head of cabbage. Place in a large saucepan and cover with water. Bring to a boil; boil until outer leaves loosen from head. Lift out cabbage; remove softened leaves. Return to boiling water to soften more leaves. Repeat until all leaves are removed. Remove tough center stalk from each leaf. Set aside 12 large leaves for rolls; reserve the balance to use as the recipe directs. Spoon half of the sauerkraut into the bottom of a Dutch oven; set aside. In a bowl, combine the beef, pork, rice, salt, pepper and egg. In a saucepan, cook bacon until crisp. Drain on paper towels. In drippings, saute onion and garlic until tender. Add bacon and half of onion mixture to meat mixture; mix well. Place about 3 tablespoons on each cabbage leaf. Roll up, tucking in sides. Place rolls, seam side down, on sauerkraut in Dutch oven. Coarsely chop any remaining cabbage leaves; place over rolls. To remaining onion mixture, add paprika, cayenne pepper, tomatoes, caraway seeds, water and remaining sauerkraut. Cook until heated through. Pour over rolls. Cover and bake at 325° for 1 hour and 45 minutes. In a small bowl, gradually stir flour into sour cream. Stir in 1-2 tablespoons hot cooking liquid; mix well. Spoon over cabbage rolls. Bake, uncovered, 15-20 minutes longer or until sauce is thickened. **Yield:** 4-6 servings.

NUTRITIOUS CATFISH. Pictured above: Lime Broiled Catfish (recipe on this page).

GRANDMA'S GLAZED HAM. Pictured above: Sugar-Glazed Ham (recipe on this page).

Cornish Pasties

Gayle Lewis of Yucaipa, California relates, "Years ago, when bakeries in my Midwestern hometown made pasties, people scrambled to get there before they were all gone. Now I make my own... filled with meat, potatoes and vegetables."

FILLING:
- 1 pound boneless top round steak, cut into 1/2-inch pieces
- 2 to 3 medium potatoes, peeled and cut into 1/2-inch cubes
- 1 cup chopped carrots
- 1/2 cup finely chopped onion
- 2 tablespoons chopped fresh parsley
- 1 teaspoon salt
- 1/2 teaspoon pepper
- 1/4 cup butter *or* margarine, melted

PASTRY:
- 3 cups all-purpose flour
- 1 teaspoon salt
- 1 cup shortening
- 8 to 9 tablespoons ice water
- 1 egg, beaten, optional

In a bowl, combine round steak, potatoes, carrots, onion, parsley, salt and pepper; mix well. Add butter and toss to coat; set aside. For pastry, combine flour and salt in a mixing bowl. Cut in shortening until mixture forms pea-size crumbs. Sprinkle with water, 1 tablespoon at a time. Toss lightly with a fork until dough forms a ball. *Do not overmix.* Divide dough into fourths. Roll out one portion into a 9-in. circle; transfer to a greased baking sheet. Mound about 1-1/4 cups of meat filling on half of circle. Moisten edges with water; fold dough over mixture and press edges with fork to seal. Repeat with remaining pastry and filling. Cut slits in the top of each pasty. Brush with beaten egg if desired. Bake at 375° for 50-60 minutes or until golden brown. **Yield:** 4 servings.

Sage Pot Roast

"Sage in this pot roast recipe really adds a unique flavor that the whole family will love," assures Naomi Giddis from her Grawn, Michigan home.

✓ This tasty dish uses less sugar, salt and fat. Recipe includes *Diabetic Exchanges.*

- 1 lean boneless beef chuck roast (about 5 pounds)
- 1 tablespoon cooking oil
- 1 to 2 teaspoons rubbed dried sage
- 1/2 teaspoon salt, optional
- 1/4 teaspoon pepper
- 1 cup beef broth
- 6 medium red potatoes (about 2 pounds), cut in half
- 3 to 4 carrots, cut into 2-inch pieces
- 2 medium onions, quartered
- 1/4 cup water
- 5 teaspoons cornstarch

In a Dutch oven, brown roast on both sides in oil. Season with sage, salt if desired and pepper. Add beef broth. Cover and bake at 325° for 2-1/2 hours. Add potatoes, carrots and onions. Cover and bake 1 hour longer or until the meat is tender and vegetables are cooked. Remove roast and vegetables to a serving platter and keep warm. Combine water and cornstarch; stir into pan juices. Cook until thickened and bubbly. Serve with the roast. **Yield:** 12 servings. **Diabetic Exchanges:** One serving (prepared with low-sodium beef broth and without added salt) equals 3 lean meat, 1 starch, 1 vegetable; also, 301 calories, 59 mg sodium, 82 mg cholesterol, 16 gm carbohydrate, 27 gm protein, 14 gm fat.

Sugar-Glazed Ham

(PICTURED ON THIS PAGE)

"This old-fashioned sugar glaze gives your ham a pretty, golden-brown coating just like Grandma used to make," comments Carol Strong Battle of Heathsville, Virginia. "The mustard and vinegar complement the brown sugar and add tangy flavor."

- 1 fully cooked bone-in ham (5 to 7 pounds)
- 1 cup packed brown sugar
- 2 teaspoons prepared mustard
- 1 to 2 tablespoons cider vinegar

Score ham about 1/2 in. deep with a sharp knife. Place ham on a rack in a shallow baking pan. Bake at 325° for 2 to 2-1/2 hours (20 minutes per pound). Combine brown sugar, mustard and enough vinegar to make a thick paste. During the last hour of baking, brush glaze on ham every 15 minutes. **Yield:** 10-14 servings.

Sage Dressing For Chicken

"My family just loves this chicken stuffed with delicious sage dressing," reports Bobbie Talbott of Venetta, Oregon. "They always ask for seconds."

✓ This tasty dish uses less sugar, salt and fat. Recipe includes *Diabetic Exchanges.*

- 2 cups unseasoned dry bread cubes
- 1/2 cup chopped onion
- 1/4 cup chopped fresh parsley
- 3 tablespoons chopped fresh sage *or* 1 tablespoon rubbed dried sage
- 1 egg, beaten
- 1/2 to 3/4 cup chicken broth
- 1 roasting chicken (3 to 4 pounds)
- Melted butter *or* margarine, optional

In a large bowl, combine bread cubes, onion, parsley, sage and the egg. Add enough broth until stuffing is moistened and holds together. Stuff loosely into chicken. Fasten with skewers to close. Place with breast side up on a shallow rack in roasting pan. Brush with butter if desired. Bake, uncovered, at 375° for 1-3/4 to 2-1/4 hours or until juices run clear. Baste several times with pan juices or butter. Prepare gravy if desired. **Yield:** 6 servings. **Diabetic Exchanges:** One serving (prepared with egg substitute and low-sodium chicken broth, without butter or margarine, and skin removed after baking) equals 4 lean meat, 2 starch, 1 vegetable; also, 359 calories, 128 mg sodium, 85 mg cholesterol, 26 gm carbohydrate, 42 gm protein, 8 gm fat.

Wild Goose with Giblet Stuffing

(PICTURED ON THIS PAGE)

"This recipe is one of our favorite ways to prepare goose and it's especially nice for the holidays. My husband does a lot of hunting, so I'm always looking for new ways to fix game," says Louise Laginess of East Jordan, Michigan.

　　1 wild goose (6 to 8 pounds dressed)
Lemon wedges
Salt
STUFFING:
Goose giblets
　　2 cups water
　　10 cups crumbled corn bread
　　2 large Granny Smith apples, chopped
　　1 large onion, chopped
　　1/3 cup minced fresh parsley
　　1 to 2 tablespoons rubbed sage
　　1 teaspoon salt
　　1/4 teaspoon pepper
　　1/4 teaspoon garlic powder
Butter *or* margarine, softened

Rub inside goose cavity with lemon and salt; set aside. In a saucepan, cook giblets in water until tender, about 20-30 minutes. Remove giblets with a slotted spoon and reserve liquid. Chop giblets and place in a large bowl with the corn bread, apples, onion, parsley, sage, salt, pepper and garlic powder. Add enough of the reserved cooking liquid to make a moist stuffing; toss gently. Stuff the body and neck cavity; truss openings. Place goose, breast side up, on a rack in a shallow roasting pan. Spread with softened butter. Bake, uncovered, at 325° for 25 minutes *per pound* or until fully cooked and tender. If goose is an older bird, add 1 cup of water to pan and cover for the last hour of baking. **Yield:** 6-8 servings.

Mexican Turkey Roll-Ups

"This is the perfect recipe when you're hungry for a dish with Mexican flavor and want to use turkey," says Marlene Muckenhirn of Delano, Minnesota.

　　2-1/2 cups cubed cooked turkey
　　1-1/2 cups (12 ounces) sour cream, *divided*
　　3 teaspoons taco seasoning, *divided*
　　1 can (10-3/4 ounces) condensed cream of mushroom soup, undiluted, *divided*
　　1-1/2 cups (6 ounces) shredded cheddar cheese, *divided*
　　1 small onion, chopped
　　1/2 cup salsa
　　1/4 cup sliced ripe olives
　　10 flour tortillas (7 inches)
Shredded lettuce
Chopped tomatoes
Additional salsa, optional

In a bowl, combine turkey, 1/2 cup sour cream, 1-1/2 teaspoons taco seasoning, half of the soup, 1 cup of cheese, onion, salsa and olives. Place 1/3 cup filling on each tortilla. Roll up and place, seam side down, in a greased 13-in. x 9-in. x 2-in. baking dish. Combine remaining sour cream, taco seasoning and soup; pour over tortillas. Cover and bake at 350° for 30 minutes or until heated through. Sprinkle with remaining cheese. Serve with shredded lettuce and chopped tomatoes. Top with additional salsa if desired. **Yield:** about 5 servings.

Ham Buns

"These tasty sandwiches are a great way to use leftover ham. Friends with whom I've shared the recipe tell me that ham buns disappear fast at potlucks or parties," informs Esther Shank of Harrisonburg, Virginia. "You can make them ahead for an easy meal."

　　1/2 cup butter *or* margarine, softened
　　1 small onion, grated
　　1 tablespoon poppy seed
　　2 teaspoons Worcestershire sauce
　　2 teaspoons prepared mustard
　　1-1/4 cups finely chopped fully cooked ham (about 8 ounces)
　　1 cup (4 ounces) shredded Swiss cheese
　　6 to 8 hamburger buns *or* 16 to 20 mini buns

In a bowl, mix butter, onion, poppy seed, Worcestershire sauce and mustard until well blended. Add ham and cheese; mix well. Divide evenly among buns. Place in a shallow baking pan and cover with foil. Bake at 350° for 15-20 minutes or until hot. **Yield:** 6-8 main dish *or* 16-20 appetizer servings.

GOOSE & GIBLETS. Pictured above: Wild Goose with Giblet Stuffing (recipe on this page).

SIDE DISHES

WHEN you need to feed your hungry clan, the fruit and vegetable dishes featured here will fill the bill!

Tomato Bread Salad

(PICTURED ON OPPOSITE PAGE)

"We look forward to tomato season each year so we can make this unique and tasty recipe. It's a great way to use your fresh garden vegetables," reports Dodi Hardcastle from Harlingen, Texas.

✓ This tasty dish uses less sugar, salt and fat. Recipe includes *Diabetic Exchanges*.

   3 large tomatoes, finely chopped and seeded
   1 medium cucumber, finely chopped and seeded
  1/2 large sweet onion, finely chopped
   1 cup loosely packed fresh basil, minced
  1/4 cup olive oil
   1 tablespoon cider vinegar
   1 garlic clove, minced
  1/2 teaspoon salt
  1/4 teaspoon pepper
   1 large loaf white *or* French bread

In a large bowl, combine tomatoes, cucumber and onion. In a small bowl, combine basil, oil, vinegar, garlic, salt and pepper. Pour over tomatoes and toss. Refrigerate for at least 1 hour. Before serving, allow salad to come to room temperature. Cut bread into thick slices; toast under broiler until lightly browned. Top with salad. Serve immediately. **Yield:** 18 servings. **Diabetic Exchanges:** One serving (with a 1-inch slice of white bread) equals 1-1/2 starch, 1 vegetable, 1 fat; also, 188 calories, 262 mg sodium, 0 cholesterol, 28 gm carbohydrate, 5 gm protein, 7 gm fat.

Spinach-Topped Tomatoes

(PICTURED ON OPPOSITE PAGE)

Ila Alderman of Galax, Virginia says, "The spinach and tomato, combined with the Parmesan cheese, give this dish a fabulous fresh flavor."

   1 package (10 ounces) frozen chopped spinach
   2 chicken bouillon cubes
Salt
   3 large tomatoes, halved
   1 cup soft bread crumbs
  1/2 cup grated Parmesan cheese
  1/2 cup chopped onion
  1/2 cup butter *or* margarine, melted
   1 egg, beaten
   1 garlic clove, minced
  1/4 teaspoon pepper
  1/8 teaspoon cayenne pepper
Shredded Parmesan cheese, optional

In a saucepan, cook spinach according to package directions with bouillon; drain well. Cool slightly; press out excess liquid. Lightly salt tomato halves; place with cut side down on a paper towel for 15 minutes to absorb excess moisture. Meanwhile, in a small bowl, combine spinach with bread crumbs, Parmesan cheese, onion, butter, egg, garlic, pepper and cayenne pepper. Mix well. Place tomato halves, cut side up, in a shallow baking dish. Divide the spinach mixture over tomatoes. Sprinkle with shredded Parmesan cheese if desired. Bake at 350° for about 15 minutes or until heated through. **Yield:** 6 servings.

Chivey Potato Topper

"I've always had chives growing just outside my back door so I can snip some anytime I need them," explains Ruth Andrewson of Leavenworth, Washington.

   1 package (8 ounces) cream cheese, softened
  1/3 cup light cream
   1 to 3 tablespoons snipped fresh chives
 1-1/2 teaspoons lemon juice
  1/2 teaspoon garlic salt
Baked potatoes

In a small bowl, beat cream cheese and cream. Blend in chives, lemon juice and garlic salt; mix well. Serve on baked potatoes. **Yield:** 1 cup.

Western Beans

"These beans are hearty and zippy with chili peppers and the extra flavor of lentils," reports Arthur Morris of Washington, Pennsylvania.

   4 bacon strips, diced
   1 large onion, chopped
 1-1/3 cups water
  1/3 cup dry lentils
   2 tablespoons ketchup
   1 teaspoon garlic powder
  3/4 teaspoon chili powder
  1/2 teaspoon ground cumin
  1/4 teaspoon dried red pepper flakes
   1 bay leaf
   1 can (16 ounces) whole tomatoes with liquid, chopped
   1 can (15 ounces) pinto beans, drained
   1 can (16 ounces) kidney beans, drained

Lightly fry bacon in a heavy 3-qt. saucepan. Add onion; cook until transparent. Stir in remaining ingredients. Cook over medium heat for 45 minutes or until lentils are tender, stirring once or twice. Remove bay leaf before serving. **Yield:** 8-10 servings.

Best Broccoli Casserole

Cindy Kolberg of Syracuse, Indiana states, "Many kids claim to not like broccoli but they'll love this!"

   1 cup water
  1/2 teaspoon salt
   1 cup instant rice
  1/4 cup butter *or* margarine
  1/4 cup chopped onion
  1/4 cup chopped celery
   1 can (10-3/4 ounces) condensed cream of mushroom soup, undiluted
   1 can (10-3/4 ounces) condensed cream of celery soup, undiluted
   1 package (10 ounces) frozen chopped broccoli, thawed
  1/2 cup diced process American cheese

Bring water and salt to a boil. Add rice; cover and remove from heat. Let sit for 5 minutes. Melt butter in skillet; saute onion and celery until tender. In large mixing bowl, combine rice, celery and onion with remaining ingredients. Pour into a greased 1-1/2-qt. casserole. Bake at 350° for 1 hour. **Yield:** 6 servings.

Candy-Coated Carrots

"This recipe easily dresses up carrots with a sweet, tangy glaze," says LaVonne Hartel of Williston, North Dakota.

   1 pound baby carrots, peeled
  1/4 cup butter *or* margarine
  1/4 cup packed brown sugar
   1 teaspoon lemon juice
  1/8 to 1/4 teaspoon hot pepper sauce
  1/8 teaspoon salt

In a saucepan, cook carrots in a small amount of water until crisp-tender; drain and keep warm. In the same saucepan, cook butter and brown sugar until bubbly. Stir in lemon juice, hot pepper sauce and salt. Return carrots to pan and heat through. **Yield:** 4-6 servings.

TEMPTING TOMATOES. Pictured clockwise from bottom right: Spinach-Topped Tomatoes, Tomato Bread Salad (both recipes on page 70) and Tomato Vegetable Juice (recipe on page 48).

HOT & CREAMY POTATOES. Pictured above: Confetti Scalloped Potatoes (recipe on this page).

stock, garlic powder and pepper; pour over potatoes. Dot with butter. Cover and bake at 400° for 1 hour and 15 minutes. Remove cover during last 15 minutes to brown. **Yield:** 4-6 servings.

Confetti Scalloped Potatoes

(PICTURED ON THIS PAGE)

"I first tasted this casserole at a church supper. It's now one of my family's most-requested dishes," reports Frances Anderson of Boise, Idaho.

- 1/2 cup butter *or* margarine
- 1/2 cup chopped onion
- 1 package (16 ounces) frozen hash brown potatoes
- 1 can (10-3/4 ounces) condensed cream of mushroom soup, undiluted
- 1 soup can milk
- 1 cup (4 ounces) shredded cheddar cheese
- 1 small green pepper, cut into strips
- 2 tablespoons chopped pimientos

Dash pepper
- 1 cup cheese cracker crumbs, *divided*

In a skillet, melt butter over medium heat. Saute onion until tender. Stir in potatoes, soup and milk. Add cheese, green pepper, pimientos, pepper and 1/2 cup of the crumbs. Pour into a shallow casserole; top with remaining crumbs. Bake at 375° for 35-40 minutes. **Yield:** 6-8 servings.

Company Brussels Sprouts

"The combination of flavorful ingredients dresses up ordinary brussels sprouts and makes an extra-special vegetable side dish," says Donald Roberts of Amherst, New Hampshire.

- 4 bacon strips, diced
- 1 dozen brussels sprouts, trimmed and halved
- 1 medium onion, chopped
- 2 tablespoons snipped fresh chives
- 1 carrot, thinly sliced
- 10 stuffed green olives, sliced
- 1/2 teaspoon dried basil
- 1/3 cup chicken broth *or* dry white wine
- 1 teaspoon olive oil
- 1/2 teaspoon pepper

Pinch salt

In a skillet, fry bacon just until cooked. Drain, reserving 2 tablespoons drippings. Add remaining ingredients; cook and stir over medium-high heat for 10-

Lima Bean Casserole

"Growing up, my daughter would only eat vegetables covered with cheese," relates Tickle Ragland of Hodgenville, Kentucky. "Now that she's grown, it's still her favorite way to eat them!"

- 2 cups frozen baby lima beans
- 1 can (10-3/4 ounces) condensed cream of mushroom soup, undiluted
- 1/2 cup chopped celery
- 1/2 cup milk
- 1 cup (4 ounces) shredded cheddar cheese
- 1/4 cup seasoned bread crumbs

In a bowl, combine lima beans, soup, celery and milk. Pour into a greased 11-in. x 7-in. x 2-in. baking dish. Sprinkle with cheese and bread crumbs. Cover and bake at 350° for 25 minutes. Uncover; bake 10 minutes longer or until the bread crumbs are lightly browned. **Yield:** 6-8 servings.

Herbed Spinach Bake

Nancy Frank of Lake Ariel, Pennsylvania shares, "This is a special side dish my mother liked to serve at church dinners. She was recognized by family and friends as an outstanding cook."

- 2 packages (10 ounces *each*) frozen chopped spinach
- 2 cups cooked rice
- 2 cups (8 ounces) shredded cheddar cheese
- 4 eggs, beaten
- 2/3 cup milk
- 1/4 cup butter *or* margarine, softened
- 1/4 cup chopped onion
- 2 teaspoons salt
- 1 teaspoon Worcestershire sauce
- 1 teaspoon ground thyme

Cook spinach according to package directions; drain well, squeezing out excess liquid. Combine spinach with remaining ingredients in a large bowl. Pour into a greased 13-in. x 9-in. x 2-in. baking dish. Cover and bake at 350° for 20 minutes. Uncover and bake 5 minutes more or until set. **Yield:** 16 servings.

Roasted Potatoes

"These potatoes are a perfect side dish for any meat," assures Christopher Gordon of Springfield, Missouri.

- 5 large potatoes, peeled and sliced
- 1 cup chicken stock
- 1 teaspoon garlic powder

Pepper to taste
- 4 tablespoons butter *or* margarine

Place potatoes in a greased 13-in. x 9-in. x 2-in. baking pan. Combine chicken

15 minutes or until brussels sprouts are crisp-tender. **Yield:** 4 servings.

Hot Fruit Compote

(PICTURED ON THIS PAGE AND PAGE 3)

"This simple-to-prepare compote is a tasty way to get fruit into your meal, especially when fresh fruit is not plentiful," explains Judy Kimball of Haverhill, Massachusetts.

- 1 can (12 ounces) frozen orange juice concentrate, thawed
- 2 tablespoons cornstarch
- 2 pounds apples, peeled, cored and sliced
- 1 can (8 ounces) pineapple chunks, drained
- 1 can (16-1/2 ounces) pitted Bing cherries, drained
- 1-1/2 cups fresh *or* frozen cranberries
- 1 package (6 ounces) dried apricots, cooked and drained
- 1/4 cup white wine, optional

In a large bowl, combine orange juice concentrate and cornstarch; stir until smooth. Add fruit; stir to coat. Pour into a buttered 3-qt. casserole. If desired, pour wine over all. Cover and bake at 350° for 50-60 minutes or until hot and bubbly. **Yield:** 12 servings.

> **BAKE POTATOES** in half the time by letting them stand in boiling water for 15 minutes before popping them into a hot oven.

Broccoli with Red Pepper

"This colorful, crisp vegetable dish gets its great flavor from the added water chestnuts," informs Karen Davies of Wanipigow, Manitoba.

✓ This tasty dish uses less sugar, salt and fat. Recipe includes *Diabetic Exchanges*.

- 2 tablespoons vegetable oil
- 4 cups broccoli florets
- 2 teaspoons minced fresh gingerroot
- 2 garlic cloves, minced
- 1 sweet red pepper, cut into strips
- 1 can (8 ounces) sliced water chestnuts, drained

In a skillet, heat oil over high. Stir-fry broccoli, ginger and garlic until broccoli is crisp-tender, about 2 minutes. Add red pepper and water chestnuts; stir-fry just until heated through, about 1 minute. Serve immediately. **Yield:** 4 servings. **Diabetic Exchanges:** One serving equals 2 vegetable, 1-1/2 fat; also, 117 calories, 28 mg sodium, 0 mg cholesterol, 17 gm carbohydrates, 3 gm protein, 7 gm fat.

Broccoli Bake

"This tasty side dish is always a big hit when my family comes for dinner or when I'm hosting a shower or party," says Carolyn Griffin of Macon, Georgia. *"At Easter, it's a great way to use up hard-cooked eggs."*

- 2 packages (10 ounces *each*) frozen cut broccoli
- 1/2 cup chopped onion
- 1 tablespoon butter *or* margarine
- 1 can (10-3/4 ounces) condensed cream of mushroom soup, undiluted
- 1/2 teaspoon dry mustard
- 1/2 teaspoon salt
- 4 hard-cooked eggs, chopped
- 1-1/2 cups (6 ounces) shredded cheddar cheese
- 1 can (2.8 ounces) french-fried onions

Cook broccoli according to package directions; drain and set aside. In a skillet or saucepan, saute onion in butter until tender. Stir in soup, mustard and salt; heat until bubbly. In a 1-1/2-qt. casserole, arrange half of broccoli; top with half of the eggs, half of the cheese and half of the mushroom sauce. Repeat layers. Bake at 350° for 20 minutes. Sprinkle onions on top and bake 5 minutes more. **Yield:** 6 servings.

Continental Zucchini

"This colorful and easy recipe wins raves at church and school gatherings," shares Martha Fehl of Brookville, Indiana.

✓ This tasty dish uses less sugar, salt and fat. Recipe includes *Diabetic Exchanges*.

- 1 tablespoon cooking oil
- 1 pound zucchini (about 3 small), cubed
- 1 to 2 garlic cloves, minced
- 1 jar (2 ounces) chopped pimientos, drained
- 1 can (15-1/2 ounces) whole kernel corn, drained
- 1 teaspoon salt, optional
- 1/4 teaspoon lemon pepper
- 1/2 cup shredded mozzarella cheese

Heat oil in a large skillet. Saute zucchini and garlic for 3-4 minutes. Add pimientos, corn, salt if desired and lemon pepper; cook and stir for 2-3 minutes or until zucchini is tender. Sprinkle with cheese and heat until cheese melts. **Yield:** 6 servings. **Diabetic Exchanges:** One serving (prepared with low-fat mozzarella cheese and without added salt) equals 1 vegetable, 1 meat, 1/2 starch; also, 131 calories, 107 mg sodium, 10 mg cholesterol, 15 gm carbohydrate, 8 gm protein, 6 gm fat.

> **SLIGHTLY SWEET SIDE DISH.** Pictured above: Hot Fruit Compote (recipe on this page).

DESSERTS

NOTHING tops off a meal like a delicious dessert. And with this assorted selection of pies, cookies, cakes and more, you're sure to keep your family's sweet tooth satisfied!

Citrus Cheesecake

(PICTURED ON OPPOSITE PAGE)

Marcy Cella of L'Anse, Michigan shares, "This cheesecake is perfect for spring or anytime of year! The cookie-like crust and creamy citrus filling are a wonderful surprise."

- 1 cup sifted all-purpose flour
- 1/4 cup sugar
- 1 teaspoon grated lemon peel
- 1/2 teaspoon vanilla extract
- 1 egg yolk
- 1/4 cup butter, softened

FILLING:
- 5 packages (8 ounces *each*) cream cheese, softened
- 1-3/4 cups sugar
- 3 tablespoons all-purpose flour
- 1-1/2 teaspoons grated lemon peel
- 1-1/2 teaspoons grated orange peel
- 1/4 teaspoon vanilla extract
- 5 eggs
- 2 egg yolks
- 1/4 cup whipping cream

TOPPING:
- 1-1/2 cups (12 ounces) sour cream
- 3 tablespoons sugar
- 1 teaspoon vanilla extract

In a bowl, combine flour, sugar, peel and vanilla. Make well; add yolk and butter. Mix with hands until ball is formed. Wrap with plastic wrap; chill at least 1 hour. Grease bottom and sides of a 9-in. springform pan. Remove sides. Divide dough in half. Between waxed paper, roll half of dough to fit bottom of pan. Peel off top paper; invert dough onto bottom of pan. Remove paper; trim dough to fit pan. Bake at 400° for 6-8 minutes or until lightly browned. Cool. Divide remaining dough into thirds. Fold a piece of waxed paper in half; place one-third inside folded paper. Roll dough into 9-1/2-in. x 2-1/2-in. strip. Trim and patch as needed. Repeat with remaining dough to make two more strips. Tear away top layer of paper from strips. Put together pan with crust on bottom. Fit dough strips to side of pan, overlapping ends. Press ends of dough together; press sides of dough to bottom crust to seal. Chill. Beat cream cheese, sugar, flour, peels and vanilla until mixed. Beat in eggs and yolks. Add cream; beat just until mixed. Pour into crust. Bake at 500° for 10 minutes. Reduce heat to 250°; bake 1 hour. Cool slightly. Combine topping ingredients; spread over cake. Chill overnight. **Yield:** 12-16 servings.

Raspberry Trifle

(PICTURED ON OPPOSITE PAGE)

"Beautiful and luscious, this trifle is an impressive way to use your fresh raspberries," says Marcy Cella of L'Anse, Michigan.

- 1 package (16 ounces) pound cake, cut into 18 slices *or*
- 2 packages (3 ounces *each*) ladyfingers
- 2 packages (3.4 ounces *each*) instant vanilla pudding mix
- 1 jar (18 ounces) raspberry jam
- 1-1/2 pints fresh raspberries
- Whipped cream and fresh raspberries for garnish

Arrange one-third of sliced cake in the bottom of a trifle dish or large decorative bowl. Prepare pudding according to package directions. Place one-third more cake pieces around inside of bowl, using half of pudding to hold them in place. Gently stir together jam and raspberries; spoon half over pudding. Cover with remaining cake pieces. Layer remaining pudding and raspberry mixture. Chill. Garnish with whipped cream and fresh raspberries. **Yield:** 8-10 servings.

Idaho Potato Cake

"Potatoes in dessert? Many cooks never think of the possibility. But this cake gets its moist texture from Idaho spuds," assures LaRene Reed of Idaho Falls, Idaho.

- 1 cup butter *or* margarine, softened
- 2 cups sugar
- 2 eggs
- 1 cup cold mashed potatoes
- 1 teaspoon vanilla extract
- 2 cups all-purpose flour
- 1/4 cup baking cocoa
- 1 teaspoon baking soda
- 1 cup milk
- 1 cup chopped nuts

In a mixing bowl, cream butter and sugar until fluffy. Add eggs, one at a time, beating well after each addition. Blend in potatoes and vanilla. Combine flour, cocoa and baking soda; add alternately with milk, blending well after each addition. Stir in nuts. Pour into a greased 13-in. x 9-in. x 2-in. baking pan. Bake at 350° for 40-45 minutes or until cake tests done. Cool on a wire rack. **Yield:** 12-16 servings.

Dipped Peanut Butter Sandwich Cookies

Jackie Howell from Gordo, Alabama states, "A tin of these chocolate-coated cookies is a tempting treat you'll love to give. The recipe is too simple to believe!"

- 1/2 cup creamy peanut butter
- 1 sleeve (4 ounces) round butter-flavored crackers
- 1 cup (6 ounces) white, semisweet *or* milk chocolate chips
- 1 tablespoon shortening

Spread peanut butter on half of the crackers; top with remaining crackers to make sandwiches. Refrigerate. In a double boiler over simmering water, melt chocolate chips and shortening, stirring until smooth. Dip sandwiches and place on waxed paper until chocolate hardens. **Yield:** 1-1/2 dozen.

Raspberry Crunch Brownies

"These moist, rich brownies with dark-chocolate flavor and nut-like crunch prove that desserts don't have to be full of fat to be delicious," informs Rita Winterberger of Huson, Montana.

✓ This tasty dish uses less sugar, salt and fat. Recipe includes *Diabetic Exchanges*.

- 1/4 cup vegetable oil
- 1-1/4 cups sugar
- 4 egg whites
- 1 cup all-purpose flour
- 2/3 cup baking cocoa
- 1/2 teaspoon baking powder
- 1/4 teaspoon salt
- 1-1/2 teaspoons vanilla extract
- Nonstick vegetable spray
- 1/4 cup raspberry jam
- 2 tablespoons Grape-Nuts cereal

In a mixing bowl, beat oil and sugar. Add egg whites and continue beating until well mixed. Combine flour, cocoa, baking powder and salt; add to mixing bowl and beat until moistened. Stir in vanilla. Batter will be thick. Coat a 9-in. square pan with vegetable spray. Spread batter into pan. Bake at 350° for 20-25 minutes or until a toothpick inserted in the center comes out clean. Cool 10 minutes on a wire rack. Spread with jam and sprinkle with Grape-Nuts if desired. Cool completely. **Yield:** 2 dozen. **Diabetic Exchanges:** One serving equals 1 starch, 1/2 fat; also, 105 calories, 47 mg sodium, 0 mg cholesterol, 19 gm carbohydrates, 2 gm protein, 3 gm fat.

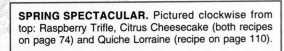

SPRING SPECTACULAR. Pictured clockwise from top: Raspberry Trifle, Citrus Cheesecake (both recipes on page 74) and Quiche Lorraine (recipe on page 110).

APPLE OF YOUR EYE. Pictured above: Upside-Down Apple Gingerbread (recipe on this page).

Chocolate Monster Cookies

Helen Hilbert of Liverpool, New York states, "This is my grandson's favorite recipe. He has fun making them and is always delighted with the results."

- 2 cups butter *or* margarine
- 2 cups sugar
- 2 cups packed brown sugar
- 4 eggs
- 2 teaspoons vanilla extract
- 4 cups all-purpose flour
- 1 tablespoon baking powder
- 2 teaspoons baking soda
- 1 teaspoon salt
- 2 cups cornflakes
- 2 cups rolled oats
- 1 package (8 ounces) flaked coconut
- 1 package (12 ounces) semisweet chocolate chips
- 1 cup chopped walnuts

In a large mixing bowl, cream butter and sugars. Add eggs and vanilla; mix well. In a small bowl, combine flour, baking powder, baking soda and salt; gradually add to creamed mixture, mixing well after each addition. Stir in cornflakes, oats and coconut. (It may be necessary to transfer to a larger bowl to stir in the cornflakes, oats and coconut.) Stir in chocolate chips and nuts. Divide dough into six sections. On a piece of waxed paper, shape each section into a 7-in. x 1-1/2-in. roll. Refrigerate several hours or overnight. Cut into 1/2-in. slices. Place 3 in. apart on ungreased cookie sheets. Bake at 350° for 13-15 minutes. **Yield:** 7-1/2 dozen.

Upside-Down Apple Gingerbread

(PICTURED ON THIS PAGE)

"Don't expect any leftovers when you serve this moist cake. People love its wonderful flavor. Try it for your next gathering," encourages Florence Palmer of Marshall, Illinois.

- 1/4 cup butter *or* margarine, melted
- 2 large apples, peeled, cored and sliced
- 1/3 cup packed brown sugar

GINGERBREAD:
- 1/2 cup butter *or* margarine, melted
- 1/2 cup molasses
- 1/2 cup sugar
- 1/3 cup packed brown sugar
- 1 egg
- 2 cups all-purpose flour
- 1 teaspoon baking soda
- 1 teaspoon ground cinnamon
- 1 teaspoon ground ginger
- 1/2 teaspoon ground cloves
- 1/2 teaspoon salt
- 1/4 teaspoon ground nutmeg
- 3/4 cup hot tea

Pour butter into a 9-in. square baking pan. Arrange apples over butter; sprinkle with brown sugar and set aside. For gingerbread, combine butter, molasses, sugars and egg in a mixing bowl; mix well. Combine dry ingredients; add to sugar mixture alternately with hot tea. Mix well; pour over apples. Bake at 350° for 45-50 minutes or until the cake tests done. Cool for 3-5 minutes. Loosen sides and invert onto a serving plate. Serve warm. **Yield:** 9 servings.

Wyoming Cowboy Cookies

"These cookies are very popular here," reports Patsy Faye Steenbock of Shoshoni, Wyoming. "They're great for munching anytime."

- 1 cup flaked coconut
- 3/4 cup chopped pecans
- 1 cup butter *or* margarine, softened
- 1-1/2 cups packed brown sugar
- 1/2 cup sugar
- 2 eggs
- 2 cups all-purpose flour
- 1 teaspoon baking soda
- 1/2 teaspoon salt
- 1-1/2 teaspoons vanilla extract
- 2 cups rolled oats
- 2 cups (12 ounces) chocolate chips

Place coconut and pecans on a jelly roll pan. Place in a 350° oven for 6-8 minutes or until toasted brown, stirring every 2 minutes. Set aside to cool. In a large mixing bowl, cream butter and sugars. Add eggs and beat well. Add dry ingredients and vanilla. Stir in oats, chocolate chips and toasted coconut and pecans. Drop by rounded teaspoonfuls onto greased cookie sheets. Bake at 350° for about 12 minutes or until browned. **Yield:** 6 dozen.

Amaretto Dream Cupcakes

"My family just loves cupcakes, so I often make plenty and freeze some for a quick dessert," informs Annette Stevens of Olds, Alberta.

- 2 cups all-purpose flour
- 1-1/2 teaspoons baking powder
- 1/2 teaspoon baking soda
- 1/4 teaspoon salt
- 3/4 cup butter *or* margarine
- 1-1/2 cups packed brown sugar
- 2 eggs
- 1/2 cup buttermilk
- 1/4 cup Amaretto
- 1/3 cup slivered almonds

FROSTING:
- 3 cups confectioners' sugar

1/4 cup butter *or* margarine, melted
3 to 4 tablespoons whipping cream
2 to 3 tablespoons Amaretto

In a medium bowl, sift together flour, baking powder, baking soda and salt; set aside. In a large mixing bowl, beat butter and brown sugar until creamy. Add eggs, one at a time, beating well after each. Alternately add 1/3 of flour and all of the buttermilk, then 1/3 of flour and the Amaretto, beating well after each addition. Add remaining flour; mix until smooth. Stir in almonds. Line regular or mini muffin cups with baking papers. Fill each 2/3 full. Bake at 375° for 14-16 minutes or until muffins test done. Cool in pans for 5 minutes. Remove and cool completely. For frosting, beat confectioners' sugar and butter in a small mixing bowl. Add 3 tablespoons cream and 2 tablespoons Amaretto; beat until smooth. Add remaining cream and Amaretto if needed to achieve spreading consistency. Spread over cool cupcakes. **Yield:** 24 regular or 48 mini cupcakes.

Homemade Pudding Mix

"Whole milk and butter give this delicious pudding its rich, creamy flavor," explains Gayle Becker of Mt. Clemens, Michigan. *"For a fat-free version, leave out the butter and substitute water for the 2 cups milk in the pudding."*

DRY MIX:
4 cups nonfat dry milk solids
2-2/3 cups sugar
1-1/3 cups cornstarch
1 to 1-1/3 cups baking cocoa
1/2 teaspoon salt
PUDDING:
2 cups milk
1 tablespoon butter *or* margarine
1/2 teaspoon vanilla extract

For mix, sift together all ingredients. Store in an airtight container or plastic bag. For pudding, combine 1 cup mix with milk in a saucepan. Bring to a boil, stirring constantly. Stir in butter and vanilla. Pour into individual serving dishes. Serve warm. **Yield:** 9 batches (4 servings per batch).

Fluffy Cranberry Cheese Pie

(PICTURED ON THIS PAGE AND PAGE 3)

"This easy-to-prepare pie has a light texture and a zippy flavor that matches its vibrant color," says Mary Parkonen of West Wareham, Massachusetts.

CRANBERRY TOPPING:
1 package (3 ounces) raspberry-flavored gelatin
1/3 cup sugar
1-1/4 cups cranberry juice
1 can (8 ounces) jellied cranberry sauce
FILLING:
1 package (3 ounces) cream cheese, softened
1/4 cup sugar
1 tablespoon milk
1 teaspoon vanilla extract
1/2 cup whipped topping
1 pastry shell (9 inches), baked

In a mixing bowl, combine gelatin and sugar; set aside. In a saucepan, bring cranberry juice to a boil. Remove from the heat and pour over gelatin mixture, stirring to dissolve. Stir in the cranberry sauce. Chill until slightly thickened. Meanwhile, in another mixing bowl, beat cream cheese, sugar, milk and vanilla until fluffy. Fold in the whipped topping. Spread evenly into pie shell. Beat cranberry topping until frothy; pour over filling. Chill overnight. **Yield:** 6-8 servings.

> **TRY SPRAYING** your beaters with non-stick cooking spray before mixing cake and cookie batters to prevent clumping.

Dream Bars

"These bar cookies are a family favorite and travel well," explains Hillary Lawson of Plummer, Idaho. *"Wonderfully moist and chewy, they're definite winners with everyone in my family."*

CRUST:
1 cup all-purpose flour
1/2 cup packed brown sugar
1/2 cup butter *or* margarine
FILLING:
2 eggs, lightly beaten
1 cup packed brown sugar
1 teaspoon vanilla extract
2 tablespoons all-purpose flour
1/2 teaspoon salt
1 cup flaked coconut
1 cup chopped walnuts

In a small bowl, combine flour and brown sugar; cut in butter until crumbly. Pat into a 13-in. x 9-in. x 2-in. baking pan. Bake at 350° for 10 minutes. Meanwhile, in a mixing bowl, beat eggs and brown sugar; stir in vanilla. Combine flour and salt; add to egg mixture. Fold in coconut and walnuts. Spread over baked crust. Return to oven and bake 20-25 minutes longer or until golden brown. Cool in pan on a wire rack. **Yield:** about 32 servings.

> **IT'S BERRY DELICIOUS!** Pictured above: Fluffy Cranberry Cheese Pie (recipe on this page).

Dairy Hollow House Almond Pie

Crescent Dragonwagon of Eureka Springs, Arkansas reports, "I like serving food that goes beyond one region. California almonds add a delicious twist and crunchy texture to this recipe."

- 1/2 cup butter (no substitutes)
- 3 eggs
- 1 cup sugar
- 3/4 cup light corn syrup
- 1/4 cup honey
- 1 teaspoon vanilla extract
- 1/4 teaspoon almond extract
- 1/8 teaspoon salt
- 1 cup chopped almonds, toasted
- 1 unbaked pastry shell (9 inches)
- Lightly sweetened whipped cream, optional

In a saucepan, melt butter over low heat until golden brown. Cool. In a mixing bowl, beat eggs. Add sugar, corn syrup, honey, extracts, salt and melted butter. Stir in almonds; pour into pastry shell. Bake at 425° for 10 minutes. Reduce heat to 325°; bake 35-40 minutes longer or until a knife inserted near center comes out clean. Cool. Garnish with whipped cream if desired. **Yield:** 8 servings.

Sugarless Apple Cookies

(PICTURED ON PAGE 53)

"These soft, chewy cookies are so moist and delicious you'll never miss the sugar," exclaims Martha Gradeless of Garrett, Indiana.

✓ This tasty dish uses less sugar, salt and fat. Recipe includes *Diabetic Exchanges*.

- 3/4 cup chopped dates
- 1/2 cup finely chopped peeled apple
- 1/2 cup raisins
- 1/2 cup water
- 1 cup plus 1 tablespoon all-purpose flour
- 1 teaspoon ground cinnamon
- 1 teaspoon baking soda
- 1/2 teaspoon salt, optional
- 2 eggs
- 1 teaspoon liquid sweetener

In a large saucepan, combine dates, apple, raisins and water. Bring to a boil; reduce heat and simmer for 3 minutes. Remove from the heat; cool. Combine flour, cinnamon, baking soda, and salt if desired. Stir into apple mixture and mix well. Combine eggs and sweetener; add to batter. Drop by tablespoonfuls onto a nonstick baking sheet. Bake at 350°

for 10-12 minutes. **Yield:** 2 dozen. **Diabetic Exchanges:** One serving (prepared without added salt) equals 1/2 starch, 1/2 fruit; also, 54 calories, 24 mg sodium, 18 mg cholesterol, 11 gm carbohydrate, 1 gm protein, 1 gm fat.

Scotch Shortbread

"This simple three-ingredient recipe makes wonderfully rich cookies. Serve them with fresh berries for a nice, light dessert," suggests Marlene Hellickson of Big Bear City, California.

- 4 cups all-purpose flour
- 1 cup sugar
- 1 pound cold butter (no substitutes)

In a large mixing bowl, combine flour and sugar. Cut in butter until mixture resembles fine crumbs. Knead dough until smooth, about 6-10 minutes. Pat dough into an ungreased 15-in. x 10-in. x 1-in. baking pan. Pierce with a fork. Bake at 325° for 25-30 minutes or until lightly browned. While warm, cut into squares. Cool. **Yield:** 4 dozen. **Editor's Note:** This recipe makes a dense, crisp cookie, so it does not call for baking powder or soda.

Raspberry Delight

"Most folks are surprised to learn that pretzels are the 'secret ingredient' in this tasty dessert," explains Warren Knudtson of Las Vegas, Nevada.

- 2 cups crushed pretzels
- 2 tablespoons sugar
- 1/3 cup chopped pecans
- 3/4 cup butter *or* margarine, softened

FILLING:
- 1 package (8 ounces) cream cheese, softened
- 3/4 cup sugar
- 1 carton (8 ounces) frozen whipped topping, thawed
- 1 package (6 ounces) raspberry-flavored gelatin
- 2 cups boiling water
- 2 packages (10 ounces *each*) unsweetened frozen raspberries (do not thaw)

In a bowl, combine pretzels, sugar, pecans and butter. Press into the bottom of an ungreased 13-in. x 9-in. x 2-in. baking pan. Bake at 350° for 10 minutes or until lightly browned; cool. In a mixing bowl, beat cream cheese and sugar until smooth. Fold in whipped topping; spread over crust. In another bowl, dissolve gelatin in boiling water. Stir in frozen raspberries until gelatin is almost set. Spread over filling. Chill several hours or overnight. **Yield:** 12-16 servings.

Delicious Apple Pie

"This apple pie my mother taught me to make is my favorite—I haven't found a recipe that tops hers yet!" says Howard Haug of Hewitt, Texas.

- 3 tablespoons water
- 4 teaspoons cornstarch
- 1 egg, beaten
- 3/4 cup light cream
- 3/4 cup sugar
- 1 teaspoon ground cinnamon
- 1/4 teaspoon ground nutmeg
- 4 medium Red Delicious apples, peeled and sliced
- Pastry for double-crust pie (9 inches)
- 2 tablespoons butter *or* margarine
- 1 tablespoon milk
- 1 tablespoon cinnamon-sugar

In a small bowl, mix water and cornstarch until dissolved. Add egg, cream, sugar, cinnamon and nutmeg. Place apples in a large bowl; pour cream mixture over and stir to coat. Line a 9-in. pie pan with the bottom pastry. Pour apple mixture into crust; dot with butter. Top with remaining pastry; flute edges and cut slits in top. Brush with milk and sprinkle with cinnamon-sugar. Bake at 350° for 55 minutes or until golden brown. **Yield:** 6-8 servings.

Granny's Spice Cookies

(PICTURED ON OPPOSITE PAGE)

"Granny always had a batch of these delicious, crispy cookies waiting for us at her house," recalls Valerie Hudson of Mason City, Iowa.

- 1 cup butter *or* margarine, softened
- 1-1/2 cups sugar
- 1 egg, lightly beaten
- 2 tablespoons light corn syrup
- 2 tablespoons grated orange peel
- 1 tablespoon cold water
- 3-1/4 cups all-purpose flour
- 2 teaspoons baking soda
- 2 teaspoons ground cinnamon
- 1 teaspoon ground ginger
- 1/2 teaspoon ground cloves
- Red hot candies, nonpareils *and/or* sprinkles

In a mixing bowl, cream butter and sugar. Add egg, corn syrup, orange peel and cold water. Combine flour, baking soda, cinnamon, ginger and cloves; add to creamed mixture and mix well. Chill for at least 1 hour. On a lightly floured surface, roll dough, a portion at a time, to 1/8-in. thickness. Cut into desired shapes. Place on greased baking sheets. Decorate as desired. Bake at 375° for 6-8 minutes or until lightly browned. **Yield:** about 4 dozen (3-inch cookies).

Cutout Christmas Cookies

(PICTURED ON THIS PAGE)

"These old-fashioned cookies have been a holiday tradition in my family for many years," reveals Carolyn Moseley of Dayton, Ohio. "It was always a joy to make these cookies for my children."

      1 cup butter *or* margarine,
        softened
      1 cup sugar
      2 eggs
  1-1/2 teaspoons vanilla extract
  3-1/2 cups all-purpose flour
      1 teaspoon ground cinnamon
    1/2 teaspoon baking powder
    1/2 teaspoon salt
    1/4 teaspoon ground cloves
    1/4 teaspoon ground nutmeg
      1 egg white, beaten
  Colored decorating sugars

In a mixing bowl, cream butter and sugar. Add eggs and vanilla. Combine flour, cinnamon, baking powder, salt, cloves and nutmeg; gradually add to creamed mixture and mix well. Chill for at least 1 hour. On a lightly floured surface, roll dough, a portion at a time, to 1/8-in. thickness. Cut into desired shapes. Place on ungreased baking sheets. Bake at 350° for 12-14 minutes or until edges begin to brown. Carefully brush with egg white; sprinkle with colored sugar. Return to the oven for 3-5 minutes or until lightly browned. **Yield:** about 6 dozen (2-inch cookies).

Date Swirls

(PICTURED ON THIS PAGE)

"My 3-year-old granddaughter nicknamed my mother 'Cookie Grandma' because she made wonderful cookies like these," shares Donna Grace of Clancy, Montana.

FILLING:
      2 cups chopped dates
      1 cup water
      1 cup sugar
      1 cup chopped nuts
      2 teaspoons lemon juice
DOUGH:
      1 cup butter *or* margarine
      1 cup packed brown sugar
      1 cup sugar
      3 eggs
      1 teaspoon lemon extract
      4 cups all-purpose flour
      1 teaspoon salt
    3/4 teaspoon baking soda

GRANDMA'S BEST. Pictured above, clockwise from the top: Cutout Christmas Cookies, Date Swirls (recipes on this page) and Granny's Spice Cookies (recipe on page 78).

In a saucepan, combine filling ingredients. Cook over medium-low heat, stirring constantly, until mixture becomes stiff, about 15-20 minutes. Chill. For dough, cream butter and sugars in a mixing bowl. Add eggs, one at a time, beating well after each addition. Add extract. Combine flour, salt and baking soda; gradually add to creamed mixture and mix well. Chill for at least 1 hour. On a lightly floured surface, roll out half of the dough to a 12-in. x 9-in. rectangle, about 1/4 in. thick. Spread with half of the filling. Roll up, starting with the long end. Repeat with remaining dough and filling. Wrap with plastic wrap; chill overnight. Cut rolls into 1/4-in. slices. Place 2 in. apart on greased baking sheets. Bake at 375° for 8-10 minutes or until lightly browned. Cool on wire racks. **Yield:** 4 dozen.

No-Bake Raisin Bars

"These hearty bars are easy to make and taste delicious," Dawn Fagerstrom of Warren, Minnesota reports.

      3 cups miniature
        marshmallows
    1/4 cup butter *or* margarine
      5 cups multi-grain puffed
        rice cereal
      1 cup raisins
    1/2 cup chopped walnuts
    1/4 teaspoon ground cinnamon

In a large saucepan or microwave-safe bowl, heat marshmallows and butter over low until melted; mix well. Stir in the cereal, raisins, walnuts and cinnamon. Pat into a greased 13-in. x 9-in. x 2-in. baking pan. Cool. Cut into bars. **Yield:** 2 dozen.

Picnic Cupcakes

"These moist cupcakes don't need frosting, so they're perfect for picnics or traveling," informs Florence Leinweber of Endicott, Washington.

        1 package (18-1/2 ounces)
           chocolate *or* yellow cake mix
    FILLING:
        1 package (8 ounces) cream
           cheese, softened
        1 egg, lightly beaten
    1/3 cup sugar
        1 cup (6 ounces) semisweet
           chocolate chips

Mix cake according to package directions. Spoon batter into 24 greased or paper-lined muffin cups, filling two-thirds full. In a mixing bowl, beat cream cheese, egg and sugar until smooth. Fold in the chips. Drop by tablespoonfuls into batter. Bake at 350° for 20 minutes or until cupcakes test done. **Yield:** 2 dozen.

Persimmon Rice Pudding

Opal Amidon of Garden Grove, California shares, "I love to serve this unique dish for fall and winter holidays."

        4 cups cooked long grain rice
        2 cups ripe persimmon pulp
    1-1/4 cups sugar
    1-1/4 cups milk
    1/3 cup all-purpose flour
        1 egg, beaten
        1 teaspoon vanilla extract
    1/4 cup chopped walnuts
    1/4 cup raisins

In a large bowl, combine rice and persimmon pulp; set side. Combine sugar, milk, flour, egg and vanilla; add to rice mixture and mix well. Stir in walnuts and raisins. Pour into a greased 3-qt. baking dish. Bake, uncovered, at 350° for 45 minutes or until pudding is set. Serve warm or cold. **Yield:** 10-12 servings.

Pecan Squares

(PICTURED ON THIS PAGE)

"These bars are good for snacking when you're on the road or for taking to gatherings," Sylvia Ford of Kennett, Missouri states. *"If you love pecan pie, you'll likely find them irresistible!"*

    CRUST:
        3 cups all-purpose flour
    1/2 cup sugar
        1 cup butter *or* margarine,
           softened
    1/2 teaspoon salt
    FILLING:
        4 eggs
    1-1/2 cups light *or* dark corn syrup

    1-1/2 cups sugar
        3 tablespoons butter *or*
           margarine, melted
    1-1/2 teaspoons vanilla extract
    2-1/2 cups chopped pecans

In a large mixing bowl, blend together flour, sugar, butter and salt until mixture resembles coarse crumbs. Press firmly and evenly into a greased 15-in. x 10-in. x 1-in. baking pan. Bake at 350° for 20 minutes. Meanwhile, in another bowl, combine first five filling ingredients. Stir in pecans. Spread evenly over hot crust. Bake at 350° for 25 minutes or until set. Cool on a wire rack. **Yield:** 4 dozen.

NICE AND NUTTY. Pictured above: Pecan Squares (recipe on this page).

Watermelon Bombe

"This sherbet dessert looks like actual watermelon slices—complete with 'seeds' —when cut. It's fun to eat and refreshing, too!" shares Renae Moncur of Burley, Idaho.

    About 1 pint lime sherbet
    About 1 pint pineapple sherbet
    About 1-1/2 pints raspberry sherbet
    1/4 cup miniature semisweet
           chocolate chips

Line a 1-1/2-qt. metal mixing bowl with plastic wrap. Press slightly softened lime sherbet against the bottom and sides of bowl. Freeze, uncovered, until firm. Spread pineapple sherbet evenly over lime sherbet layer. Freeze, uncovered,

until firm. (Lime and pineapple sherbet layers should be thin.) Pack raspberry sherbet in center of sherbet-lined bowl. Smooth the top to resemble a cut watermelon. Cover and freeze until firm, about 8 hours. Just before serving, uncover bowl of molded sherbet. Place a serving plate on the bowl and invert. Remove bowl and peel off plastic wrap. Cut the bombe into wedges; press a few chocolate chips into the raspberry section of each wedge to resemble watermelon seeds. **Yield:** 8 servings.

Whole Wheat Snickerdoodles

"These soft, chewy cookies make a super dessert," relates Jana Horsfall from Garden City, Kansas. *"Their light cinnamon taste goes great with a cold glass of milk."*

        1 cup butter *or* margarine,
           softened
    1-1/2 cups sugar
        1 egg plus 1 egg white
    1-1/2 cups whole wheat flour
    1-1/4 cups all-purpose flour
        1 teaspoon baking soda
    1/4 teaspoon salt
    TOPPING:
        2 tablespoons sugar
        2 teaspoons ground cinnamon

In a mixing bowl, cream butter and sugar until fluffy. Add egg and egg white; beat well. Combine the dry ingredients; add to creamed mixture and beat well. In a small bowl, combine topping ingredients. Shape dough into walnut-sized balls; roll in cinnamon-sugar. Place 2 in. apart on ungreased baking sheets. Bake at 400° for 8-10 minutes. Cookies will puff up and flatten as they bake. **Yield:** about 5 dozen.

Salted Peanut Chews

"I took these great treats to a reunion," reports Irene Yoder of Millersburg, Ohio. *"They disappeared fast, and soon people were asking for the recipe."*

    1-1/2 cups all-purpose flour
    1/2 cup packed brown sugar
    3/4 cup butter *or* margarine,
           softened, *divided*
        3 cups miniature
           marshmallows
        2 cups peanut butter-flavored
           baking chips
    2/3 cup corn syrup
        2 teaspoons vanilla extract
        2 cups crisp rice cereal
        2 cups salted peanuts

In a mixing bowl, combine flour, brown sugar and 1/2 cup butter; mix well. Press into an ungreased 13-in. x 9-in. x 2-in. baking pan. Bake at 350° for 12-15 minutes or until lightly browned. Sprinkle marshmallows over top and return to the oven for 3-5 minutes or until marshmallows begin to melt; set aside. In a large saucepan, cook and stir peanut butter chips, corn syrup, vanilla and remaining butter until chips are melted and smooth. Remove from the heat; stir in cereal and peanuts. Pour over prepared crust, spreading to cover. Cool before cutting into bars. **Yield:** about 2 dozen.

Creamy Raspberry Dessert

(PICTURED ON THIS PAGE)

"Do-ahead and delicious, this refreshing dessert is a favorite because of its pretty color, creamy texture and terrific flavor," says Julianne Johnson of Grove City, Minnesota.

      1 cup graham cracker crumbs
      3 tablespoons sugar
   1/4 cup butter *or* margarine, melted
FILLING:
      1 package (10 ounces) frozen
         raspberries, thawed
   1/4 cup cold water
      1 envelope unflavored gelatin
      1 package (8 ounces) cream
         cheese, softened
   1/2 cup sugar
      1 cup whipping cream,
         whipped
**Fresh raspberries and whipped
   cream for garnish**

Combine crumbs, 3 tablespoons sugar and butter. Press onto the bottom of an 8-in. or 9-in. springform pan. Bake at 350° for 10 minutes. Cool. Meanwhile, for filling, drain raspberries and reserve juice. Set berries aside. In a small saucepan, combine juice, cold water and gelatin. Let stand for 5 minutes. Cook and stir over low heat until gelatin dissolves. Remove from the heat; cool for 10 minutes. In a mixing bowl, beat cream cheese and sugar until blended. Add berries and gelatin mixture; beat on low until thoroughly blended. Chill until partially set. Watch carefully, as mixture will set up quickly. By hand, gently fold in whipped cream. Spoon into the crust. Chill for 6 hours or overnight. Just before serving, run knife around edge of pan to loosen. Remove sides of pan. Top with fresh raspberries and whipped cream. **Yield:** 10 servings.

Carrot Cake

(PICTURED ON PAGE 92)

"You'll love the texture this pretty, moist cake gets from pineapple, coconut and, of course, carrots! Its traditional cream cheese frosting adds just the right touch of sweetnes," says Debbie Jones of California, Maryland.

      2 cups all-purpose flour
      2 cups sugar
      2 teaspoons ground cinnamon
      1 teaspoon baking soda
   1/2 teaspoon salt
      3 eggs
      2 cups finely grated carrots
1-1/2 cups vegetable oil
      1 teaspoon vanilla extract
      1 cup well-drained crushed
         pineapple
      1 cup shredded coconut
      1 cup chopped nuts, *divided*
CREAM CHEESE FROSTING:
      2 packages (3 ounces *each*)
         cream cheese, softened
      3 cups confectioners' sugar
      6 tablespoons butter *or*
         margarine, softened
      1 teaspoon vanilla extract

In a mixing bowl, combine dry ingredients. Add eggs, carrots, oil and vanilla; beat until combined. Stir in pineapple, coconut and 1/2 cup nuts. Pour into a greased 13-in. x 9-in. x 2-in. baking pan. Bake at 350° for 50-60 minutes or until cake tests done. Cool. Combine frosting ingredients in a small bowl; mix until well blended. Frost cooled cake. Sprinkle with remaining nuts. Store in refrigerator. **Yield:** 12-16 servings.

Whoopie Pies

"These moist little treats have been a favorite of my friends and family for many years," relates Ruth Ann Stelfox of Raymond, Alberta.

      1 cup butter *or* margarine,
         softened
1-1/2 cups sugar
      2 teaspoons vanilla extract
      2 eggs
      4 cups all-purpose flour
   3/4 cup baking cocoa
      2 teaspoons baking soda
   1/2 teaspoon salt
      1 cup water
      1 cup buttermilk
FILLING:
      2 cups marshmallow creme
      2 cups confectioners' sugar
   1/2 cup butter *or* margarine,
         softened
      2 teaspoons vanilla extract

In a mixing bowl, beat butter, sugar, vanilla and eggs until well mixed. Combine dry ingredients; add to butter mixture alternately with water and buttermilk. Drop by teaspoonfuls onto greased baking sheets. Bake at 375° for 5-7 minutes or until done. Cool completely. In a small mixing bowl, beat filling ingredients until fluffy. Spread filling on half of the cookies, then top with remaining cookies. **Yield:** about 3 dozen.

COOL AND CREAMY. Pictured above: Creamy Raspberry Dessert (recipe on this page).

Rhubarb Upside-Down Cake

(PICTURED ON PAGE 59)

"I've baked this cake every spring for years, and my family just loves it," explains Helen Breman of Mattydale, New York. *"At potlucks it disappears quickly, drawing compliments even from those who normally don't care for rhubarb."*

TOPPING:
- 3 cups fresh rhubarb, cut into 1/2-inch slices
- 1 cup sugar
- 2 tablespoons all-purpose flour
- 1/4 teaspoon ground nutmeg
- 1/4 cup butter *or* margarine, melted

BATTER:
- 1-1/2 cups all-purpose flour
- 3/4 cup sugar
- 2 teaspoons baking powder
- 1/2 teaspoon ground nutmeg
- 1/4 teaspoon salt
- 1/4 cup butter *or* margarine, melted
- 2/3 cup milk
- 1 egg

Sweetened whipped cream, optional

Place rhubarb in a greased 10-in. heavy skillet. Combine sugar, flour and nutmeg; sprinkle over rhubarb. Drizzle with butter. For batter, combine flour, sugar, baking powder, nutmeg and salt in a mixing bowl. Add butter, milk and egg; beat until smooth. Spread over rhubarb mixture. Bake at 350° for 35 minutes or until the cake tests done. Loosen edges immediately and invert onto serving dish. Serve warm, topped with whipped cream if desired. **Yield:** 8-10 servings.

Washington State Apple Pie

(PICTURED ON THIS PAGE)

"This pie looks traditional, but making your own filling gives it a different flair and great taste," comments Dolores Scholz of Tonasket, Washington.

- 6 cups sliced peeled baking apples (5 to 6 medium)
- 2 tablespoons water
- 1 tablespoon lemon juice
- 1/2 cup sugar
- 1/2 cup packed brown sugar
- 3 tablespoons all-purpose flour
- 1 teaspoon ground cinnamon
- 1/4 teaspoon ground nutmeg
- 1/8 teaspoon ground ginger
- 1/8 teaspoon salt

Pastry for double-crust pie (9 inches)

In a saucepan, combine apples, water and lemon juice; cook over medium-low heat just until the apples are tender. Remove from the heat and cool (do not drain). In a large bowl, combine sugars, flour, cinnamon, nutmeg, ginger and salt; add apples and toss to coat. Place bottom pastry in pie plate; add apple mixture. Cover with top pastry; seal and flute edges. Cut slits in top crust. Bake at 450° for 10 minutes. Reduce heat to 350°; bake 35-45 minutes longer or until golden brown. **Yield:** 6-8 servings.

Apricot Almond Bars

"Each year I host a cookie exchange with close friends," states Arliene Hillinger of Rancho Palos Verdes, California. *"I've shared this recipe too many times to count!"*

CRUST:
- 1-1/2 cups all-purpose flour
- 3/4 cup confectioners' sugar
- 1/2 cup butter *or* margarine, softened
- 1/4 cup shortening

TOPPING:
- 1 egg, lightly beaten
- 1/2 cup sugar
- 1/2 cup apricot preserves
- 1 tablespoon butter *or* margarine, softened
- 1/2 teaspoon vanilla extract
- 1 cup sliced almonds

In a mixing bowl, beat flour, sugar, butter and shortening. Pat into the bottom and 1/2 in. up the sides of an ungreased 13-in. x 9-in. x 2-in. baking pan. Bake at 350° for 15-18 minutes or until lightly browned. For topping, beat egg, sugar, preserves, butter and vanilla in a mixing bowl until smooth. Spread over hot crust. Sprinkle with almonds. Bake at 350° for 15-20 minutes. Cool. **Yield:** 2-1/2 to 3 dozen.

Golden Apple Bundles

(PICTURED ON THIS PAGE)

"I usually make these bundles on Fridays, so when family drops in on the weekend, I have a nice dessert to serve," relates Lila Eller of Everett, Washington. *"They bake flaky and golden brown outside and moist inside."*

- 2 cups chopped peeled apples
- 1/3 cup chopped walnuts
- 1/4 cup packed brown sugar
- 1/4 cup raisins
- 1 tablespoon all-purpose flour
- 1/2 teaspoon lemon peel
- 1/2 teaspoon ground cinnamon

Pastry for double-crust pie
Milk
Sugar

In a bowl, combine the apples, walnuts, brown sugar, raisins, flour, lemon peel and cinnamon; set aside. Roll pastry to 1/8-in. thickness. Cut into 5-in. circles. Spoon about 1/4 cup apple mixture into center of each circle. Moisten edges of pastry with water. Fold over and seal edges with a fork. Place on a greased baking sheet. Bake at 450° for 10 minutes. Reduce heat to 400°; bake 10 minutes longer. Brush each with milk and sprinkle with sugar; return to oven for 5 minutes. **Yield:** 10-12 servings.

APPEALING APPLES. Pictured above, clockwise from top right, Apple Raisin Bread (recipe on page 98), Golden Apple Bundles and Washington State Apple Pie (both recipes on this page).

White Texas Sheet Cake

(PICTURED ON PAGE 64)

"This cake gets better the longer it sits, so I make it a day ahead. With its creamy frosting, no one can resist it," says Joanie Ward of Brownsburg, Indiana.

- 1 cup butter *or* margarine
- 1 cup water
- 2 cups all-purpose flour
- 2 cups sugar
- 2 eggs, beaten
- 1/2 cup sour cream
- 1 teaspoon almond extract
- 1 teaspoon salt
- 1 teaspoon baking soda

FROSTING:
- 1/2 cup butter *or* margarine
- 1/4 cup milk
- 4-1/2 cups confectioners' sugar
- 1/2 teaspoon almond extract
- 1 cup chopped walnuts

In a large saucepan, bring butter and water to a boil. Remove from the heat; stir in flour, sugar, eggs, sour cream, almond extract, salt and baking soda until smooth. Pour into a greased 15-in. x 10-in. x 1-in. baking pan. Bake at 375° for 20-22 minutes or until cake is golden brown and tests done. Cool for 20 minutes. Meanwhile, for frosting, combine butter and milk in a saucepan. Bring to a boil. Remove from the heat; add sugar and extract and mix well. Stir in walnuts; spread over warm cake. **Yield:** 16-20 servings.

Pineapple Cheese Torte

Diane Bradley of Sparta, Michigan informs, *"This light, yummy pineapple dessert looks prettiest when it's garnished with fresh strawberries."*

PAT-IN-THE-PAN CRUST:
- 1 cup all-purpose flour
- 1/4 cup confectioners' sugar
- 1/4 cup finely chopped almonds
- 1/3 cup butter *or* margarine, softened

FILLING:
- 2 packages (8 ounces *each*) cream cheese, softened
- 1/2 cup sugar
- 2 eggs
- 2/3 cup unsweetened pineapple juice

PINEAPPLE TOPPING:
- 1/4 cup all-purpose flour
- 1/4 cup sugar
- 1 can (20 ounces) crushed pineapple, juice drained and reserved
- 1/2 cup whipping cream
Fresh strawberries, optional

Combine crust ingredients; pat into the bottom of a 11-in. x 7-in. x 2-in. baking dish. Bake at 350° for 20 minutes. Beat cream cheese in a mixing bowl until fluffy; beat in sugar and eggs. Stir in juice. Pour filling over hot crust. Bake at 350° for 25 minutes or until center is set. Cool. For topping, combine flour and sugar in a saucepan. Stir in 1 cup of reserved pineapple juice. Bring to a boil, stirring constantly. Boil and stir 1 minute. Remove from heat; fold in pineapple. Cool. Whip cream until stiff peaks form; fold into topping. Spread carefully over dessert. Refrigerate 6 hours or overnight. Garnish with strawberries if desired. **Yield:** 12-16 servings.

Kiwifruit Danish

"You might like to try this recipe for an easy, pretty treat," suggests Debbie Shick of McFarland, California.

- 1 package (3 ounces) refrigerator crescent dinner rolls
- 1 package (3 ounces) cream cheese, softened
- 1 egg yolk
- 2 tablespoons sugar
- 1/2 teaspoon almond extract
- 1/2 cup apricot jam
- 2 to 3 kiwifruit, pared and sliced

Unroll crescent roll dough and shape into eight triangles with equal sides. Combine cream cheese, egg yolk, sugar and almond extract; blend well. Place 1 tablespoon cream cheese mixture in center of each triangle; top with kiwifruit slice. Pull points of triangle to center and pinch to seal. Bake on greased baking sheet at 375° for 12-15 minutes or until golden brown. Cool on rack. Heat jam. Top each Danish with another kiwifruit slice; brush with jam. **Yield:** 8 servings.

Buttery Black Walnut Brittle

"For my family's favorite holiday candy, I use black walnuts from trees in our own backyard," reveals Anne Medlin of Bolivar, Missouri.

- 1 cup sugar
- 1/2 cup corn syrup
- 1/4 cup water
- 1/2 cup butter (no substitutes)
- 1 to 1-1/2 cups black walnuts
- 1/2 teaspoon baking soda

In a saucepan, cook sugar, corn syrup and water until sugar dissolves and mixture comes to a boil. Add butter; cook until mixture reaches 280° on a candy thermometer. Stir in walnuts; cook until 300° (hard crack stage). Remove from the heat and stir in baking soda. Spread immediately into a greased 15-in. x 10-in. x 1-in. baking pan. When cool, break into pieces. **Yield:** 1-1/4 pounds.

Peppermint Candy

"Try these soon...and enjoy the cool, tingly taste of mint!" Kandy Clarke of Columbia Falls, Montana urges.

- 1 cup (6 ounces) semisweet chocolate chips
- 1 can (14 ounces) sweetened condensed milk, *divided*
- 1 cup (6 ounces) vanilla-flavored baking chips
- 1 tablespoon peppermint extract
- 2 to 3 drops green food coloring

In a saucepan, melt chocolate chips and 3/4 cup condensed milk over low heat, stirring occasionally. Line an 8-in. square baking pan with waxed paper; butter the paper. Spread half of melted chocolate mixture into pan; chill for 5-10 minutes (keep remaining melted chocolate at room temperature). In another saucepan, melt vanilla chips. Stir in remaining condensed milk and mix well. Remove from the heat; add extract and food coloring. Chill. Spread over chocolate layer; spread reserved melted chocolate on top. Chill. Cut into 1-in. pieces. **Yield:** 5 dozen.

Mom's Soft Raisin Cookies

"With four sons in service during WWII, my mother sent these favorite cookies as a taste from home to 'her boys' in different parts of the world," shares Pearl Cochenour of Williamsport, Ohio.

- 2 cups raisins
- 1 cup water
- 1 cup shortening
- 1-3/4 cups sugar
- 2 eggs, lightly beaten
- 1 teaspoon vanilla extract
- 3-1/2 cups all-purpose flour
- 1 teaspoon baking powder
- 1 teaspoon baking soda
- 1 teaspoon salt
- 1/2 teaspoon ground cinnamon
- 1/2 teaspoon ground nutmeg
- 1/2 cup chopped walnuts

Combine raisins and water in a small saucepan; bring to a boil. Cook for 3 minutes; remove from the heat and let cool (do not drain). In a mixing bowl, cream shortening; gradually add sugar. Add eggs and vanilla. Combine dry ingredients; gradually add to creamed mixture and blend thoroughly. Stir in nuts and raisins. Drop by teaspoonfuls 2 in. apart on greased baking sheets. Bake at 350° for 12-14 minutes. **Yield:** about 6 dozen.

ALL-TIME FAVORITES. Pictured above, clockwise from bottom: Salted Nut Squares (recipe on this page), Classic Beef Stew (recipe on page 90) and Nutty O's (recipe on page 51).

Chocolate Chip Date Cake

"This bar-like cake travels well because there's no messy frosting to melt," assures Pam Jennings of Prairie City, Iowa. *"It also stays moist—if there's any left over!"*

> 1 cup water
> 1 cup chopped dates
> 1 cup sugar
> 1 cup shortening
> 2 eggs, lightly beaten
> 1 teaspoon vanilla extract
> 1-3/4 cups all-purpose flour
> 1 tablespoon unsweetened baking cocoa
> 1/2 teaspoon salt
> 1/2 cup semisweet chocolate chips
> 1/2 cup chopped walnuts

In a small saucepan, bring water and dates to a boil. Remove from heat; cool. In a mixing bowl, cream together sugar and shortening. Add eggs and vanilla; mix well. Combine flour, cocoa and salt; add to creamed mixture. Add dates and cooking liquid; mix well. Place in a greased 13-in. x 9-in. x 2-in. baking pan. Sprinkle with chocolate chips and walnuts. Bake at 350° for 30-35 minutes. Remove to a wire rack to cool. **Yield:** about 32 servings.

Lemon Custard Pudding Cake

Deborah Hill of Coffeyville, Kansas reveals, "This recipe originated in a 1949 cookbook that my mom had thrown out, but I fished out of the trash can and saved! I was only 10 then, but already had an interest in cooking."

> 6 tablespoons all-purpose flour
> 6 tablespoons butter *or* margarine, melted
> 2 cups sugar, *divided*
> 4 eggs, *separated*
> 1-1/2 cups milk
> Grated peel of 1 lemon
> 2 tablespoons fresh lemon juice
> Confectioners' sugar

In a large mixing bowl, combine flour, butter and 1-1/2 cups sugar. Beat egg yolks; add to mixing bowl along with milk and lemon peel. Mix well. Add lemon juice. In another bowl, beat egg whites until stiff, slowly adding remaining 1/2 cup sugar while beating. Fold into batter. Pour into a greased 2-qt. baking dish or individual ramekins. Place in a shallow pan of hot water and bake at 350° for 55-60 minutes or until lightly browned. Serve warm or chilled with confectioners' sugar dusted on top. **Yield:** 6-8 servings.

Creamy Mocha Frozen Dessert

"Light as a feather, this cool, satisfying dessert is delicious and impressive to serve," shares Launa Shoemaker of Midland City, Alabama. *"It's an excellent dessert to take to a potluck because it can be made ahead and stored in the freezer."*

> 2 teaspoons instant coffee granules
> 1 tablespoon hot water
> 1 cup cream-filled chocolate cookie crumbs
> 3/4 cup chopped pecans, *divided*
> 1/4 cup butter *or* margarine, melted
> 2 packages (8 ounces *each*) cream cheese, softened
> 1 can (14 ounces) sweetened condensed milk
> 1/2 cup chocolate-flavored syrup
> 1 carton (8 ounces) frozen whipped topping, thawed

In a small bowl, dissolve coffee granules in hot water; set aside. In another bowl, combine cookie crumbs, 1/2 cup pecans and butter. Pat into the bottom of a 13-in. x 9-in. x 2-in. baking pan. In a mixing bowl, beat cream cheese until light and fluffy. Blend in coffee mixture, milk and chocolate syrup. Fold in whipped topping and spread over crust. Sprinkle the remaining pecans on top. Freeze. **Yield:** 24 servings.

> **FOR SWEETER,** richer bread pudding, use day-old cinnamon rolls instead of bread.

Salted Nut Squares

(PICTURED ON THIS PAGE)

"This recipe came from my sister-in-law. It's easy to prepare and delicious. No need to keep it warm or cold, so it's perfect to take to a potluck," informs Kathy Tremel of Earling, Iowa.

> 3 cups salted peanuts without skins, *divided*
> 2-1/2 tablespoons butter *or* margarine
> 2 cups (12 ounces) peanut butter chips
> 1 can (14 ounces) sweetened condensed milk
> 2 cups miniature marshmallows

Place half of the peanuts in an ungreased 11-in. x 7-in. x 2-in. baking pan; set aside. In a saucepan, melt butter and peanut butter chips over low heat. Remove from the heat. Add milk and marshmallows; stir until melted. Pour over peanuts. Sprinkle the remaining peanuts on top. Cover and refrigerate. Cut into bars. **Yield:** 5-6 dozen.

84

Pumpkin Spice Cake

"Pumpkin Spice Cake is a moist treat also called Thanksgiving Cake. We don't relegate it to that holiday, however—it's delicious anytime of year," says Kathy Rhoads of Circleville, Ohio.

   1 package (18-1/4 ounces) spice cake mix
   3 eggs
   1 cup cooked *or* canned pumpkin
  1/2 cup water
  1/2 cup vegetable oil
   1 package (3.4 ounces) instant vanilla pudding mix
   1 teaspoon ground cinnamon
  1/2 cup chopped pecans
Favorite cream cheese frosting *or* whipped cream

In a mixing bowl, combine cake mix, eggs, pumpkin, water, oil, pudding mix and cinnamon. Beat at medium speed for 5 minutes. Stir in pecans. Pour into a greased and floured 10-in. fluted tube pan. Bake at 350° for 45-55 minutes or until cake tests done. Let cool in pan 10 minutes before removing to a wire rack. Frost cake or serve with whipped cream. **Yield:** 16-20 servings.

Triple-Layer Cookie Bars

(PICTURED ON THIS PAGE)

"My family just loves these chewy chocolate and peanutty bars," professes Diane Bradley of Sparta, Michigan. *"They're perfect for dessert and snacks. I make them whenever I get a craving for something sweet and special."*

CRUST:
1-1/4 cups all-purpose flour
  2/3 cup sugar
  1/3 cup baking cocoa
  1/4 cup packed brown sugar
   1 teaspoon baking powder
  1/4 teaspoon salt
  1/2 cup butter *or* margarine
   2 eggs, lightly beaten
TOPPING:
   1 package (7 ounces) flaked coconut
   1 can (14 ounces) sweetened condensed milk
   2 cups (12 ounces) semisweet chocolate chips
  1/2 cup creamy peanut butter

In a mixing bowl, combine the first six ingredients. Cut in butter until crumbly. Add eggs; mix well. Spread in a greased 13-in. x 9-in. x 2-in. baking pan. Bake at 350° for 8 minutes. Sprinkle coconut on top. Drizzle sweetened condensed milk evenly over coconut. Return to the oven for 20-25 minutes or until lightly browned. In a saucepan over low heat, melt chocolate chips and peanut butter, stirring until smooth. Spread over bars. Cool. **Yield:** 2-3 dozen.

Caramel Apple Crisp

Janet Siciak of Bernardston, Massachusetts comments, "This is a great dessert to prepare when you want something typical of New England or when you just want something delicious!"

  1/2 cup all-purpose flour
  1/2 cup sugar
  1/2 teaspoon ground cinnamon
  1/4 teaspoon ground nutmeg
  40 caramels, quartered
   9 cups sliced peeled baking apples
  1/4 cup orange juice
TOPPING:
  1/2 cup sugar
  1/3 cup all-purpose flour
   3 tablespoons butter *or* margarine
  2/3 cup quick-cooking oats
  1/2 cup chopped walnuts

In a bowl, combine flour, sugar, cinnamon and nutmeg; add caramels and stir to coat. In another bowl, toss apples with orange juice. Add caramel mixture and mix. Spread into a greased 13-in. x 9-in. x 2-in. baking pan. For topping, combine sugar and flour in a small bowl; cut in butter until crumbly. Add oats and walnuts; sprinkle over apples. Bake at 350° for 45 minutes or until apples are tender. **Yield:** 16-20 servings.

Sopaipillas

(PICTURED ON PAGE 57)

"Light, crispy pastry puffs, sopaipillas are a sweet way to round out a spicy meal," informs Mary Anne McWhirter of Pearland, Texas. *"They're great served warm and topped with sugar."*

   1 cup all-purpose flour
1-1/2 teaspoons baking powder
  1/4 teaspoon salt
   1 tablespoon shortening
  1/3 cup warm water
Cooking oil for deep-fat frying
Honey, optional
Confectioners' sugar, optional

In a bowl, combine flour, baking powder and salt. Cut in shortening until mixture resembles fine crumbs. Gradually add water, stirring with a fork. The dough will be crumbly. On a lightly floured surface, knead the dough for 3 minutes or until smooth. Cover and let rest for 10 minutes. Roll out into a 12-in. x 10-in. rectangle. Cut into 12 squares. In a deep-fat fryer, heat 2 in. of oil to 375°. Fry sopaipillas for 1-2 minutes per side. Drain on paper towels; keep hot in a warm oven. Serve with honey or dust with confectioners' sugar if desired. **Yield:** 6-8 servings.

GIFTS FROM THE KITCHEN. Pictured above, left to right: Triple-Layer Cookie Bars (recipe on this page) and Puffed Wheat Balls (recipe on page 52).

PLEASING PIZZAS...FOR DESSERT! Pictured above: Mini Apple Pizzas (recipe on this page).

Fold in chocolate chips and nuts. Drop by teaspoonfuls 2 in. apart onto greased baking sheets. Bake at 350° for 10-12 minutes or until golden. Cool on a wire rack. For glaze, melt the caramels and cream in a saucepan over low heat, stirring until smooth. Drizzle over cooled cookies. **Yield:** 2 dozen.

Mini Apple Pizzas

(PICTURED ON THIS PAGE)

"My children are now grown, but they still enjoy snacking on these sweet little pizzas," reports Helen Lamb of Seymour, Missouri. "We use fresh apples from the orchard on our farm."

> 1 tube refrigerator biscuits
>   (10 biscuits)
> 1/2 cup packed brown sugar
> 2 tablespoons all-purpose flour
> 1 teaspoon ground cinnamon
> 2 cooking apples, peeled,
>   cored and shredded
> 1 cup (4 ounces) shredded
>   cheddar cheese, optional

Roll or pat biscuits into 3-1/2-in. circles; place on a lightly greased baking sheet. In a mixing bowl, combine brown sugar, flour and cinnamon; mix well. Add apples and mix well; spoon rounded tablespoonfuls onto biscuits. Bake at 350° for 15-20 minutes or until edges begin to brown. If desired, sprinkle each pizza with 1 tablespoon cheese. Serve warm. **Yield:** 10 servings.

Fudge-Nut Oatmeal Bars

States Kim Stoller of Smithville, Ohio, "When I make these bars for lunches and snacks, they're gone in a jiffy!"

> 1 cup butter *or* margarine,
>   softened
> 2 cups packed brown sugar
> 2 eggs
> 2 teaspoons vanilla extract
> 3 cups quick-cooking oats
> 2-1/2 cups all-purpose flour
> 1 teaspoon baking soda
> 1 teaspoon salt
> **FUDGE FILLING:**
> 1 can (14 ounces) sweetened
>   condensed milk
> 2 cups (12 ounces) semisweet
>   chocolate chips
> 2 tablespoons butter *or*
>   margarine
> 1/2 teaspoon salt
> 2 teaspoons vanilla extract
> 1 cup chopped walnuts

In a mixing bowl, cream butter and brown sugar. Add eggs and vanilla; mix well. Combine oats, flour, baking soda and salt; add to the creamed mixture. Spread two-thirds in the bottom of an ungreased 15-in. x 10-in. x 1-in. baking pan; set aside. For filling, heat milk, chocolate chips, butter and salt in a saucepan or microwave-safe bowl until melted. Remove from the heat; stir in vanilla and walnuts. Spread over oat mixture in pan. Drop remaining oat mixture by tablespoonfuls over chocolate. Bake at 350° for 20-25 minutes. **Yield:** 2-1/2 to 3 dozen.

Chocolate Macadamia Nut Cookies

"Macadamia nuts really add a unique flavor to these delicious cookies," reveals Arliene Hillinger of Rancho Palos Verdes, California. "I know your family will love them."

> 10 tablespoons butter (no
>   substitutes), softened
> 3/4 cup packed brown sugar
> 1 teaspoon vanilla extract
> 1 egg, lightly beaten
> 1 cup all-purpose flour
> 3/4 teaspoon baking powder
> 1/8 teaspoon baking soda
> 1/8 teaspoon salt
> 1-1/2 cups semisweet chocolate
>   chips
> 3/4 cup coarsely chopped
>   macadamia nuts
> 3/4 cup coarsely chopped pecans
> **CARAMEL GLAZE:**
> 12 caramel candies
> 2 tablespoons whipping cream

In a mixing bowl, cream butter, sugar and vanilla. Add egg. Combine flour, baking powder, baking soda and salt; add to creamed mixture and mix well.

Crisp Sugar Cookies

(PICTURED ON PAGE 102)

"Grandmother always had sugar cookies in her pantry," recalls Evelyn Poteet of Hancock, Maryland. "We grandchildren would empty that jar quickly!"

> 1 cup butter *or* margarine,
>   softened
> 2 cups sugar
> 2 eggs
> 1 teaspoon vanilla extract
> 5 cups all-purpose flour
> 1-1/2 teaspoons baking powder
> 1 teaspoon baking soda
> 1/2 teaspoon salt
> 1/4 cup milk

In a mixing bowl, cream butter and sugar. Add eggs and vanilla. Combine flour, baking powder, baking soda and salt; add to creamed mixture alternately with the milk. Cover and refrigerate for 15-30 minutes. On a floured surface, roll out dough to 1/8-in. thickness. Cut out cookies into desired shapes and place 2 in. apart on a greased baking sheet. Bake at 350° for 10 minutes or until edges are lightly browned. **Yield:** 8 dozen (2-1/2-inch cookies).

Carrot Fruitcake

"Even those who don't care for fruit-cake will love this special dessert," assures Ann Parden of Chunchula, Alabama. "It's a great way to 'dress up' carrot cake."

- **1-1/2 cups chopped nuts**
- **1 cup chopped mixed candied fruit**
- **1 cup chopped dates**
- **1 cup raisins**
- **3 cups all-purpose flour, *divided***
- **2 cups sugar**
- **1-1/2 cups vegetable oil**
- **4 eggs**
- **2 teaspoons baking powder**
- **2 teaspoons baking soda**
- **2 teaspoons ground cinnamon**
- **1 teaspoon salt**
- **3 cups finely shredded carrots**
- **Confectioners' sugar icing, optional**

Combine nuts, fruit, dates and raisins with 1/2 cup flour; set aside. In a large mixing bowl, combine sugar and oil; mix well. Add eggs, one at a time, beating well after each addition. Combine baking powder, baking soda, cinnamon, salt and remaining flour; gradually add to sugar mixture, beating until smooth. (Batter will be stiff.) Fold in carrots and fruit mixture. Spoon into a greased and floured 10-in. tube pan. Bake at 350° for 1 hour and 20 minutes or until cake tests done. Cool for 15 minutes before removing from pan to cool on a wire rack. If desired, drizzle with confectioners' sugar icing when cooled. **Yield:** 12-16 servings.

Apple Walnut Cake

"This cake is perfect for brunch. It gets its appeal from chunks of sweet apples, nutty flavor and creamy frosting," shares Renae Moncur of Burley, Idaho.

- **1-2/3 cups sugar**
- **2 eggs**
- **1/2 cup vegetable oil**
- **2 teaspoons vanilla extract**
- **2 cups all-purpose flour**
- **2 teaspoons baking soda**
- **1-1/2 teaspoons ground cinnamon**
- **1 teaspoon salt**
- **1/2 teaspoon ground nutmeg**
- **4 cups chopped unpeeled apples**
- **1 cup chopped walnuts**
- **FROSTING:**
- **2 packages (3 ounces *each*) cream cheese, softened**
- **3 tablespoons butter *or* margarine, softened**
- **1 teaspoon vanilla extract**
- **1-1/2 cups confectioners' sugar**

In a mixing bowl, beat sugar and eggs. Add oil and vanilla; mix well. Combine flour, baking soda, cinnamon, salt and nutmeg; gradually add to sugar mixture, mixing well. Stir in apples and walnuts. Pour into a greased and floured 13-in. x 9-in. x 2-in. baking pan. Bake at 350° for 50-55 minutes or until cake tests done. Cool on a wire rack. For frosting, beat cream cheese, butter and vanilla in a mixing bowl. Gradually add confectioners' sugar until the frosting has reached desired spreading consistency. Frost cooled cake. **Yield:** 16-20 servings.

Chocolate Sauce

"I make different toppings so we can enjoy our favorite snack—ice cream sundaes," explains Nancy McDonald of Burns, Wyoming. "This smooth chocolate sauce is always a hit."

- **1/2 cup butter *or* margarine**
- **2 squares (1 ounce *each*) unsweetened chocolate**
- **2 cups sugar**
- **1 cup light cream *or* evaporated milk**
- **1/2 cup light corn syrup**
- **1 teaspoon vanilla extract**

In a saucepan, melt butter and chocolate. Add sugar, cream, corn syrup and vanilla. Bring to a boil, stirring constantly. Boil for 1-1/2 minutes. Remove from the heat. Serve warm or cold over ice cream or pound cake. Refrigerate leftovers. **Yield:** about 3-1/3 cups.

Mini-Choco Cupcakes

"I like to make these mini muffins for a change of pace," claims Annette Stevens of Olds, Alberta. "People love the hint of chocolate in each bite."

- **2-1/2 cups all-purpose flour**
- **2-1/2 teaspoons baking powder**
- **1/2 teaspoon salt**
- **1 cup butter *or* margarine, softened**
- **1-1/2 cups sugar**
- **1-1/2 teaspoons vanilla extract**
- **4 eggs**
- **1 cup milk**
- **1 cup semisweet mini chocolate chips**
- **Confectioners' sugar**

In a medium bowl, sift together flour, baking powder and salt; set aside. In a large bowl, beat butter and sugar. Add vanilla. Add eggs, one at a time, beating well after each addition. Alternately add dry ingredients and milk, beginning and ending with dry ingredients; beat well after each addition. Stir in chocolate chips. Line regular or mini muffin cups with baking papers. Fill each two-thirds full. Bake at 400° for 14-16 minutes or until muffins test done. Cool. Dust with confectioners' sugar. **Yield:** 24 regular or 48 mini cupcakes.

Make-Ahead S'mores

"These are perfect little desserts to keep on hand for when unexpected company drops in," says Anne Sherman of Orangeburg, South Carolina.

- **8 ounces semisweet chocolate**
- **1 can (14 ounces) sweetened condensed milk**
- **1 teaspoon vanilla extract**
- **1 box (16 ounces) graham crackers**
- **2 cups miniature marshmallows**

In a heavy saucepan, melt chocolate over low heat. Stir in milk and vanilla; cook and stir until smooth. Making 1 s'more at a time, spread 1 tablespoon each of chocolate mixture on two whole graham crackers. Place 5-6 marshmallows on one cracker; gently press the other cracker on top. Repeat with remaining chocolate, crackers and marshmallows. Wrap with plastic wrap; store at room temperature. **Yield:** 16 s'mores.

Old-Fashioned Oatmeal Cookies

Michelle Wise of Spring Mills, Pennsylvania says, "These are my favorite cookies to take on a trip because they stay moist and aren't too sweet."

- **1 cup raisins**
- **1 cup water**
- **3/4 cup shortening**
- **1-1/2 cups sugar**
- **2 eggs**
- **1 teaspoon vanilla extract**
- **2-1/2 cups all-purpose flour**
- **1 teaspoon baking soda**
- **1 teaspoon salt**
- **1 teaspoon ground cinnamon**
- **1/2 teaspoon baking powder**
- **1/4 teaspoon ground cloves**
- **2 cups quick-cooking oats**
- **1/2 cup chopped walnuts, optional**

In a saucepan, cook raisins in water over medium heat until plump, about 15 minutes. Drain, reserving liquid. Add enough water to liquid to measure 1/2 cup. In a mixing bowl, cream shortening, sugar, eggs and vanilla. Stir in raisin liquid. Blend in dry ingredients. Stir in raisins and oats. Add nuts if desired. Drop by teaspoonfuls about 2 in. apart onto ungreased cookie sheets. Bake at 375° for 10-12 minutes or until light brown. **Yield:** 5 dozen.

SOUPS & SALADS

WHAT goes together better than soup and salad? The hot, hearty soups and cool, refreshing salads featured in this chapter are sure to complement any meal. Or serve them alone for a light, yet pleasing, entree.

Pizza Salad

(PICTURED ON OPPOSITE PAGE)

"This is a different salad that tastes as good as it looks. I love to take it to parties—the wonderful zesty flavor really complements a barbecue," explains Debbie Jones of California, Maryland.

- 1 pound spiral macaroni, cooked and drained
- 3 medium tomatoes, diced and seeded
- 1 pound cheddar cheese, cubed
- 1 to 2 bunches green onions, sliced
- 3 ounces sliced pepperoni
- 3/4 cup vegetable oil
- 2/3 cup grated Parmesan cheese
- 1/2 cup red wine vinegar
- 2 teaspoons dried oregano
- 1 teaspoon garlic powder
- 1 teaspoon salt
- 1/4 teaspoon pepper
- Croutons, optional

In a large bowl, combine macaroni, tomatoes, cheddar cheese, green onions and pepperoni. In a small bowl, combine oil, Parmesan cheese, vinegar and seasonings; pour over macaroni mixture. Cover and refrigerate for several hours. Top with croutons just before serving if desired. **Yield:** 16 servings.

Sauerkraut Salad

(PICTURED ON OPPOSITE PAGE)

"I got this tangy recipe from my sister-in-law. It always gets raves at potlucks," says Diane Thompson of Nutrioso, Arizona. *"It's easy to prepare and can be made a day or two before the get-together."*

- 1 can (16 ounces) sauerkraut, drained
- 1 cup grated carrots
- 1 cup chopped celery
- 1 cup chopped green pepper
- 1 cup chopped onion
- 1 jar (4 ounces) diced pimientos, drained
- 3/4 cup sugar
- 1/2 cup vegetable oil

In a large bowl, mix sauerkraut, carrots, celery, green pepper, onion and pimien-tos. In a jar or small bowl, combine sugar and oil. Pour over vegetables and mix well. Cover and refrigerate for at least 8 hours. **Yield:** 10-12 servings.

Minestrone Soup

(PICTURED ON OPPOSITE PAGE)

"Here's the perfect soup to put fresh garden vegetables to good use," assures Lana Rutledge of Shepherdsville, Kentucky. *"It's great for a light meal served with a salad and warm bread."*

- 1 beef chuck roast (4 pounds)
- 1 gallon water
- 2 bay leaves
- 2 medium onions, diced
- 2 cups sliced carrots
- 2 cups sliced celery
- 1 can (28 ounces) tomatoes with liquid, cut up
- 1 can (15 ounces) tomato sauce
- 1/4 cup chopped fresh parsley
- Salt and pepper to taste
- 4 teaspoons dried basil
- 1 teaspoon garlic powder
- 2 packages (9 ounces *each*) frozen Italian *or* cut green beans
- 1 package (16 ounces) frozen peas
- 2 cans (15-1/2 ounces *each*) kidney beans, rinsed and drained
- 2 boxes (7 ounces *each*) shell macaroni, cooked and drained
- Grated Parmesan cheese

Place beef roast, water and bay leaves in a large kettle or Dutch oven; bring to a boil. Reduce heat; cover and simmer until meat is tender, about 3 hours. Remove meat from broth; cool. Add onions, carrots and celery to broth; cook for 20 minutes or until vegetables are tender. Cut meat into bite-size pieces; add to broth. Add tomatoes, tomato sauce, parsley, seasonings, beans, peas and kidney beans. Cook until vegetables are done, about 10 minutes. Add macaroni and heat through. Remove bay leaves. Ladle into soup bowls; sprinkle with Parmesan cheese. **Yield:** about 40 servings (10 quarts).

Cajun Corn Soup

"I prepare this dish for out-of-state guests who want to taste some Cajun food," shares Sue Fontenot of Kinder, Louisiana. *"Everyone who tries it gives it high marks. Plus, it's easy to prepare."*

- 1 cup chopped onion
- 1 cup chopped green pepper
- 6 green onions, sliced
- 1/2 cup cooking oil

- 1/2 cup all-purpose flour
- 3 cups water
- 1 can (14-1/2 ounces) Cajun-style stewed tomatoes
- 2 cups chopped peeled tomatoes
- 1 can (6 ounces) tomato paste
- 2 packages (16 ounces *each*) frozen whole kernel corn
- 3 cups cubed cooked ham
- 1-1/2 pounds fully cooked smoked sausage, sliced
- 1/8 teaspoon cayenne pepper *or* to taste
- Salt to taste
- Hot pepper sauce to taste

In a large kettle or Dutch oven, saute onion, green pepper and green onions in oil until tender, about 5 minutes. Add flour and cook until bubbly. Add water, stewed and chopped tomatoes and tomato paste; mix well. Stir in the corn, ham, sausage, cayenne pepper, salt and hot pepper sauce. Bring to a boil, stirring frequently. Reduce heat; simmer, uncovered, for 1 hour, stirring occasionally. **Yield:** 12-14 servings.

German Potato Salad

"I'd always loved my German grandmother's potato salad," says Sue Hartman of Parma, Idaho. *"So when I married a potato farmer—and had spuds in abundance—I played with several recipes that sounded similar and came up with this salad that reminds me of hers."*

- 5 bacon strips
- 3/4 cup chopped onion
- 2 tablespoons all-purpose flour
- 1 teaspoon salt
- 1/8 teaspoon pepper
- 1-1/3 cups water
- 2/3 cup cider vinegar
- 1/4 cup sugar
- 6 cups sliced cooked peeled potatoes

In a large skillet, fry bacon until crisp; remove and set aside. Drain all but 2-3 tablespoons of drippings; cook onion until tender. Stir in flour, salt and pepper; blend well. Add water and vinegar; cook and stir until bubbly and slightly thick. Add sugar and stir until it dissolves. Crumble bacon; gently stir in bacon and potatoes. Heat through, stirring lightly to coat potato slices. Serve warm. **Yield:** 6-8 servings.

Scotch Broth

Shares Ann Main of Moorefield, Ontario, "I make up big pots of this hearty soup to freeze in plastic containers. Then I can bring out one or two containers at a time. I heat the frozen soup in a saucepan on low all morning. By lunchtime, it's hot and ready to serve."

        2 pounds meaty beef soup bones
        2 quarts water
        6 whole peppercorns
    1-1/2 teaspoons salt
        1 cup chopped carrots
        1 cup chopped turnips
        1 cup chopped celery
      1/2 cup chopped onion
      1/4 cup medium pearl barley

In a large kettle, combine soup bones, water, peppercorns and salt. Cover and simmer for 2-1/2 hours or until the meat comes easily off the bones. Remove bones. Strain broth; cool and chill. Skim off fat. Remove meat from bones; dice and return to broth along with remaining ingredients. Bring to a boil. Reduce heat; cover and simmer about 1 hour or until vegetables and barley are tender. **Yield:** 6-8 servings (2 quarts).

Chicken Chili with Black Beans

"Because it looks different than traditional chili, my family was a little hesitant to try this dish at first," explains Jeanette Urbom of Overland Park, Kansas. "But thanks to full, hearty flavor, it's become a real favorite around our house. I like to serve it with warm corn bread."

✓ This tasty dish uses less sugar, salt and fat. Recipe includes *Diabetic Exchanges.*

        3 whole skinless boneless
            chicken breasts (about 1-3/4
            pounds), cubed
        2 medium sweet red peppers,
            chopped
        1 large onion, chopped
        4 garlic cloves, minced
        3 tablespoons olive oil
        1 can (4 ounces) chopped green
            chilies
        2 tablespoons chili powder
        2 teaspoons ground cumin
        1 teaspoon ground coriander
        2 cans (15 ounces *each*) black
            beans, rinsed and drained
        1 can (28 ounces) Italian plum
            tomatoes with liquid, chopped
        1 cup chicken broth *or* beer

In a Dutch oven, saute chicken, red peppers, onion and garlic in oil for 5 minutes or until chicken is no longer pink. Add green chilies, chili powder, cumin and coriander; cook for 3 minutes. Stir in beans, tomatoes and broth or beer; bring to a boil. Reduce heat and simmer, uncovered, for 15 minutes, stir-

SOUPER SOUP AND SALADS. Pictured above, top to bottom: Pizza Salad, Minestrone Soup and Sauerkraut Salad (all recipes on page 88).

ring often. **Yield:** 10 servings (3 quarts). **Diabetic Exchanges:** One serving (prepared with chicken broth) equals 1 meat, 1 vegetable, 1/2 starch; also, 149 calories, 172 mg sodium, 33 mg cholesterol, 12 gm carbohydrate, 16 gm protein, 4 gm fat.

Turkey Mandarin Salad

"A refreshing, interesting combination of turkey, pasta and fruit with a lightly sweet dressing makes this a family favorite," relates Bernice Smith of Sturgeon Lake, Minnesota.

        2 cups cubed cooked turkey
        1 tablespoon finely chopped
            onion
      1/2 teaspoon salt
        1 cup seedless red grape halves
        1 cup diced celery
        1 can (15 ounces) mandarin
            oranges, drained
        1 cup cooked macaroni
      3/4 cup mayonnaise
      3/4 cup whipping cream, whipped
      1/3 cup slivered almonds
    Toasted almonds, optional

In a large bowl, combine turkey, onion and salt; mix well. Add grapes, celery, oranges and macaroni; toss lightly to mix. Cover and refrigerate. Just before serving, combine mayonnaise and whipped cream; fold into salad along with almonds. Top with toasted almonds if desired. **Yield:** 6-8 servings.

Classic Beef Stew

(PICTURED ON PAGE 84)

"This good old-fashioned stew with rich beef gravy lets the flavor of the potatoes and carrots come through," states Alberta McKay of Bartlesville, Oklahoma. "It's the perfect hearty dish for a blustery winter day."

- 2 pounds beef stew meat, cut into 1-inch cubes
- 1 to 2 tablespoons cooking oil
- 1-1/2 cups chopped onion
- 1 can (16 ounces) tomatoes with liquid, cut up
- 1 can (10-1/2 ounces) condensed beef broth, undiluted
- 3 tablespoons quick-cooking tapioca
- 1 garlic clove, minced
- 1 tablespoon dried parsley flakes
- 1 teaspoon salt
- 1/4 teaspoon pepper
- 1 bay leaf
- 6 medium carrots, cut into 2-inch pieces
- 3 medium potatoes, peeled and cut into 2-inch pieces
- 1 cup sliced celery (1-inch pieces)

In a Dutch oven, brown the beef, half at a time, in oil. Drain. Return all meat to pan. Add onion, tomatoes, beef broth, tapioca, garlic, parsley, salt, pepper and bay leaf. Bring to a boil; remove from the heat. Cover and bake at 350° for 1-1/2 hours. Stir in carrots, potatoes and celery. Bake, covered, 1 hour longer or until meat and vegetables are tender. Remove bay leaf before serving. **Yield:** 6-8 servings.

Five-Bean Soup

"One of my family's favorite soups, this tasty recipe was one I discovered years ago," says Lynne Dodd of Mentor, Ohio. "Served with salad and bread or rolls, it makes a savory supper."

✓This tasty dish uses less sugar, salt and fat. Recipe includes *Diabetic Exchanges*.

- 5 packages (16 ounces *each*) dried beans: lima, great northern, kidney, pinto and split peas (enough for four batches of soup)
- 3 beef bouillon cubes
- 3 tablespoons dried chives
- 1 teaspoon dried savory
- 1 teaspoon salt, optional
- 1/2 teaspoon ground cumin
- 1/2 teaspoon pepper
- 1 bay leaf
- 2-1/2 quarts water

- 1 can (14-1/2 ounces) stewed tomatoes

Combine beans; divide into four equal batches, about 3-3/4 cups each. *To make one batch of soup:* Wash one batch of beans. Place in a large kettle; add enough water to cover. Bring to a boil; cook for 3-4 minutes. Remove from heat; cover and let stand 1 hour. Tie spices in a cheesecloth bag. Drain and rinse beans. Return to kettle; add bouillon, spices and water. Bring to boil. Reduce heat; cover and simmer 1-1/2 hours or until beans are tender, stirring occasionally. Remove spices. Add tomatoes and heat through. **Yield:** one batch makes 14 servings (3-1/2 quarts). **Diabetic Exchanges:** One serving (1 cup) equals 2 starch, 1 vegetable, 1/2 meat; also, 191 calories, 293 mg sodium, 0 mg cholesterol, 35 gm carbohydrate, 13 gm protein, 1 gm fat.

Zesty Potato Salad

"A new, zippy version of the old favorite, this refreshing potato salad is sure to please! Horseradish gives it a delightfully different flavor," relates Aney Chatterton of Soda Springs, Idaho.

- 2 pounds red potatoes
- 1/2 cup mayonnaise
- 1/2 cup sour cream
- 2 tablespoons prepared horseradish
- 1 tablespoon chopped fresh parsley
- 1/2 teaspoon salt
- 1/2 teaspoon pepper
- 3 bacon strips, cooked and crumbled
- 4 hard-cooked eggs, chopped
- 2 green onions, sliced

Peel potatoes; cook in boiling salted water for 20 minutes or until done. Drain and cool. Cut potatoes into cubes. In a large bowl, combine mayonnaise, sour cream, horseradish, parsley, salt and pepper; mix until smooth. Stir in potatoes, bacon, eggs and onions. Cover and chill up to 24 hours. **Yield:** 6 servings.

Cheesy Chicken Chowder

"I like to serve this hearty chowder with garlic bread and a salad. It's a wonderful dish to prepare when company drops in. The rich, mild flavor and tender chicken and vegetables appeal even to children and picky eaters," assures Hazel Fritchie of Palestine, Illinois.

- 3 cups chicken broth
- 2 cups diced peeled potatoes
- 1 cup diced carrots

- 1 cup diced celery
- 1/2 cup diced onion
- 1-1/2 teaspoons salt
- 1/4 teaspoon pepper
- 1/4 cup butter *or* margarine
- 1/3 cup all-purpose flour
- 2 cups milk
- 2 cups (8 ounces) shredded cheddar cheese
- 2 cups diced cooked chicken

In a 4-qt. saucepan, bring chicken broth to a boil. Reduce heat; add potatoes, carrots, celery, onion, salt and pepper. Cover and simmer for 15 minutes or until vegetables are tender. Meanwhile, melt butter in a medium saucepan; add flour and mix well. Gradually stir in milk; cook over low heat until slightly thickened. Stir in cheese and cook until melted; add to broth along with chicken. Cook and stir over low heat until heated through. **Yield:** 6-8 servings.

> **SERVE TUNA** or egg salad a new way by cutting off the top of a hard roll, "hollowing" it out and filling it with the salad. Add onion, tomato and lettuce and put the "top" back on.

Chinese Chicken Salad

"Here's a cool, easy entree perfect for steamy summer days! The crispy lettuce and wonton skins keep this dish light, while the chicken and dressing give it wonderful flavor," shares Shirley Smith of Yorba Linda, California.

- 1/2 package wonton skins, cut into 1/4-inch strips
- Oil for deep-fat frying
- 3 cups cubed cooked chicken
- 1 head lettuce, shredded
- 4 green onions with tops, sliced
- 4 tablespoons sesame seeds, toasted

DRESSING:
- 1/3 cup white wine vinegar
- 1/4 cup sugar
- 3 tablespoons vegetable oil
- 2 tablespoons sesame oil
- 1 teaspoon salt
- 1 teaspoon monosodium glutamate, optional
- 1/2 teaspoon pepper

Deep-fry wonton skins in oil until brown and crisp. Drain on paper towels; set aside. In a large salad bowl, combine chicken, lettuce, green onions and sesame seeds; mix gently. In a small bowl, whisk together all dressing ingredients. Just before serving, add fried wonton skins to salad; pour dressing over and toss to coat. **Yield:** 6-8 servings. **Editor's Note:** For faster preparation, a can of chow mein noodles can be substituted for the wonton skins.

Gazpacho Salad

"This fresh, colorful salad is great to make ahead and take to a potluck later, after the flavors have had a chance to blend. It's sure to be a success,"assures Florence Jacoby of Granite Falls, Minnesota.

    4 tomatoes, diced and seeded
    2 cucumbers, peeled and diced
    2 green peppers, seeded and
      diced
    1 medium onion, diced
    1 can (2-1/4 ounces) sliced ripe
      olives, drained
    1 teaspoon salt
    1/2 teaspoon pepper
DRESSING:
    1/2 cup olive oil
    1/4 cup vinegar
Juice of 1 lemon (about 1/4 cup)
    1 tablespoon chopped fresh
      parsley
    2 garlic cloves, minced
    2 teaspoons chopped green
      onions
    1/2 teaspoon salt
    1/4 teaspoon ground cumin

In a 1-1/2-qt. glass jar or bowl, layer one-third to one-half of the tomatoes, cucumbers, green peppers, onion, olives, salt and pepper. Repeat layers two or three more times. In a small bowl, combine all dressing ingredients. Pour over vegetables. Cover and chill several hours or overnight. **Yield:** 10-12 servings.

Easy Low-Fat Chili

(PICTURED ON THIS PAGE)

"This zesty chili really hits the spot on cool fall days," confirms Janet Moore of Ogdensburg, New York.

✓ This tasty dish uses less sugar, salt and fat. Recipe includes *Diabetic Exchanges*.

    1 medium onion, chopped
    1/4 cup chopped green pepper
    4 cups water, *divided*
    1 can (15 to 16 ounces) great
      northern beans, rinsed and
      drained
    1 can (15 ounces) navy beans,
      rinsed and drained
    1 can (6 ounces) salt-free
      tomato paste
    1 can (14-1/2 ounces) low-salt
      diced tomatoes, undrained
    2 to 4 teaspoons chili powder
    1 teaspoon salt, optional
    1/2 teaspoon pepper

In a large saucepan, cook the onion and green pepper in 1/2 cup water until tender. Add beans, tomato paste and tomatoes. Stir in chili powder, salt if desired, pepper

and remaining water; bring to a boil. Reduce heat; cover and simmer for 20 minutes. **Yield:** 7 servings. **Diabetic Exchanges:** One 1-cup serving (prepared without added salt) equals 2 starch, 1-1/2 vegetable; also, 198 calories, 295 mg sodium, 0 cholesterol, 38 gm carbohydrate, 11 gm protein, 1 gm fat.

Creamy Sliced Tomatoes

Explains Doris Smith of Woodbury, New Jersey, "This is a family favorite that's also popular with friends. The basil and cool creamy dressing make this pretty dish tasty and refreshing."

    1 cup mayonnaise
    1/2 cup light cream
    3/4 teaspoon dried basil *or* 1-1/2
      teaspoons chopped fresh
      basil, *divided*
Lettuce leaves
    6 medium tomatoes, sliced
    1 medium red onion, thinly
      sliced into rings

In a small bowl, combine mayonnaise, cream and half of the basil; mix well. Refrigerate. Just before serving, arrange lettuce, tomatoes and onions on individual salad plates. Drizzle dressing over. Sprinkle with remaining basil. **Yield:** 12 servings.

Garden Bean Salad

"My mother gave me this crunchy bean salad recipe years ago. It looks especially attractive served in a glass bowl to show off the colorful vegetables," comments Bernice McFadden of Dayton, Ohio.

    1 can (16 ounces) cut green
      beans
    2 cans (17 ounces *each*) lima
      beans
    1 can (16 ounces) kidney beans
    1 can (16 ounces) wax beans
    1 can (15 ounces) garbanzo
      beans
    1 large green pepper, chopped
    3 celery ribs, chopped
    1 jar (2 ounces) sliced pimientos,
      drained
    1 bunch green onions, sliced
    2 cups vinegar
    2 cups sugar
    1/2 cup water
    1 teaspoon salt

Drain all cans of beans; place in a large bowl. Add green pepper, celery, pimientos and green onions; set aside. Bring remaining ingredients to a boil in a heavy saucepan; boil for 5 minutes. Remove from heat and immediately pour over vegetables. Refrigerate several hours or overnight. **Yield:** 12-16 servings.

FABULOUS FIXIN'S. Pictured above: Easy Low-Fat Chili (recipe on this page) and Cinnamon Mini-Muffins (recipe on page 104).

SATISFYING MEAL. Pictured above, clockwise from the top: Herbed Beef Stew (recipe on this page), Angel Biscuits (recipe on page 103), Emily's Spinach Salad (recipe on this page) and Carrot Cake (recipe on page 81).

sary. Stir in remaining ingredients; cover and simmer 20 minutes. **Yield:** 10-12 servings.

Emily's Spinach Salad

(PICTURED ON THIS PAGE)

Emily Fields of Santa Ana, California relates, "I was delighted when this original colorful, tangy salad took the grand prize at a spinach cooking contest!"

   2/3 cup vegetable oil
   1/4 cup red wine vinegar
   2 teaspoons lemon juice
   2 teaspoons soy sauce
   1 teaspoon sugar
   1 teaspoon dry mustard
   1/2 teaspoon curry powder
   1/2 teaspoon salt
   1/2 teaspoon seasoned pepper
   1/4 teaspoon garlic powder
   1 package (10 ounces) fresh spinach, torn
   5 bacon strips, cooked and crumbled
   2 hard-cooked eggs, sliced

Combine first 10 ingredients in a jar; cover tightly and shake until well mixed; set aside. Place spinach in a large salad bowl. Just before serving, pour dressing over spinach and toss gently. Garnish with crumbled bacon and egg slices. **Yield:** 6-8 servings.

Cucumber Potato Soup

"This soup never fails to delight the taste buds! It's simple to make and has a nice dill flavor," shares Robert Breno of Strongsville, Ohio.

✓ This tasty dish uses less sugar, salt and fat. Recipe includes *Diabetic Exchanges*.

   4 medium potatoes, peeled and diced
   1 teaspoon salt
   2 cups water
   1 medium cucumber, peeled, diced and seeded
   1/4 teaspoon white pepper
   1 cup heavy cream *or* milk
   1/2 cup milk
   1 green onion, sliced
   1 teaspoon dill weed *or* 1 tablespoon chopped fresh dill
Additional salt and pepper to taste

In a large saucepan, cook potatoes in salted water until very soft. Place sieve over a large bowl. Pour potatoes and liquid into sieve and force potatoes through. Return to saucepan. Stir in cucumber, pepper, cream, milk and onion. Simmer gently for about 5 minutes or until cucumber is tender. Add dill, salt and pepper. Serve hot or cold. **Yield:** 4 servings. **Diabetic Exchanges:** One serving (prepared with skim milk) equals

Herbed Beef Stew

(PICTURED ON THIS PAGE)

"This stew looks as terrific as it tastes! It's flavored with a variety of herbs and chock-full of vegetables," explains Marlene Severson of Everson, Washington.

   2 pounds beef stew meat, cut into 1-inch cubes
   2 tablespoons cooking oil
   3 cups water
   1 large onion, chopped
   2 teaspoons pepper
   1 to 2 teaspoons salt, optional
1-1/2 teaspoons garlic powder
   1 teaspoon rosemary, crushed
   1 teaspoon dried oregano
   1 teaspoon dried basil
   1 teaspoon ground marjoram

   2 bay leaves
   1 can (6 ounces) tomato paste
   2 cups cubed peeled potatoes
   2 cups sliced carrots
   1 large green pepper, chopped
   1 package (10 ounces) frozen green beans
   1 package (10 ounces) frozen peas
   1 package (10 ounces) frozen kernel corn
   1/4 pound mushrooms, sliced
   3 medium tomatoes, chopped

Brown meat in oil in a Dutch oven. Add water, onion, seasonings and tomato paste. Cover and simmer for 1-1/2 hours or until meat is tender. Stir in potatoes, carrots and green pepper; simmer 30 minutes. Add additional water if neces-

1 starch, 1/2 skim milk, 1 vegetable; also, 131 calories, 631 mg sodium, 2 mg cholesterol, 27 gm carbohydrate, 6 gm protein, trace fat.

Pat's Potato Salad

"I developed this recipe while working at a restaurant. It tastes even better after being refrigerated," comments Patricia Maul of Bartlesville, Oklahoma.

- 12 medium red potatoes, cooked, peeled and cubed
- 1 medium red onion, chopped
- 1 cup chopped fresh parsley
- 1-1/2 cups mayonnaise
- 1 cup (8 ounces) sour cream
- 1/4 cup sugar
- 1/4 cup vinegar
- 4 teaspoons dry mustard
- 1 teaspoon salt

In a large bowl, combine potatoes, onion and parsley. In a small bowl, combine remaining ingredients. Pour over potatoes and mix well. Refrigerate at least 1 hour before serving. Salad can be prepared a day ahead. **Yield:** 12-16 servings.

Cranberry Pineapple Salad

(PICTURED ON PAGE 3)

"This fresh and fruity salad impresses family and guests with its striking rosy color," relates Dorothy Angley of Carver, Massachusetts.

- 1 package (6 ounces) raspberry-flavored gelatin
- 1-3/4 cups boiling water
- 1 can (16 ounces) jellied cranberry sauce
- 1 can (8 ounces) crushed pineapple, undrained
- 3/4 cup orange juice
- 1 tablespoon lemon juice
- 1/2 cup chopped walnuts
- Lettuce leaves
- Mayonnaise *or* salad dressing

In a bowl, dissolve gelatin in boiling water. Break up and stir in cranberry sauce. Add pineapple, orange juice and lemon juice. Chill until partially set. Stir in nuts. Pour into an 11-in. x 7-in. x 2-in. dish. Chill until firm. Cut into squares; serve each on a lettuce leaf and top with a dollop of mayonnaise. **Yield:** 12 servings.

U.S. Senate Bean Soup

"This soup is a staple served in the Senate dining room in Washington, D.C.," explains Rosemarie Forcum of White Stone, Virginia. *"Chock-full of ham, beans and celery, it makes a wonderful hearty meal anytime of year."*

- 1 pound dried great northern beans
- 1 meaty ham bone *or* 2 smoked ham hocks
- 3 medium onions, chopped
- 3 garlic cloves, minced
- 3 celery ribs, chopped
- 1 cup mashed potatoes *or* 1/3 cup instant potato flakes
- 1/4 cup chopped fresh parsley
- Salt and pepper to taste
- Parsley *or* chives for garnish

Place beans and enough water to cover in a saucepan; bring to a boil and boil for 2 minutes. Remove from the heat and soak for 1 hour. Drain and rinse beans. In a large kettle, place beans, ham bone or hocks and 3 qts. water. Bring to boil. Reduce heat; cover and simmer for 2 hours. Skim fat if necessary. Add onions, garlic, celery, parsley, potatoes, salt and pepper; simmer 1 hour longer. Remove meat and bones from the soup. Remove meat from the bones; dice and return to kettle. Heat through. Garnish with parsley or chives. **Yield:** 8-10 servings (2-1/2 quarts).

Marinated Tomatoes

"Nothing enhances the flavor of garden-fresh tomatoes like basil," says Monica Wilcott from her Sturgis, Saskatchewan home.

- 3 tomatoes, thickly sliced
- 2 tablespoons chopped fresh basil
- 2 tablespoons olive oil
- 2 tablespoons lemon juice
- 1/2 teaspoon sugar
- 1/8 teaspoon lemon pepper

Place tomato slices in a shallow serving dish; sprinkle with basil. In a small bowl, combine remaining ingredients; pour over tomatoes. Let stand at room temperature for 1 hour before serving. **Yield:** 6 servings.

Creamy Vegetable Soup

"I came up with this soup after tasting a similar version at a restaurant," states Audrey Nemeth of Mount Vernon, Maine. *"My family just loves it!"*

- 1 large onion, chopped
- 1/4 cup butter *or* margarine

- 3 medium sweet potatoes, peeled and chopped
- 3 medium zucchini, chopped
- 1 bunch broccoli, chopped
- 2 quarts chicken broth
- 2 medium potatoes, peeled and shredded
- 2 teaspoons salt
- 1 teaspoon pepper
- 1 teaspoon celery seed
- 1 to 2 teaspoons ground cumin
- 2 cups light cream

In a large kettle, saute onion in butter until transparent but not browned. Add the sweet potatoes, zucchini and broccoli; saute lightly for 5 minutes or until crisp-tender. Stir in broth; simmer for a few minutes. Add potatoes and seasonings; cook another 10 minutes or until vegetables are tender. Stir in cream and heat through. **Yield:** 12-16 servings (4 quarts).

Pork and Spinach Salad

"To get in the mood for warmer weather, I serve this hearty main-dish salad," shares Marian Platt of Sequim, Washington. *"You just can't beat a salad that tastes great and is good for you, too!"*

✓ This tasty dish uses less sugar, salt and fat. Recipe includes *Diabetic Exchanges*.

- 10 ounces fresh spinach, washed and stems removed
- 1 can (16 ounces) black-eyed peas, rinsed and drained
- 1/2 cup sliced fresh mushrooms
- 1/3 cup Italian *or* low-fat Italian dressing
- 1/4 cup sliced green onions
- 1/4 cup sliced celery
- 1 jar (2 ounces) sliced pimientos, drained
- 2 to 3 tablespoons sliced ripe olives
- 2 garlic cloves, minced
- 1 tablespoon olive oil
- 1/2 pound pork tenderloin, cut into thin strips

Line four plates with spinach leaves; set aside. In a bowl, combine peas, mushrooms, Italian dressing, green onions, celery, pimientos and olives; set aside. In a medium skillet, saute garlic in oil for 30 seconds. Add pork and stir-fry for 2-3 minutes or until no pink remains. Remove from the heat; add vegetable mixture and mix well. Divide among spinach-lined plates. Serve immediately. **Yield:** 4 servings. **Diabetic Exchanges:** One serving (prepared with low-fat dressing) equals 2 meat, 3 vegetable, 1 starch, 1 fat; also, 317 calories, 758 mg sodium, 56 mg cholesterol, 24 gm carbohydrate, 27 gm protein, 13 gm fat.

SAVORY STEW. Pictured above: Sausage and Mushroom Stew (recipe on this page).

Sausage and Mushroom Stew

(PICTURED ON THIS PAGE)

Ann Nace of Perkasie, Pennsylvania contributes, "The perfect dish for a hungry hardworking bunch, this savory stew has a hearty sausage flavor and delicious creamy sauce. Lots of vegetables add color and interest to each ladleful."

- 2 cans (10-3/4 ounces *each*) cream of mushroom soup, undiluted
- 1-1/2 pounds smoked kielbasa, cut into 1-inch rounds
- 5 medium potatoes, peeled and cut into 1-inch chunks
- 4 carrots, peeled and cut into 1-inch pieces
- 3 medium onions, coarsely chopped
- 1 cup fresh green beans, halved
- 3/4 pound fresh mushrooms, halved
- 1/2 medium head cabbage, coarsely chopped

In an ovenproof 5-qt. Dutch oven or casserole, combine all ingredients except cabbage. Cover and bake at 350° for 1-1/4 hours. Uncover and stir. Add the cabbage. Cover and bake 30 minutes longer or until vegetables are tender. Stir again before serving. **Yield:** 6-8 servings.

Vegetable Pasta Salad

"This light, multicolored salad is an original," informs Kathy Crow of Cordova, Alaska. *"When I serve it at potlucks, I'm always asked for the recipe. It's also a standby for friends who gather with us in Arizona each winter."*

- 12 ounces rotini pasta, cooked and drained
- 6 green onions, thinly sliced
- 1 to 2 small zucchini, thinly sliced
- 2 cups frozen broccoli and cauliflower, thawed and drained
- 1-1/2 cups thinly sliced carrots, parboiled
- 1 cup thinly sliced celery
- 1/2 cup frozen peas, thawed
- 1 can (2-1/4 ounces) sliced ripe olives, drained
- 1 jar (6 ounces) marinated artichoke hearts, drained and quartered

DRESSING:
- 1/2 cup mayonnaise
- 1/2 cup bottled Italian salad dressing
- 1/2 cup sour cream
- 1 tablespoon prepared mustard
- 1/2 teaspoon dried Italian seasoning

In a large bowl, combine pasta, onions, zucchini, broccoli and cauliflower, carrots, celery, peas, olives and artichoke hearts. In a small bowl, combine dressing ingredients; mix well. Pour over pasta and vegetables and toss. Cover and refrigerate for at least 1 hour. **Yield:** 16-18 servings.

Turkey Wild Rice Soup

(PICTURED ON PAGE 60)

"An area turkey grower shared this recipe with me. A rich and smooth soup, it makes great use of two Minnesota resources—turkey and wild rice," says Terri Holmgren of Swanville, Minnesota.

- 1 medium onion, chopped
- 2 celery ribs, diced
- 2 carrots, diced
- 1/2 cup butter *or* margarine
- 1/2 cup all-purpose flour
- 4 cups chicken *or* turkey broth
- 2 cups cooked wild rice
- 2 cups light cream
- 2 cups diced cooked turkey
- 1 teaspoon dried parsley flakes
- 1/2 teaspoon salt
- 1/4 teaspoon pepper

In a large kettle or Dutch oven, saute onion, celery and carrots in butter until onion is transparent. Reduce heat. Blend in flour and cook until bubbly. Gradually add broth, stirring constantly. Bring to a boil; boil for 1 minute. Reduce heat; add wild rice, cream, turkey, parsley, salt and pepper; simmer for 20 minutes. **Yield:** 10-12 servings (about 3 quarts).

Smoked Turkey and Apple Salad

"This refreshing, eye-catching dish is a great main course for a summer lunch or light dinner," states Carolyn Popwell of Lacey, Washington. *"The dressing's Dijon flavor goes nicely with turkey."*

✓ This tasty dish uses less sugar, salt and fat. Recipe includes *Diabetic Exchanges.*

DRESSING:
- 5 tablespoons olive oil
- 2 tablespoons cider vinegar
- 1 tablespoon Dijon mustard
- 1 teaspoon lemon pepper
- 1/2 teaspoon salt, optional

SALAD:
- 1 bunch watercress *or* romaine, torn into bite-size pieces
- 1 carrot, julienned
- 10 cherry tomatoes, halved
- 8 ounces smoked turkey, julienned
- 4 unpeeled apples, sliced
- 1/3 cup chopped walnuts, toasted

Whisk together dressing ingredients and set aside. Just before serving, arrange salad greens on a platter or individual plates. Top with carrot, tomatoes, turkey and apples. Drizzle dressing over salad and sprinkle with walnuts. **Yield:** 8 servings. **Diabetic Exchanges:** One serving (prepared with romaine and without added salt) equals 2 fat, 1-1/2 vegetable, 1 meat; also, 195 calories, 267 mg sodium, 8 mg cholesterol, 10 gm carbohydrate, 6 gm protein, 16 gm fat.

Hearty Potato Soup

(PICTURED ON THIS PAGE)

"I love our country life here in Idaho's 'potato country'. My favorite potato soup originally called for heavy cream and bacon fat, but I've trimmed down the recipe," shares Gladys DeBoer of Castleford, Idaho.

- 6 medium potatoes, peeled and sliced
- 2 carrots, diced
- 6 celery ribs, diced
- 2 quarts water
- 1 onion, chopped
- 6 tablespoons butter *or* margarine
- 6 tablespoons all-purpose flour
- 1 teaspoon salt
- 1/2 teaspoon pepper
- 1-1/2 cups milk

In a large kettle, cook potatoes, carrots and celery in water until tender, about 20 minutes. Drain, reserving liquid and setting vegetables aside. In the same kettle, saute onion in butter until soft. Stir in flour, salt and pepper; gradually add milk, stirring constantly until thickened. Gently stir in cooked vegetables. Add 1 cup or more of reserved cooking liquid until soup is desired consistency. **Yield:** 8-10 servings (about 2-1/2 quarts).

Tomato Dill Bisque

"When our garden tomatoes are plentiful, I make a big batch of this soup (without mayonnaise) and freeze it. Then we can enjoy it even after the garden is gone for the season," states Susan Breckbill of Lincoln University, Pennsylvania.

✓ This tasty dish uses less sugar, salt and fat. Recipe includes *Diabetic Exchanges*.

- 2 medium onions, chopped
- 1 garlic clove, minced
- 2 tablespoons butter *or* margarine
- 2 pounds tomatoes, peeled and chopped
- 1/2 cup water

- 1 chicken bouillon cube
- 1 teaspoon sugar
- 1 teaspoon dill weed
- 1/2 teaspoon salt
- 1/4 teaspoon pepper
- 1/2 cup mayonnaise, optional

In a large saucepan, saute onions and garlic in butter until tender. Add tomatoes, water, bouillon, sugar and seasonings. Cover and simmer 10 minutes or until tomatoes are tender. Remove from heat; cool. Puree in a blender or food processor. Return to saucepan. If a creamy soup is desired, stir in mayonnaise. Cook and stir over low heat until heated through. Serve warm. **Yield:** 5 servings (5 cups). **Diabetic Exchanges:** One serving (prepared with margarine and without mayonnaise) equals 2 vegetable, 1 fat; also, 108 calories, 572 mg sodium, 0 cholesterol, 14 gm carbohydrate, 3 gm protein, 5 gm fat.

Chicken and Sausage Stew

"I love to prepare delicious large one-pot meals at a reasonably low cost, which enables me to feed all my family and friends," explains Ernest Foster of Climax, New York.

- 1 broiler-fryer chicken (3 to 4 pounds)
- 2 quarts water

- 2 pounds hot Italian sausage links
- 6 bacon strips
- 2 garlic cloves, minced
- 1 tablespoon chopped fresh parsley
- 1 teaspoon dried oregano
- 1 can (16 ounces) crushed tomatoes
- 1 can (8 ounces) tomato sauce
- 8 ounces elbow macaroni, cooked and drained

Salt and pepper to taste

Place chicken and water in a large kettle; bring to a boil. Reduce heat; cover and simmer until chicken nearly falls from the bones. Remove chicken from stock. Chill stock. Remove chicken from bones and cube; set aside. Puncture skins of sausages; cover with water in a small saucepan and boil until fully cooked, 20-30 minutes. Drain; pan fry sausages until browned. Cool and cut into bite-size pieces; set aside. In a Dutch oven, cook bacon until crisp. Drain, reserving 1 teaspoon drippings. Cool and crumble bacon; set aside. In the drippings, saute garlic. Skim fat from the chicken stock; add 5 cups to Dutch oven. Add chicken, sausage, bacon, parsley and oregano. Cover and simmer for 10-15 minutes. Add tomatoes, tomato sauce, macaroni, salt and pepper; simmer 10 minutes more. **Yield:** 8-10 servings.

THIS SOUP'S SPUD-TACULAR! Pictured above: Hearty Potato Soup (recipe on this page).

Wild Rice Salad

"Since I spend part of my summers in northern Minnesota near the wild rice fields, I have tried many recipes featuring this delicious, nutty-flavored grain in the past 46 years," states Florence Jacoby of Granite Falls, Minnesota. *"This salad is often requested by family and friends."*

✓ This tasty dish uses less sugar, salt and fat. Recipe includes *Diabetic Exchanges*.

    1 cup uncooked wild rice
Seasoned salt, optional
    2 cups diced cooked chicken
1-1/2 cups halved green grapes
    1 cup sliced water chestnuts, drained
    3/4 cup light mayonnaise
    1 cup cashews, optional
Lettuce leaves

Cook rice according to package directions, omitting salt or substituting seasoned salt if desired. Drain well; cool to room temperature. Spoon into a large bowl; add chicken, grapes, water chestnuts and mayonnaise. Toss gently with a fork. Cover and chill. Just before serving, add cashews if desired. Serve on lettuce leaves or line a bowl with lettuce leaves and fill with salad. **Yield:** 6 servings. **Diabetic Exchanges:** One serving (prepared without cashews or additional salt) equals 2 lean meat, 1 starch, 1 fruit, 1 vegetable, 1 fat; also, 318 calories, 229 mg sodium, 38 mg cholesterol, 40 gm carbohydrate, 19 gm protein, 10 gm fat.

Honey Fruit Dressing

(PICTURED ON PAGE 59)

"Mix this dressing with a medley of fruits for a flavorful brunch dish," suggests Dorothy Anderson of Ottawa, Kansas.

    2/3 cup sugar
    1 teaspoon dry mustard
    1 teaspoon paprika
    1 teaspoon celery seed
    1/4 teaspoon salt
    1/3 cup honey
    1/3 cup vinegar
    1 tablespoon lemon juice
    1 teaspoon grated onion
    1 cup vegetable oil

In a mixing bowl, combine sugar, mustard, paprika, celery seed and salt. Add honey, vinegar, lemon juice and onion. Pour oil into mixture very slowly, beating constantly. Serve with fresh fruit. Store in the refrigerator. **Yield:** 2 cups.

Overnight Coleslaw

(PICTURED ON THIS PAGE)

"Before I retired, when my office had a covered-dish get-together, I was always asked to bring my tangy coleslaw. My family loves it, too," shares Fern Hammock of Garland, Texas.

    12 cups shredded cabbage
        (1 medium head)
    1 green pepper, chopped
    1 medium red onion, chopped
    2 carrots, shredded
    1 cup sugar
DRESSING:
    1 cup vinegar
    3/4 cup vegetable oil
    2 teaspoons sugar
    1 teaspoon dry mustard
    1 teaspoon celery seed
    1 teaspoon salt

In a large bowl, combine first four ingredients. Sprinkle with sugar; set aside. In a saucepan, combine dressing ingredients; bring to a boil. Remove from the heat and pour over vegetables, stirring to cover evenly. Cover and refrigerate overnight. Stir well before serving. **Yield:** 12-16 servings.

Rosemary Split Pea Soup

"This zesty soup is great served with warm rolls or French bread," says Diane Hixon of Niceville, Florida.

✓ This tasty dish uses less sugar, salt and fat. Recipe includes *Diabetic Exchanges*.

    3 celery ribs, finely chopped
    1 cup finely chopped onion
    1 garlic clove, minced
    1 tablespoon fresh rosemary, minced, *or* 1 teaspoon dried rosemary
    3 tablespoons butter *or* margarine
    6 cups chicken broth
1-1/4 cups dried split peas, rinsed
    1 teaspoon salt, optional
MEATBALLS:
    1/2 pound ground pork *or* turkey
1-1/2 teaspoons fresh rosemary, minced, *or* 1/2 teaspoon dried rosemary
    1/4 teaspoon pepper

In a large kettle or Dutch oven, saute celery, onion, garlic and rosemary in butter until tender. Add broth, peas and salt if desired; bring to a boil. Reduce heat; cover and simmer for 1-1/2 hours or until peas are soft. Remove from the heat and allow to cool. For meatballs, combine pork or turkey, rosemary and pepper. Shape into 1/2-in. balls. In a skillet, brown meatballs until no pink remains, about 5-10 minutes. Ladle half of the cooled soup into a blender or food processor; puree. Return soup to the kettle along with the meatballs and heat through. **Yield:** 5 servings. **Diabetic Exchanges:** One serving (prepared with margarine and ground turkey and without added salt) equals 2 lean meat, 2 starch, 1 vegetable, 1/2 fat; also, 359

IT'S AN OVERNIGHT SUCCESS. Pictured above: Overnight Coleslaw (recipe on this page).

calories, 1,064 mg sodium, 24 mg cholesterol, 37 gm carbohydrate, 26 gm protein, 13 gm fat.

Frozen Fruit Salad

"I use this recipe to add a healthy twist to brown-bag lunches," reports Virginia Powell of Eureka, Kansas. "I'm always in a hurry in the morning, so having a ready-made salad is a great help."

- 1 can (16 ounces) apricots in light syrup, drained
- 1 package (16 ounces) frozen sweetened sliced strawberries, thawed and drained
- 1 can (8 ounces) pineapple tidbits, drained
- 3 bananas, sliced
- 1 can (6 ounces) frozen orange juice concentrate, thawed
- 1 juice can water

In a food processor, chop apricots. In a pitcher or bowl, combine apricots, strawberries, pineapple, bananas, orange juice and water. Pour or ladle into muffin cups that have been sprayed with vegetable cooking spray. Freeze. When frozen, quickly remove salads to freezer bags or tightly covered storage containers. When packing a lunch, place salad in individual storage container in a thermal lunch bag, and it will thaw by lunchtime. **Yield:** 22-24 servings.

Dilly Potato Salad

"Each spring and fall, I make large amounts of potato salad for the festivals at our church," states Howard Haug of Hewitt, Texas. "Everyone says it goes well with the meats the other men barbecue."

- 6 large red potatoes, boiled, peeled and diced
- 4 celery ribs, diced
- 3 medium dill pickles, finely chopped
- 1 jar (4 ounces) diced pimientos, drained
- 3 hard-cooked eggs, diced
- 1 green pepper, chopped
- 1/4 cup mayonnaise
- 1 teaspoon prepared mustard
- 1 teaspoon salt

Paprika
- 6 green pepper strips (1/4 inch wide)

In a large bowl, combine the potatoes, celery, pickles, pimientos, eggs and the chopped green pepper. In a small bowl, combine mayonnaise, mustard and salt; add to the potato mixture and mix well. Spoon into a serving bowl. Sprinkle with paprika. Arrange green pepper strips in

WILD ABOUT STEW. Pictured above: Venison Stew (recipe on this page).

the center in the shape of wheel spokes. Chill. **Yield:** 8 servings.

Cranberry Pecan Salad

Janice Rogers of Gardendale, Texas relates, "I use pecans in many recipes. One that's become a family favorite is this tasty, colorful salad."

- 3 packages (3 ounces *each*) orange-flavored gelatin
- 3 cups boiling water
- 2-1/2 cups fresh *or* frozen cranberries, chopped
- 1-1/2 cups finely chopped celery
- 2 oranges, diced
- 1 can (8 ounces) crushed pineapple, undrained
- 2 tablespoons grated orange peel
- 1 cup sugar
- 2 tablespoons lemon juice

Dash salt
- 3/4 cup chopped pecans

In a bowl, dissolve gelatin in boiling water. Stir in cranberries, celery, oranges, pineapple with liquid, orange peel, sugar, lemon juice and salt. Chill until partially set. Stir in pecans. Pour into 8-cup mold. Chill until firm. **Yield:** 12-16 servings.

FAT FACT. Dropping a lettuce leaf into a pot of homemade soup will help absorb excess grease. Simply remove the saturated leaf before serving the soup.

Venison Stew

(PICTURED ON THIS PAGE)

"I had no choice but to learn to cook some years ago while my wife recuperated from surgery," says Gene Pitts of Wilsonville, Alabama. "That's how my now-famous stew recipe came to be."

- 2 tablespoons cooking oil
- 2 pounds venison stew meat
- 3 large onions, coarsely chopped
- 2 garlic cloves, crushed
- 1 tablespoon Worcestershire sauce
- 1 bay leaf
- 1 teaspoon dried oregano
- 1 tablespoon salt
- 1 teaspoon pepper
- 3 cups water
- 7 potatoes, peeled and quartered
- 1 pound carrots, cut into 1-inch pieces
- 1/4 cup all-purpose flour
- 1/4 cup cold water

Bottled browning sauce, optional

Heat oil in a Dutch oven. Brown meat. Add onions, garlic, Worcestershire sauce, bay leaf, oregano, salt, pepper and water. Simmer, covered, 1-1/2 to 2 hours or until meat is tender. Add potatoes and carrots. Continue to cook until vegetables are tender, about 30-45 minutes. Mix flour and cold water; stir into stew. Cook and stir until thickened and bubbly. Add browning sauce if desired. Remove bay leaf. **Yield:** 8-10 servings.

BREADS

THIS BOUNTY of fresh-from-the-oven quick breads, yeast breads, muffins and more will taste great with your best meals. Or slather them with your favorite spreads for an anytime snack.

Candy Cane Rolls

(PICTURED ON OPPOSITE PAGE)

"Fun and lightly sweet, these festive rolls will delight children of all ages," assures Janice Peterson of Huron, South Dakota. *"Make them as part of a holiday brunch or an evening snack."*

　　1 package (1/4 ounce) active dry yeast
　1/4 cup warm water (110° to 115°)
　3/4 cup warm milk (110° to 115°)
　1/4 cup sugar
　1/4 cup shortening
　　1 teaspoon salt
　　1 egg, lightly beaten
3-1/4 to 3-3/4 cups all-purpose flour
　　1 cup red candied cherries, quartered
　　1 cup confectioners' sugar
　　1 tablespoon milk

In a large mixing bowl, dissolve yeast in warm water. Add warm milk, sugar, shortening, salt, egg and 2 cups flour; beat until smooth. Stir in cherries. Add enough of the remaining flour to form a soft dough. Turn onto a floured board; knead until smooth and elastic, about 6-8 minutes. Place in a greased bowl, turning once to grease top. Cover and let rise in a warm place until doubled, about 1 hour. Punch dough down; let rest for 10 minutes. Divide in half. Roll each half into a 12-in. x 7-in. rectangle. Cut twelve 1-in. strips from each rectangle. Twist each strip and place 2 in. apart on greased baking sheets, shaping one end like a cane. Cover and let rise until doubled, about 45 minutes. Bake at 375° for 12-15 minutes or until golden brown. Cool completely. Combine confectioners' sugar and milk; frost rolls. **Yield:** 2 dozen.

Eggnog Bread

(PICTURED ON OPPOSITE PAGE)

"Someone always asks for the recipe when I make this delicious rich bread. It's a traditional part of Christmas at my home here in the foothills of the Blue Ridge Mountains," relates Ruth Bickel of Hickory, North Carolina.

　1/4 cup butter *or* margarine, melted
　3/4 cup sugar

　　2 eggs, beaten
2-1/4 cups all-purpose flour
　　2 teaspoons baking powder
　　1 teaspoon salt
　　1 cup dairy *or* canned eggnog
　1/2 cup chopped pecans
　1/2 cup raisins
　1/2 cup chopped red and green candied cherries

In a large bowl, combine butter, sugar and eggs; mix well. Combine the flour, baking powder and salt. Stir into butter mixture alternately with eggnog; mix only until dry ingredients are moistened. Fold in pecans, raisins and cherries. Spoon into a greased 8-1/2-in. x 4-1/2-in. x 2-1/2-in. loaf pan. Bake at 350° for 70 minutes or until bread tests done. **Yield:** 1 loaf.

HOW SWEET IT IS! Next time you bake sweet breads or muffins, try greasing and *sugaring* pans instead of greasing and flouring. Everyone will love the slight hint of added sweetness.

Christmas Stollen

(PICTURED ON OPPOSITE PAGE)

"I like to make and share this festive delight with family and friends. A slice really brightens a snowy winter day," states Sharon Hasty of New London, Missouri.

　3/4 cup raisins
　1/2 cup chopped mixed candied fruit
　1/4 cup orange juice
　　1 package (1/4 ounce) active dry yeast
　1/4 cup warm water (110° to 115°)
　3/4 cup warm milk (110° to 115°)
　1/2 cup butter *or* margarine, melted
　1/4 cup sugar
　　2 eggs, lightly beaten
　　2 tablespoons grated orange peel
　　1 tablespoon grated lemon peel
　　1 teaspoon salt
5-1/4 to 5-3/4 cups all-purpose flour
　1/2 cup chopped almonds
Confectioners' sugar

Soak raisins and fruit in orange juice; set aside. In a large mixing bowl, dissolve yeast in water. Add milk, butter, sugar, eggs, orange and lemon peel, salt and 3 cups flour; beat until smooth. Add raisin mixture and almonds. Add enough remaining flour to form a soft dough. Turn onto a floured board; knead until smooth and elastic, about 6-8 minutes. Place in a greased bowl, turning once to grease top.

Cover and let rise in a warm place until doubled, about 1-1/2 hours. Punch dough down; let rest for 10 minutes. Divide in half; roll each half into a 10-in. x 7-in. oval. Fold one of the long sides over to within 1 in. of the opposite side; press edges lightly to seal. Place on greased baking sheets. Cover and let rise until nearly doubled, about 1 hour. Bake at 375° for 25-30 minutes or until golden brown. Cool on a wire rack. Just before serving, dust with confectioners' sugar. **Yield:** 2 loaves.

Apple Raisin Bread

(PICTURED ON PAGE 82)

"I've been making this bread for many years. It smells so good in the oven and tastes even better," shares Perlene Hoekema of Lynden, Washington. *"I make this bread almost every Saturday, and it doesn't stay around long."*

　　2 packages (1/4 ounce *each*) active dry yeast
1-1/2 cups warm water (110° to 115°), *divided*
　　1 teaspoon sugar
　　3 eggs, beaten
　　1 cup applesauce
　1/2 cup honey
　1/2 cup vegetable oil
　　2 teaspoons salt
　　8 to 9 cups all-purpose flour
1-1/2 cups diced peeled apples
1-1/2 cups raisins
　　2 tablespoons lemon juice
　　2 tablespoons cornmeal
GLAZE:
　　1 egg, beaten
Sugar

In a small bowl, combine yeast, 1/2 cup water and sugar; set aside. In a large bowl, combine eggs, applesauce, honey, oil, salt and remaining water; mix well. Stir in yeast mixture. Gradually add enough flour to form a soft dough. Knead on a floured surface until smooth and elastic, about 10 minutes. Place dough in a greased bowl, turning once to grease top. Cover and let rise in a warm place until doubled, about 1 hour. Punch down and turn over in bowl. Cover and let rise 30 minutes. In a small bowl, combine apples, raisins and lemon juice. Divide dough into three parts; knead one-third of the apple mixture into each part. Shape each into round flat balls. Place each in a greased 8-in. round baking pan that has been sprinkled with cornmeal. Cover and let rise until doubled, about 1 hour. Brush each loaf with egg and sprinkle with sugar. Bake at 350° for 30-35 minutes or until bread sounds hollow when tapped. **Yield:** 3 loaves.

BEST BAKED GOODS. Pictured clockwise from top: Cherry Almond Wreath (recipe on page 106), Eggnog Bread, Candy Cane Rolls and Christmas Stollen (recipes on page 98).

Raspberry Lemon Muffins

(PICTURED ON THIS PAGE)

"These are my all-time favorite muffins, and I have a hard time eating just one," admits Sharon Shine of Bradford, Pennsylvania. *"With their pretty color and tangy flavor, they're delectable!"*

      2 cups all-purpose flour
      1 cup sugar
      1 tablespoon baking powder
  1/2 teaspoon salt
      2 eggs, lightly beaten
      1 cup light cream
  1/2 cup vegetable oil
      1 teaspoon lemon extract
1-1/2 cups fresh *or* frozen
        raspberries

In a large bowl, combine flour, sugar, baking powder and salt. Combine the eggs, cream, oil and lemon extract; stir into dry ingredients just until moistened. Fold in raspberries. Spoon into 18 greased or paper-lined muffin cups. Bake at 400° for 18-20 minutes or until golden brown. **Yield:** 1-1/2 dozen.

Lemon Cheese Braid

(PICTURED ON PAGE 107 AND BACK COVER)

"Although fairly simple to make, when you finish making this bread you'll feel a sense of accomplishment because it tastes delicious and looks impressive," states Grace Dickey of Vernonia, Oregon.

      1 package (1/4 ounce) active dry
        yeast
      3 tablespoons warm water
        (110° to 115°)
  1/4 cup sugar
  1/4 cup butter *or* margarine, melted
  1/3 cup milk
      2 eggs
  1/2 teaspoon salt
      3 to 3-1/2 cups all-purpose flour
FILLING:
      2 packages (one 8 ounces, one 3
        ounces) cream cheese,
        softened
  1/2 cup sugar
      1 egg
      1 teaspoon grated lemon peel
ICING:
  1/2 cup confectioners' sugar
      2 to 3 teaspoons milk
  1/4 teaspoon vanilla extract

In a mixing bowl, dissolve yeast in warm water; let stand for 5 minutes. Add sugar, butter, milk, eggs, salt and 2 cups flour; beat on low speed for 3 minutes. Stir in enough of the remaining flour to form a soft dough. Knead on a floured surface until smooth and elastic, about 6-8 minutes. Place in a greased bowl, turn-

RASPBERRY DELIGHT. Pictured above: Raspberry Lemon Muffins (recipe on this page).

ing once to grease top. Cover and let rise in a warm place until doubled, about 1 hour. Meanwhile, beat filling ingredients in a mixing bowl until fluffy; set aside. Punch dough down. On a floured surface, roll into a 14-in. x 12-in. rectangle. Place on a greased baking sheet. Spread filling down center third of rectangle. On each long side, cut 1-in.-wide strips, 3 in. into center. Starting at one end, fold alternating strips at an angle across filling. Seal end. Cover and let rise for 30 minutes. Bake at 375° for 25-30 minutes or until golden brown. Cool. Combine icing ingredients; drizzle over bread. **Yield:** 12-14 servings.

Winter Squash Bread

"One year my son requested I bake this bread for his birthday rather than cake, saying he liked it better!" comments Audrey Thibodeau of Mesa, Arizona. *"Nowadays, seven grandchildren relish these generous slices."*

      2 packages (1/4 ounce *each*)
        active dry yeast
      1 cup warm milk (110° to 115°)
      4 to 5 cups all-purpose flour
      2 cups whole wheat flour
      2 cups mashed winter squash
  1/4 cup sugar
      2 tablespoons butter *or*
        margarine, softened
      2 teaspoons salt

In a large mixing bowl, dissolve yeast in warm milk. Add 2 cups all-purpose flour, whole wheat flour, squash, sugar, butter and salt; beat until smooth. Add enough

remaining all-purpose flour to form a soft dough. Turn out onto a floured board; knead until smooth and elastic, about 6-8 minutes. Place in a greased bowl, turning once to grease top. Cover and let rise in a warm place until doubled, about 1 hour. Punch the dough down. Shape into two loaves and place in greased 9-in. x 5-in. x 3-in. loaf pans. Cover and let rise until doubled, about 1 hour. Bake at 375° for 30-35 minutes. Remove from pans to cool on a wire rack. **Yield:** 2 loaves.

Blueberry Oat Muffins

"Using fresh blueberries from our own farm, these are my most-requested muffins," relates Connie Sanders of Belle River, Prince Edward Island.

      1 cup quick-cooking oats
      1 cup sour milk*
      1 cup all-purpose flour
  3/4 cup packed brown sugar
      1 teaspoon baking powder
  1/2 teaspoon baking soda
  1/2 teaspoon salt
      1 egg, beaten
  1/4 cup butter *or* margarine,
        melted
      1 cup fresh blueberries

In a bowl, combine oats and milk; let stand a few minutes. In another bowl, combine flour, brown sugar, baking powder, baking soda and salt; mix well. Stir egg and butter into oat mixture. Add oat mixture all at once to dry ingredients. Stir just until moistened. Gently fold in blueberries. Fill well-greased muffin cups 3/4 full. Bake at 400° for 15-20 minutes. **Yield:** 12 muffins. (*To sour milk, place 1 tablespoon white vinegar in a measuring cup; add enough milk to equal 1 cup.)

FREEZING BLUEBERRIES is a snap! Put dry, unwashed blueberries in a container, seal and freeze up to 2 months without losing flavor or quality.

Savory Almond-Buttermilk Biscuits

Crescent Dragonwagon of Eureka Springs, Arkansas says, "Chockful of almonds, these biscuits have crunchy character. I'm sure your family will love them."

      3 tablespoons butter *or*
        margarine, *divided*
      1 small onion, finely chopped
      2 garlic cloves, minced
      2 cups all-purpose flour
      1 tablespoon baking powder
      1 teaspoon salt
  1/2 teaspoon baking soda
  1/3 cup shortening
      1 cup buttermilk

1/2 cup coarsely chopped
almonds, toasted
2 tablespoons minced fresh
parsley
1-1/2 teaspoons minced fresh sage
or 1/2 teaspoon dried sage
1-1/2 teaspoons minced fresh
rosemary *or* 1/2 teaspoon
dried rosemary
1-1/2 teaspoons minced fresh
thyme *or* 1/2 teaspoon dried
thyme

In a skillet, melt 1 tablespoon butter; saute onion and garlic until transparent, about 5 minutes. Cool completely. Combine flour, baking powder, salt and baking soda. Cut in shortening until mixture is the size of peas. Add buttermilk, almonds, parsley, sage, rosemary, thyme and onion mixture; stir just until mixed. Turn out onto a floured board; knead lightly for 1 minute. On a floured surface, roll dough to 1/2-in. thickness. Cut with a 2-in. round biscuit cutter. Place on an ungreased baking sheet. Bake at 450° for 10-15 minutes or until golden brown. Melt remaining butter and brush on warm biscuits. **Yield:** 1 dozen.

Butter Nut Twists

(PICTURED ON THIS PAGE)

Relates Joyce Hallisey of Mt. Gilead, North Carolina, "My mother has been using this recipe for the last 45 years for special occasions and the holidays. She taught my sister and me how to make the twists so we can carry on the tradition for our families."

A NEW TWIST ON BREAD. Pictured above: Butter Nut Twists (recipe on this page).

FRESH, FRUITY...FAST! Pictured above: Orange Date Bread (recipe on this page).

2 packages (1/4 ounce *each*)
active dry yeast
1/4 cup warm water (110° to 115°)
1 cup butter *or* margarine
4 cups all-purpose flour
2 eggs, beaten
3/4 cup sour milk*
1/3 cup sugar
1/2 teaspoon salt
FILLING:
1 pound ground walnuts
2 cups flaked coconut
3/4 cup sugar
3 tablespoons butter *or*
margarine, melted

Dissolve yeast in water; set aside. In a large bowl, cut butter into flour until coarse crumbs form. Add yeast mixture, eggs, milk, sugar and salt; mix lightly. Divide dough into thirds. Cover and refrigerate overnight. Take out one piece at a time from refrigerator; roll out on a sugared board to a 12-in. x 9-in. rectangle. Combine all filling ingredients. Sprinkle 1/3 cup filling on half of the 12-in. edge of dough. Fold over lengthwise and seal, forming a 12-in. x 4-1/2-in. rectangle. Pat out to press filling into dough. Sprinkle another 1/3 cup of filling on half of the 12-in. edge of dough. Fold over lengthwise, forming a 12-in. x 2-in. rectangle. Pat down to 12 in. x 4 in. Slice 1/2-in. pieces down the 12-in. side of dough. Repeat with remaining two portions of dough. Twist each slice and roll in remaining filling. Place on greased baking sheets. Bake at 350° for 15-18 minutes or until golden brown. Serve warm or cool. (*To sour milk, place 2 teaspoons white vinegar in a measuring cup. Add enough milk to equal 3/4 cup.) **Yield:** 5-6 dozen.

Orange Date Bread

(PICTURED ON THIS PAGE)

"I loved visiting my aunt—she was an excellent baker, and her kitchen always smelled great. With her inspiration, I now bake this moist yummy bread every holiday season. Christmas wouldn't be the same without it," reports Joann Wolfe of Sunland, California.

1 cup butter *or* margarine,
softened
2 cups sugar
3 eggs, beaten
4 cups all-purpose flour
1 teaspoon baking soda
1 teaspoon salt
1-1/3 cups buttermilk
1 cup chopped walnuts
1 cup chopped dates
1 tablespoon grated orange
peel
GLAZE:
1/4 cup orange juice
1/2 cup sugar
2 tablespoons grated orange
peel

In a mixing bowl, cream butter and sugar. Add eggs; mix well. Combine flour, baking soda and salt; add to creamed mixture alternately with buttermilk. Fold in walnuts, dates and orange peel. Pour into two greased and floured 8-1/2-in. x 4-1/2-in. x 2-1/2-in. loaf pans. Bake at 350° for 60-65 minutes or until done. Combine glaze ingredients; spoon half over hot bread. Cool for 10 minutes. Remove from pans; spoon remaining glaze over bread. **Yield:** 2 loaves.

FRESH FROM THE OVEN. Pictured above: left to right: Crisp Sugar Cookies (recipe on page 86) and Grandma Russell's Bread (recipe on this page).

Rosemary Raisin Bread

"On a whim," reports Clarice Schweitzer of Sun City, Arizona, "I decided to add rosemary to my raisin bread recipe. We were really happy with the result. The bread is very tasty toasted."

- 1 package (1/4 ounce) active dry yeast
- 1/4 cup warm water (110° to 115°)
- 3 cups all-purpose flour, *divided*
- 1/2 cup warm milk (110° to 115°)
- 1/4 cup olive oil
- 3 tablespoons sugar
- 1 teaspoon dried rosemary
- 1 teaspoon salt
- 1 egg plus 1 egg white
- 1/2 cup raisins

GLAZE:

Olive oil
- 1 egg yolk
- 1 tablespoon water

In a large mixing bowl, dissolve yeast in warm water. Let stand for 5 minutes. Add 1 cup flour, milk, oil, sugar, rosemary, salt, egg and egg white. Beat on low for about 30 seconds. Increase speed to medium and continue beating for 2 minutes. Stir in the raisins and remaining flour. Turn out onto a floured surface and knead until smooth and elastic, about 6-8 minutes. Place in a greased bowl, turning once to grease top. Cover and let rise in a warm place until doubled, about 1 hour. Punch down and shape into a flat 8-1/2-in. round. Place on a greased baking sheet; brush with olive oil. Cover and let rise until doubled, about 30 minutes. With a sharp knife, cut a cross in top of loaf. Combine egg yolk with water and brush over loaf. Bake at 350° for 35 minutes or until golden brown. **Yield:** 1 loaf.

Grandma Russell's Bread

(PICTURED ON THIS PAGE)

"I remember as a child always smelling fresh homemade bread and rolls whenever I walked into Grandma's house," shares Janet Polito of Nampa, Idaho. "The warm slices were delicious and melted in my mouth!"

- 1 package (1/4 ounce) active dry yeast
- 1/3 cup warm water (110° to 115°)
- 1/2 cup sugar, *divided*
- 1 cup milk
- 1/2 cup butter *or* margarine
- 1 tablespoon salt
- 1 cup mashed potatoes
- 2 eggs, beaten
- 5 to 6 cups all-purpose flour

CINNAMON FILLING:
- 1/4 cup butter *or* margarine, melted
- 3/4 cup sugar
- 1 tablespoon ground cinnamon

In a large bowl, combine yeast, warm water and 1 teaspoon sugar; set aside. In a saucepan, heat milk, butter, salt and remaining sugar until butter melts. Remove from the heat; stir in potatoes until smooth. Cool to lukewarm; add eggs and mix well. To yeast mixture add the potato mixture and 5 cups flour. Stir in enough remaining flour to form a soft dough. Turn out onto a floured surface and knead until smooth and elastic, about 6-8 minutes. Place in a greased bowl, turning once to grease top. Cover and let rise in a warm place until doubled, about 1-1/2 hours. Punch down and divide in half. *For white bread:* Shape two loaves and place in greased 8-1/2-in. x 4-1/2-in. x 2-1/2-in. loaf pans. *For cinnamon bread:* Roll each half into a 16-in. x 8-in. rectangle. Brush with melted butter; combine sugar and cinnamon and sprinkle over butter. Starting at the narrow end, roll up into a loaf, sealing the edges and ends. Place in greased 8-1/2-in. x 4-1/2-in. x 2-1/2-in. loaf pans. *For cinnamon rolls:* Roll each half into an 18-in. x 12-in. rectangle. Brush with melted butter; sprinkle with cinnamon-sugar. Starting at the narrow end, roll up and seal edges and ends. Cut each into 12 pieces of 1-1/2 in. Place in greased 9-in. round baking pans. *To bake:* Cover and let rise until doubled. Bake loaves at 375° for 20 minutes; bake rolls at 375° for 25-30 minutes. Cover with foil if they brown too quickly. **Yield:** 2 loaves or 2 dozen rolls.

Garlic-Parmesan Rolls

"Garlic is one of the world's most widely-used culinary herbs. If you're not using it in your cooking, your family just may be missing something," states Loretta Ruda of Kennesaw, Georgia.

- 1 loaf (1 pound) frozen bread dough, thawed
- 6 tablespoons grated Parmesan cheese
- 1 teaspoon garlic powder
- 1/2 cup butter *or* margarine, melted

Cut dough into 16 pieces; shape into balls. Place on a floured surface; cover and let rise in a warm place for 10 minutes. In a bowl, stir Parmesan cheese and garlic powder into butter. Using a spoon, roll balls in butter mixture; arrange loosely in a 9-in. round baking pan. Cover and let rise in a warm place until doubled. Bake at 375° for 10-15 minutes or until golden brown. Warm leftover butter mixture; when rolls are baked, pull them apart and dip them again. Serve warm. **Yield:** 16 rolls.

Angel Biscuits

(PICTURED ON PAGE 92)

"These biscuits are perfect with sausage gravy or served with butter and honey," informs Faye Hintz of Springfield, Missouri.

- **2 packages (1/4 ounce *each*) active dry yeast**
- **1/4 cup warm water (110° to 115°)**
- **2 cups warm buttermilk (110° to 115°)**
- **5 cups all-purpose flour**
- **1/3 cup sugar**
- **1 tablespoon salt**
- **2 teaspoons baking powder**
- **1 teaspoon baking soda**
- **1 cup shortening**
- **Melted butter *or* margarine**

Dissolve yeast in warm water. Let stand 5 minutes. Stir in the buttermilk; set aside. In a large mixing bowl, combine flour, sugar, salt, baking powder and soda. Cut in shortening with a pastry blender until mixture resembles coarse meal. Stir in yeast/buttermilk mixture; mix well. Turn out onto a lightly floured surface; knead lightly 3-4 times. Roll to a 1/2-in. thickness. Cut with a 2-1/2-in. biscuit cutter. Place on a lightly greased baking sheet. Cover and let rise in a warm place about 1-1/2 hours. Bake at 450° for 8-10 minutes. Lightly brush tops with melted butter. **Yield:** about 2-1/2 dozen.

Potato Herb Bread

"Everyone agrees my garden-fresh chives add special flavor to this moist and tasty bread," reveals Carol Mead of Los Alamos, New Mexico.

- **2 packages (1/4 ounce *each*) active dry yeast**
- **2 tablespoons plus 1 teaspoon sugar, *divided***
- **1/2 cup warm water (110° to 115°)**
- **1 can (10-3/4 ounces) condensed cream of potato soup, undiluted**
- **1 cup hot water**
- **1/2 cup nonfat dry milk powder**
- **1/2 cup sour cream**
- **1/2 cup snipped fresh chives**
- **2 tablespoons butter *or* margarine, melted**
- **2 teaspoons salt**
- **1 teaspoon dried tarragon, crushed**
- **6 to 6-1/2 cups all-purpose flour**

In a small bowl, dissolve yeast and 1 teaspoon sugar in warm water. Let stand for 5 minutes. In a large mixing bowl, combine soup and hot water. Stir in yeast mixture, milk powder, sour cream, chives, butter, salt, tarragon and remaining sugar. Mix well. Add enough flour to make a stiff dough. Turn dough onto a floured surface; knead until smooth and elastic, about 6-8 minutes. Place in a greased bowl, turning once to grease top. Cover and let rise in warm place until doubled, about 1 hour. Punch dough down. Divide in half. Shape into two loaves and place in greased 9-1/4-in. x 5-1/4-in. x 2-3/4-in. loaf pans. Cover and let rise until doubled, about 30 minutes. Bake at 400° for 30 minutes or until golden. **Yield:** 2 loaves.

Chewy Bread Pretzels

Marilyn Strickland of Williamson, New York relates, "I used this recipe to introduce my grandsons to the thrill of baking. They enjoy measuring and stirring, kneading the dough and shaping their pretzels any way they want."

- **1 package (1/4 ounce) active dry yeast**
- **1-1/2 cups warm water (110° to 115°)**
- **1 tablespoon sugar**
- **2 teaspoons salt**
- **4 cups all-purpose flour**
- **1 egg, beaten**
- **Coarse salt, optional**

In a large bowl, dissolve yeast in water. Add sugar and salt. Blend in flour, 1 cup at a time, to form a soft dough. Turn out onto a floured surface; knead until smooth and elastic, about 5 minutes. Place dough in a greased bowl, turning once to grease top. Cover and let rise in a warm place until doubled, about 1 hour. Punch dough down and divide into 15 equal portions. Roll each portion into a 14-in. rope. Shape into the traditional pretzel shape and place on a greased baking sheet. Brush pretzels with egg and sprinkle with salt if desired. Cover and let rise 15 minutes. Bake at 425° for 15 minutes. **Yield:** 15 pretzels.

Orange Biscuits

(PICTURED ON THIS PAGE)

"These biscuits are a special treat with a ham dinner, but they're also delicious just by themselves. I've been enjoying them since the 1940's," states Winifred Brown of Wilmette, Illinois.

- **1/2 cup orange juice**
- **3/4 cup sugar, *divided***
- **1/4 cup butter *or* margarine**
- **2 teaspoons grated orange peel**
- **2 cups all-purpose flour**
- **1 tablespoon baking powder**
- **1/2 teaspoon salt**
- **1/4 cup shortening**
- **3/4 cup milk**
- **Melted butter *or* margarine**
- **1/2 teaspoon ground cinnamon**

In a saucepan, combine orange juice, 1/2 cup sugar, butter and orange peel. Cook and stir over medium heat for 2 minutes. Divide among 12 muffin cups; set aside. In a large bowl, combine flour, baking powder and salt. Cut in shortening until mixture resembles coarse crumbs. With a fork, stir in milk until mixture forms a ball. On a lightly floured surface, knead the dough 1 minute. Roll into a 9-in. square, about 1/2 in. thick. Brush with melted butter. Combine the cinnamon and remaining sugar; sprinkle over butter. Roll up. Cut into 12 slices, about 3/4 in. thick. Place slices, cut side down, over orange mixture in muffin cups. Bake at 450° for 12-16 minutes. Cool for 2-3 minutes; remove from pan. **Yield:** 1 dozen.

THE BEST BREAKFAST BISCUITS. Pictured above: Orange Biscuits (recipe on this page).

A BETTER BREAD TOPPING. Pictured above: Spinach Garlic Bread (recipe on this page).

Finnish Easter Bread

Ben Middleton of Walla Walla, Washington points out, "These round loaves, baked in coffee cans, are fun to make and they slice attractively."

- 3 packages (1/4 ounce *each*) active dry yeast
- 1/2 cup water (110° to 115°)
- 1-1/2 cups warm light cream (110° to 115°)
- 6 to 7 cups all-purpose flour, *divided*
- 5 egg yolks
- 1 cup sugar
- 1 cup milk
- 1 cup butter *or* margarine, melted
- 2 teaspoons ground cardamom
- 2 tablespoons grated orange peel
- 2 teaspoons grated lemon peel
- 1-1/2 teaspoons salt
- 2 cups rye flour
- 1 cup golden raisins
- 1 cup chopped blanched almonds

Additional melted butter *or* margarine

In a mixing bowl, dissolve yeast in water. Stir in cream and 2 cups all-purpose flour; beat until smooth. Cover and let rise in a warm place until doubled, about 1-1/2 hours. Dough will be very soft and spongy in texture. Punch dough down. Stir in egg yolks, sugar, milk, butter, cardamom, orange and lemon peel and salt. Beat until thoroughly combined. Stir in rye flour until well blended. Stir in raisins and almonds; mix well. By hand, add enough remaining flour to make a stiff dough. Turn out onto a lightly floured surface.

Knead until smooth and elastic, about 6-8 minutes. Place dough in a greased bowl, turning once to grease top. Cover and let rise in a warm place until doubled, about 1 to 1-1/2 hours. Punch dough down; shape into a smooth ball. Divide into two pieces. Place each piece into a well-greased large (6-in. x 7-in.) coffee can. Cover and let rise in a warm place until the dough reaches the top of the can, about 45 minutes. Do not let breads rise over top of coffee cans. Bake at 350° for 55-60 minutes or until breads sound hollow when tapped. Cover breads loosely with foil during last 15 minutes if tops are browning too fast. Remove from oven; brush tops with melted butter. Let cool in coffee cans about 20 minutes; remove to cool on wire racks. **Yield:** 2 loaves.

Poppy Seed Bread

"This moist, rich bread is so delicious—it's very popular in our area. It gets golden brown and looks great sliced for a buffet," says Faye Hintz of Springfield, Missouri.

- 3 cups all-purpose flour
- 2-1/4 cups sugar
- 1-1/2 tablespoons poppy seeds
- 1-1/2 teaspoons baking powder
- 1-1/2 teaspoons salt
- 3 eggs, lightly beaten
- 1-1/2 cups milk
- 1 cup vegetable oil
- 1-1/2 teaspoons vanilla extract
- 1-1/2 teaspoons almond extract
- 1-1/2 teaspoons butter extract

GLAZE:
- 3/4 cup sugar
- 1/4 cup orange juice

- 1/2 teaspoon vanilla extract
- 1/2 teaspoon almond extract
- 1/2 teaspoon butter extract

In a large bowl, combine first five ingredients. Add eggs, milk, oil and extracts. Pour into two greased 8-1/2-in. x 4-1/2-in. x 2-1/2-in. loaf pans. Bake at 350° for 60-65 minutes. Cool completely in pans. In a saucepan, bring all glaze ingredients to a boil. Pour over bread in pans. Cool for 5 minutes; remove from pans and cool completely. **Yield:** 2 loaves.

Spinach Garlic Bread

(PICTURED ON THIS PAGE)

"I've found that this pretty bread goes great with any Italian meal," informs Ruby Williams of Bogalusa, Louisiana.

- 1 loaf French *or* Italian bread (about 1 pound)
- 1 medium onion, chopped
- 2 garlic cloves, minced
- 3 tablespoons olive oil
- 1 package (10 ounces) frozen chopped spinach, thawed and well drained
- 1 tablespoon grated Parmesan cheese
- 1 teaspoon Italian seasoning
- 1/2 teaspoon fennel seed, crushed
- 1 large tomato, chopped and seeded
- 1-1/2 cups (6 ounces) shredded mozzarella cheese
- 1 tablespoon dried basil

Chopped fresh parsley, optional

Cut bread in half lengthwise. Place with cut side up on a baking sheet; set aside. In a skillet, saute onion and garlic in oil until tender. Add spinach and stir until heated through, about 1 minute. Remove from the heat. Stir in Parmesan cheese, Italian seasoning and fennel seed; mix well. Spread evenly over bread halves. Sprinkle with tomato, mozzarella and basil. Bake at 400° for 8-10 minutes or until cheese is melted. Garnish with parsley if desired. Cut into slices and serve immediately. **Yield:** 8-10 servings.

Cinnamon Mini-Muffins

(PICTURED ON PAGE 91)

"These mini muffins are wonderful with a bowl of fresh fruit for breakfast or anytime," relates Bonni Larson of New Berlin, Wisconsin.

- 1-1/2 cups all-purpose flour
- 1/2 cup sugar
- 2 teaspoons baking powder
- 1/2 teaspoon salt
- 1/2 teaspoon ground nutmeg
- 1/2 teaspoon ground allspice
- 1 egg, lightly beaten

1/2 cup skim milk
1/3 cup margarine, melted
TOPPING:
   2 tablespoons sugar
   1/2 teaspoon ground cinnamon
   1/4 cup margarine, melted

In a large bowl, combine flour, sugar, baking powder, salt, nutmeg and all-spice. Combine the egg, milk and margarine; mix well. Stir into dry ingredients just until moistened. Spoon into greased or paper-lined mini muffin cups. Bake at 400° for 12-14 minutes or until muffins test done. For topping, combine sugar and cinnamon. Brush the tops of warm muffins with margarine; sprinkle with cinnamon-sugar. **Yield:** 2 dozen. **Nutritional Information:** 96 calories, 128 mg sodium, 9 mg cholesterol, 12 gm carbohydrate, 1 gm protein, 5 gm fat.

Cranberry Fruit Bread

(PICTURED ON THIS PAGE)

"My family looks forward to this combination of cranberry bread and fruit-cake for the holidays. Baked in smaller pans, the loaves make nice gifts," says Ellen Puotinen of Tower, Minnesota.

   1 bag (12 ounces) fresh *or* frozen cranberries, halved
   2 cups pecan halves
   1 cup chopped mixed candied fruit
   1 cup chopped dates
   1 cup golden raisins
   1 tablespoon grated orange peel
   4 cups all-purpose flour, *divided*
   2 cups sugar

FESTIVE FARE. Pictured above: Cranberry Fruit Bread (recipe on this page).

   1 tablespoon baking powder
   1 teaspoon baking soda
   1/4 teaspoon salt
   2 eggs
   1 cup orange juice
   1/4 cup shortening, melted
   1/4 cup warm water

Combine cranberries, pecans, fruit, dates, raisins and orange peel with 1/4 cup flour; set aside. In another bowl, combine sugar, baking powder, baking soda, salt and remaining flour; set aside. In a large mixing bowl, beat eggs. Add orange juice, shortening and water. Add flour mixture; stir just until combined. Fold in cranberry mixture. Spoon into three greased and waxed paper-lined 8-1/2-in. x 4-1/2-in. x 2-1/2-in. loaf pans. Bake at 350° for 60-65 minutes or until breads test done. Cool 10 minutes in the pans. Remove to a wire rack. Remove waxed paper and continue to cool on the rack. **Yield:** 3 loaves.

Parmesan Herb Bread

"This zesty bread was an experiment that ended up winning grand prize in a local baking contest," recalls Audrey Thibodeau of Mesa, Arizona. "The herbs really add a savory filling."

   2-1/4 cups water
   3/4 cup butter *or* margarine, *divided*
   6 to 7 cups all-purpose flour
   2 packages (1/4 ounce *each*) active dry yeast
   2 tablespoons sugar
   1 teaspoon salt
FILLING:
   1/2 cup grated Parmesan cheese
   2 tablespoons dried chives
   2 tablespoons dried parsley flakes
   1 teaspoon garlic powder
   1/2 teaspoon dried savory
   1/2 teaspoon dried thyme
Cornmeal

In a saucepan, heat water and 1/4 cup butter to 120°-130°. In a large bowl, combine 3 cups flour, yeast, sugar and salt. Add water mixture and beat until smooth. Add enough remaining flour to form a soft dough. Turn out onto a floured board; knead until smooth and elastic, about 6-8 minutes. Place in a greased bowl, turning once to grease top. Cover and let rise in a warm place until doubled, about 1 hour. Punch dough down and divide in half; roll each half into an 18-in. x 15-in. rectangle. Soften remaining butter; spread on rectangles. In a small bowl, combine first six filling ingredients; sprinkle over butter. Starting at the wide end, roll up each rectangle into a loaf, sealing edges and ends. Sprinkle two ungreased baking sheets with cornmeal; place the loaves with seam side down on cornmeal. Use a knife to cut four or five slashes in the top of each loaf; sprinkle with cornmeal. Cover and let rise until doubled, about 1 hour. Bake at 375° for 15 minutes. Reduce heat to 350°; bake 20-25 minutes longer. Serve warm or cold. **Yield:** 2 loaves.

MOIST MUFFINS. Pictured above: Feather-Light Muffins (recipe on this page).

Feather-Light Muffins

(PICTURED ON THIS PAGE)

"Pretty as well as tasty, these muffins will brighten breakfast, brunch or lunch for family or company," shares Sonja Blow of Groveland, California.

   1/3 cup shortening
   1/2 cup sugar
   1 egg
   1-1/2 cups cake flour
   1-1/2 teaspoons baking powder
   1/2 teaspoon salt
   1/4 teaspoon ground nutmeg
   1/2 cup milk
TOPPING:
   1/2 cup sugar
   1 teaspoon ground cinnamon
   1/2 cup butter *or* margarine, melted

In a mixing bowl, cream shortening, sugar and egg. Combine dry ingredients; add to creamed mixture alternately with milk. Fill greased muffin cups two-thirds full. Bake at 325° for 20-25 minutes or until golden. Let cool for 3-4 minutes. Meanwhile, combine sugar and cinnamon in a small bowl. Roll warm muffins in melted butter, then in sugar mixture. Serve warm. **Yield:** 8-10 muffins.

EARLY-MORNING entertaining is a breeze with this mouth-watering selection of easy egg dishes, flavorful coffee cakes and hot-off-the-griddle goodies. Try them today…your family will surely thank you!

Cherry Almond Wreath

(PICTURED ON PAGE 99)

"My daughter and I enjoy making specialty breads like this one and find they make excellent Christmas gifts," shares Gwen Roffler of Grassy Butte, North Dakota.

- 1 package (1/4 ounce) active dry yeast
- 1/2 cup warm milk (110° to 115°)
- 1/4 cup warm water (110° to 115°)
- 3 to 4-1/4 cups all-purpose flour
- 2 eggs
- 1/4 cup butter *or* margarine, softened
- 3 tablespoons sugar
- 1-1/2 teaspoons salt
- 1 teaspoon grated lemon peel
- 1/2 teaspoon ground cardamom

FILLING:
- 1/4 cup butter *or* margarine, softened
- 1/4 cup all-purpose flour
- 2 tablespoons sugar
- 1 teaspoon almond extract
- 1/2 teaspoon grated lemon peel
- 2/3 cup finely chopped blanched almonds
- 1/2 cup chopped red and green candied cherries

GLAZE:
- 2/3 cup confectioners' sugar
- 2 teaspoons lemon juice
- 1 teaspoon water

In a large mixing bowl, dissolve yeast in milk and water. Add 2 cups flour, eggs, butter, sugar, salt, lemon peel and cardamom; beat until smooth. Add enough remaining flour to form a soft dough. Turn onto a floured surface; knead until smooth and elastic, about 6-8 minutes. Place in a greased bowl, turning once to grease top. Cover and let rise in a warm place until doubled, about 1-1/2 hours. In a small mixing bowl, beat butter, flour, sugar, extract and lemon peel. Stir in almonds and cherries. Refrigerate if needed. Punch dough down. Roll into a 30-in. x 9-in. rectangle. Crumble filling over dough. Starting with the 30-in. edge, roll up and seal edge. Place, seam side down, on a greased baking sheet. With a sharp knife, cut roll in half lengthwise; carefully turn cut sides up. Loosely twist strips around each other, keeping cut sides up. Shape into a ring and pinch ends together. Cover and let rise 1 hour. Bake at 350° for 35-40 minutes or until browned. Cool 15 minutes. Combine glaze ingredients; drizzle over warm coffee cake. Cool completely. **Yield:** 1 coffee cake.

Morning Mix-Up

Kim Scholting of Springfield, Nebraska states, "This filling dish of eggs, cheese, hash browns and ham is super to serve for breakfast or supper. It's one of my family's favorites."

- 2 cups frozen hash browns
- 1 cup chopped fully cooked ham
- 1/2 cup chopped onion
- 2 tablespoons cooking oil
- 6 eggs
- Salt and pepper to taste
- 1 cup (4 ounces) shredded cheddar cheese
- Minced fresh chives

In a large skillet, saute potatoes, ham and onion in oil for 10 minutes or until potatoes are tender. In a small bowl, beat eggs, salt and pepper. Add to the skillet; cook, stirring occasionally, until eggs are set. Remove from the heat and gently stir in cheese. Spoon onto a serving platter; sprinkle with chives. **Yield:** 4 servings.

Oat Pancakes

"My daughter brought this recipe home from school one day, and we loved it," says Linda Hicks of Pinconning, Michigan. *"Since then, these pancakes have been a regular part of Sunday morning breakfast."*

✓ This tasty dish uses less sugar, salt and fat. Recipe includes *Diabetic Exchanges*.

- 1 cup quick-cooking oats
- 1 cup all-purpose flour
- 2 tablespoons sugar
- 2 teaspoons baking powder
- 1 teaspoon salt
- 2 eggs, lightly beaten
- 1-1/2 cups milk
- 1/4 cup vegetable oil
- 1 teaspoon lemon juice

Combine oats, flour, sugar, baking powder and salt in a mixing bowl. Make a well in the center. Combine egg, milk, oil and lemon juice; pour into well and stir just until moistened. Pour batter by 1/4 cupfuls onto a lightly greased hot griddle; turn when bubbles form on top of pancakes. Cook until second side is golden brown. **Yield:** 6 servings. **Diabetic Exchanges:** One serving (2 pancakes, prepared with skim milk) equals 1-1/2 starch, 1/2 skim milk, 1 fat; also, 241 calories, 581 mg sodium, 71 mg cholesterol, 25 gm carbohydrate, 8 gm protein, 12 gm fat.

Apricot Almond Coffee Cake

"This coffee cake looks beautiful and is absolutely delicious. It won a blue ribbon at the Oklahoma State Fair," relates Peggy Phelps of Oklahoma City, Oklahoma.

TOPPING:
- 1 cup sliced *or* slivered toasted almonds
- 2 tablespoons sugar
- 1 teaspoon ground cinnamon

CAKE:
- 1 cup butter *or* margarine, softened
- 2 cups sugar
- 2 eggs
- 1 teaspoon almond extract
- 1-1/2 cups cake flour
- 1-1/2 teaspoons baking powder
- 1/2 teaspoon salt
- 1 cup (8 ounces) sour cream
- 1 jar (6 ounces) apricot preserves
- Additional toasted almonds, optional

Combine topping ingredients; sprinkle a third of mixture in the bottom of a well-greased and floured 9-in. springform pan with a *flat* bottom tube pan insert (not fluted). In a mixing bowl, cream butter and sugar. Add eggs and extract; mix well. Combine flour, baking powder and salt; add to creamed mixture alternately with sour cream. Spoon half over topping in pan. Sprinkle with another third of the topping; cover with remaining batter and topping. Bake at 350° for 60-65 minutes or until done. Cool for 10 minutes. Loosen edges and remove sides of pan. Run a knife around the bottom of the tube pan. Cool for 10 minutes on a wire rack. Carefully invert onto a serving platter. Spread preserves over top. Garnish with toasted almonds if desired. Serve warm. **Yield:** 10-12 servings. **Editor's Note:** Only a springform pan with tube insert will work for this recipe. Do not use a bundt or angel food cake pan.

Hash Brown Quiche

(PICTURED ON THIS PAGE AND BACK COVER)

"This is a great dish to serve for breakfast. To save time in the morning, I make the hash brown crust and chop the ham, cheese and peppers the night before," explains Jan Peters of Chandler, Minnesota.

        3 cups frozen loose-pack
           shredded hash browns, thawed
    1/3 cup butter *or* margarine, melted
        1 cup diced fully cooked ham
        1 cup (4 ounces) shredded
           cheddar cheese
    1/4 cup diced green pepper
        2 eggs
    1/2 cup milk
    1/2 teaspoon salt
    1/4 teaspoon pepper

Press hash browns between paper towel to remove excess moisture. Press into the bottom and up the sides of an ungreased 9-in. pie plate. Drizzle with butter. Bake at 425° for 25 minutes. Combine the ham, cheese and green pepper; spoon over crust. In a small bowl, beat eggs, milk, salt and pepper. Pour over all. Reduce heat to 350°; bake for 25-30 minutes or until a knife inserted near the center comes out clean. Allow to stand for 10 minutes before cutting. **Yield:** 6 servings.

RISE AND SHINE! Pictured above, left to right: Lemon Cheese Braid (recipe on page 100) and Hash Brown Quiche (recipe on this page).

Poteca Nut Roll

"My mother-in-law brought this recipe from Yugoslavia in the early 1900's," informs Mrs. Anthony Setta of Saegertown, Pennsylvania. *"It was a tradition in her family to serve it for holidays and special occasions. Now it's my tradition."*

        1 package (1/4 ounce) active
           dry yeast
    1/4 cup warm water (110° to 115°)
    3/4 cup warm milk (110° to 115°)
    1/4 cup sugar
    1/4 cup shortening
        1 teaspoon salt
        1 egg, lightly beaten
        3 to 3-1/2 cups all-purpose flour
FILLING:
    1/2 cup butter *or* margarine,
           softened
        1 cup packed brown sugar
        2 eggs, lightly beaten
        1 teaspoon vanilla extract
        1 teaspoon lemon extract,
           optional
        4 cups ground *or* finely
           chopped walnuts
Confectioners' sugar icing, optional

In a mixing bowl, dissolve yeast in water. Add milk, sugar, shortening, salt, egg and 1-1/2 cups flour; beat until smooth. Add enough remaining flour to form a soft dough. Turn onto a floured surface; knead until smooth and elastic, about 6-8 minutes. Place in a greased bowl, turning once to grease top. Cover and let rise in a warm place until doubled, about 1 hour. Combine butter, brown sugar, eggs, vanilla, lemon extract if desired and nuts. Add milk until mixture is of spreading consistency, about 1/2 cup; set aside. Punch dough down. Roll into a 30-in. x 20-in. rectangle. Spread filling to within 1 in. of edges. Roll up from one long side; pinch seams and ends to seal. Place on a greased baking sheet; shape into a tight spiral. Cover and let rise until nearly doubled, about 1 hour. Bake at 350° for 35 minutes or until golden brown. Cool on a wire rack. If desired, brush with confectioners' sugar icing when cooled. **Yield:** 1 coffee cake.

Cinnamon Rolls

"I relish my role as family bread maker," says Ben Middleton of Walla Walla, Washington. *"And so do family and friends who get to sample the results of my work!"*

        2 packages (1/4 ounce *each*)
           active dry yeast
    1/2 cup sugar, *divided*
        1 cup warm water (110° to 115°)
        1 cup milk
        6 tablespoons butter *or*
           margarine
        7 to 7-1/2 cups all-purpose
           flour, *divided*
        3 eggs, beaten
        1 teaspoon salt
FILLING:
    1/4 cup butter *or* margarine,
           softened
        5 teaspoons ground cinnamon
    3/4 cup packed brown sugar
    3/4 cup raisins *or* currants
Confectioners' sugar icing, optional

In a large mixing bowl, dissolve yeast and 1 tablespoon sugar in water. In a saucepan, heat milk and butter to 110°-115°; add to yeast mixture. Stir in 3 cups flour, eggs, salt and remaining sugar. Stir in enough remaining flour to make a soft dough. Turn out onto a lightly floured surface. Knead until smooth and elastic, about 6-8 minutes. Place in a greased bowl, turning once to grease top. Cover and let rise in a warm place until doubled, about 1 hour. Punch dough down and divide in half. Roll each half into a 15-in. x 12-in. rectangle. Brush with softened butter. Combine cinnamon, sugar and raisins or currants; sprinkle evenly over each rectangle. Roll up tightly, jelly-roll style, starting with the long side. Slice each roll into 12 pieces. Place in two greased 13-in. x 9-in. x 2-in. baking pans. Cover and let rise until doubled, about 30 minutes. Bake at 350° for 25-30 minutes or until golden brown. Cool in pans for 5 minutes; invert onto a wire rack. Frost with icing if desired. Serve warm. **Yield:** 2 dozen.

Peanut Butter and Jelly French Toast

"My grandson thinks cooking is a lot of fun," reports Flo Burtnett of Gage, Oklahoma. "With this easy-to-prepare recipe, he took third prize in a children's cooking contest!"

- **12 slices bread**
- **3/4 cup peanut butter**
- **6 tablespoons jelly *or* jam**
- **3 eggs**
- **3/4 cup milk**
- **1/4 teaspoon salt**
- **2 tablespoons butter *or* margarine**

Spread peanut butter on six slices of bread; spread jelly on other six slices of bread. Put one slice of each together to form sandwiches. In mixing bowl, lightly beat eggs; add milk and salt and mix together. Melt butter in a large skillet over medium heat. Dip sandwiches in egg mixture, coating well. Place in skillet and brown both sides. Serve immediately. **Yield:** 6 servings.

Egg and Sausage Strata

(PICTURED ON THIS PAGE)

"I especially like to make this breakfast dish when we have weekend guests," informs Gail Carney of Arlington, Texas. "I fix it the night before, and the next morning I can sit, eat and enjoy their company."

- **12 slices white bread, crusts removed, cubed**
- **1-1/2 pounds bulk pork sausage**
- **1/3 cup chopped onion**
- **1/4 cup chopped green pepper**
- **1 jar (2 ounces) chopped pimientos, drained**
- **6 eggs**
- **3 cups milk**
- **2 teaspoons Worcestershire sauce**
- **1 teaspoon dry mustard**
- **1/2 teaspoon salt**
- **1/4 teaspoon pepper**
- **1/4 teaspoon dried oregano**

Line a greased 13-in. x 9-in. x 2-in. pan with bread cubes; set aside. In a skillet, brown sausage with the onion and green pepper; drain. Stir in pimientos; sprinkle over bread. In a bowl, beat eggs, milk, Worcestershire sauce, mustard, salt, pepper and oregano. Pour over sausage mixture. Cover and refrigerate overnight. Bake, covered, at 325° for 1 hour and 20 minutes. Uncover and bake 10 minutes longer or until a knife inserted near the center comes out clean. Let stand 10 minutes before serving. **Yield:** 12-15 servings.

Bacon and Cheese Breakfast Pizza

"An area fire fighter shared this recipe with me," says Dina Davis of Madison, Florida. "It's good for breakfast and even a light dinner. I'm a big fan of this easy recipe."

- **Pastry for single-crust pie (9 inches)**
- **1/2 pound bacon, cooked and crumbled**
- **2 cups (8 ounces) shredded Swiss cheese**
- **4 eggs**
- **1-1/2 cups (12 ounces) sour cream**
- **2 tablespoons chopped fresh parsley**

Roll pastry to fit a 12-in. pizza pan. Bake at 425° for 5 minutes. Sprinkle bacon and cheese evenly over crust. In a bowl, beat eggs, sour cream and parsley until smooth; pour over pizza. Bake for 20-25 minutes or until pizza is puffy and lightly browned. **Yield:** 6 main-dish or 18 appetizer servings.

Buttermilk Pecan Waffles

Edna Hoffman of Hebron, Indiana states, "These nutty waffles are my husband's favorite, so we enjoy them often. They're easy to prepare and their unique taste makes them exceptional."

- **2 cups all-purpose flour**
- **1 tablespoon baking powder**
- **1 teaspoon baking soda**
- **1/2 teaspoon salt**
- **4 eggs**
- **2 cups buttermilk**
- **1/2 cup butter *or* margarine, melted**
- **3 tablespoons chopped pecans**

Combine the flour, baking powder, baking soda and salt; set aside. In a mixing bowl, beat eggs until light. Add buttermilk; mix well. Add dry ingredients and beat until batter is smooth. Stir in butter. Pour about 3/4 cup batter onto a lightly greased preheated waffle iron. Sprinkle with a few pecans. Bake according to manufacturer's directions until golden brown. Repeat until batter and pecans are gone. **Yield:** 7 waffles (about 8 inches each).

Lo-Cal Blueberry Jam

"My family loves this slightly-sweet jam on homemade breads, pancakes and French toast," says Connie Sanders of Belle River, Prince Edward Island. "You won't miss the calories!"

- **5 cups fresh blueberries *or* 2 packages (12 ounces *each*) unsweetened frozen blueberries, thawed**
- **1 package (1-3/4 ounces) fruit pectin powder**
- **2 tablespoons lemon juice**
- **3-1/2 teaspoons liquid artificial sweetener**

In a saucepan, mash blueberries. Stir in pectin and lemon juice. Bring to a boil; boil 1 minute. Remove from the heat; stir in the sweetener. Stir for 2 minutes. Spoon into jars. Cool. Cover, seal and refrigerate. **Yield:** 1-1/2 pints. **Calories:** 9 per tablespoon.

MAKE-AHEAD MORNING MEAL. Pictured above: Egg and Sausage Strata (recipe on this page).

Stuffed Apricot French Toast

(PICTURED ON THIS PAGE)

"In our family, this special recipe is often served for our Christmas Day brunch," reports Deb Leland of Three Rivers, Michigan. "I was always looking for something unique to serve, and this rich, colorful dish certainly fills the bill."

- 1 package (8 ounces) cream cheese, softened
- 1-1/2 teaspoons vanilla extract, *divided*
- 1/2 cup finely chopped walnuts
- 1 loaf (1-1/2 pounds) French bread
- 4 eggs
- 1 cup heavy cream
- 1/2 teaspoon ground nutmeg
- 1 jar (12 ounces) apricot preserves
- 1/2 cup orange juice

In a mixing bowl, beat cream cheese and 1 teaspoon vanilla until fluffy. Stir in nuts; set aside. Cut bread into 1-1/2-in. slices; cut a pocket in the top of each slice. Fill each pocket with about 2 tablespoons of cream cheese mixture. In another bowl, beat eggs, cream, nutmeg and remaining vanilla. Dip both sides of bread into egg mixture, being careful not to squeeze out the filling. Cook on a lightly greased griddle until golden brown on both sides. Place on an ungreased baking sheet; bake at 300° for 20 minutes. Meanwhile, combine preserves and orange juice in a small saucepan; heat through. Drizzle over hot French toast. **Yield:** about 8 servings.

Breakfast Burritos

"I discovered this different recipe at a workshop on holiday breakfasts offered at our church. It was a big hit with everyone!" exclaims Catherine Allan of Twin Falls, Idaho.

- 1 bag (16 ounces) frozen Southern-style hash browns
- 12 eggs
- 1 large onion, chopped
- 1 green pepper, chopped
- 1/2 pound bulk pork sausage, browned and drained
- 12 flour tortillas (10 inches), warmed
- 3 cups (12 ounces) shredded cheddar cheese

Salsa, optional

In a large skillet, fry hash browns according to package directions; remove and set aside. In a large bowl, beat eggs; add onions and green pepper. Pour into

FANCY FRENCH TOAST. Pictured above: Stuffed Apricot French Toast (recipe on this page).

the same skillet; cook and stir until eggs are set. Remove from heat. Add hash browns and sausage; mix gently. Place about 3/4 cup of filling on each tortilla and top with about 1/4 cup cheese. Roll up and place on a greased baking sheet. Bake at 350° for 15-20 minutes or until heated through. Serve with salsa if desired. **Yield:** 12 servings.

Oatmeal Waffles

"This recipe can be used to make pancakes as well as waffles. Both are delicious because of their hearty, whole-grain flavor," shares Mrs. Francis Stoops of Stoneboro, Pennsylvania.

- 2 eggs, beaten
- 2 cups buttermilk
- 1 cup quick-cooking oats
- 1 tablespoon molasses
- 1 tablespoon vegetable oil
- 1 cup whole wheat flour
- 1 teaspoon baking soda
- 1 teaspoon baking powder
- 1/2 teaspoon salt

Milk, optional

In a large bowl, mix eggs and buttermilk. Add oats and mix well. Stir in molasses and oil. Combine flour, baking soda, baking powder and salt; stir into the egg mixture. If batter becomes too thick, thin with a little milk. Pour about 3/4 cup batter onto a greased preheated waffle maker. Bake according to manufacturer's di-

rections. **To make pancakes:** Drop batter by 1/4 cupfuls onto a hot greased griddle. Turn when bubbles begin to form on top of pancake. **Yield:** 5 waffles (7 inches) or about 15 standard-size pancakes.

> **BETTER BATTER.** Add leftover sausages, thinly sliced, to your pancake batter to make a new breakfast treat.

Sausage Quiche

"I started cooking years ago when a back injury kept me home for several months," explains Ernest Foster of Climax, New York. "This quiche is a family favorite."

- 1 package (8 ounces) breakfast sausage links
- 1 unbaked pie pastry (9 inches)
- 1 cup (4 ounces) shredded cheddar cheese
- 4 eggs
- 1 pint heavy cream
- 1/8 to 1/4 teaspoon ground nutmeg

In a skillet, brown sausages until done. Drain and cut into small pieces; place in the bottom of pie shell. Sprinkle with cheese. In a mixing bowl, beat eggs; add cream and nutmeg. Pour over cheese. Bake at 350° for 55-60 minutes or until a knife inserted near the center comes out clean. **Yield:** 6-8 servings.

AN APPLE A DAY. Pictured above: Apple Pecan Pancakes topped with Apple Spice Syrup (recipes on this page).

Apple Pecan Pancakes

(PICTURED ON THIS PAGE)

"The combination of apples and pecans adds a light crunch to these fluffy pancakes," shares Renae Moncur of Burley, Idaho. *"They have a nice cinnamon flavor and make a hearty, easy-to-prepare breakfast."*

- **1 cup all-purpose flour**
- **2 tablespoons brown sugar**
- **2 teaspoons baking powder**
- **1/2 teaspoon salt**
- **1/2 teaspoon ground cinnamon**
- **3/4 cup plus 2 tablespoons milk**
- **2 eggs, *separated***
- **1 teaspoon vanilla extract**
- **1/2 cup finely chopped peeled apple**
- **1/2 cup finely chopped pecans**

In a bowl, combine flour, brown sugar, baking powder, salt and cinnamon. Stir in milk, egg yolks and vanilla. Add apple and pecans. Beat egg whites until stiff peaks form; fold into batter. Pour batter by 1/4 cupfuls onto a hot greased griddle or skillet. Turn when bubbles begin to form and the edges are golden. Cook until the second side is golden. **Yield:** 12 pancakes.

Apple Spice Syrup

(PICTURED ON THIS PAGE)

Renae Moncur of Burley, Idaho states, "This spicy apple syrup has just the right sweetness to complement your favorite pancakes or waffles."

- **1/4 cup packed brown sugar**
- **2 tablespoons cornstarch**
- **1/4 teaspoon ground allspice**
- **1/8 teaspoon ground nutmeg**
- **1-3/4 cups apple juice *or* cider**

In a saucepan, combine brown sugar, cornstarch, allspice and nutmeg; mix well. Add juice or cider. Cook and stir over medium heat until syrup is bubbly and slightly thickened. **Yield:** 1-3/4 cups.

Baked Peach Pancake

"This dish makes for a dramatic presentation. I usually take it right from the oven to the table, fill it with peaches and sour cream and serve with bacon or ham," relates Nancy Wilkinson of Princeton, New Jersey.

- **2 cups fresh *or* frozen sliced peeled peaches**
- **4 teaspoons sugar**
- **1 teaspoon lemon juice**
- **3 eggs**
- **1/2 cup all-purpose flour**
- **1/2 cup milk**
- **1/2 teaspoon salt**
- **2 tablespoons butter *or* margarine**
- **Ground nutmeg**
- **Sour cream, optional**

In a bowl, combine peaches with sugar and lemon juice; set aside. In a mixing bowl, beat eggs until fluffy. Add flour, milk and salt; beat until smooth. Place butter in a 10-in. skillet; bake at 400° for 3-5 minutes or until melted. Immediately pour batter into hot skillet. Bake for 20-25 minutes or until pancake has risen and is puffed all over. Fill with peach slices and sprinkle with nutmeg. Serve immediately with sour cream if desired. **Yield:** 4-6 servings.

Quiche Lorraine

(PICTURED ON PAGE 75)

"Try serving a wedge of this classic recipe with fresh fruit and homemade muffins for a plate that will look as good as the food tastes!" suggests Marcy Cella of L'Anse, Michigan.

CRUST:
- **2 cups sifted unbleached *or* bleached all-purpose flour**
- **1/2 teaspoon salt**
- **3/4 cup butter-flavored shortening**
- **3 to 4 tablespoons cold water**

FILLING:
- **12 bacon strips, cooked and crumbled**
- **4 eggs**
- **2 cups light cream**
- **1/4 teaspoon salt**
- **1/8 teaspoon ground nutmeg**
- **1-1/4 cups shredded Swiss cheese**

Combine flour and salt in a mixing bowl. Cut in shortening with pastry blender until mixture resembles peas. Add water, a little at a time, until dough comes away from the bowl. Form dough into a ball. Divide in half. On a lightly floured surface, roll half of dough to fit a 9-in. pie plate; transfer to pie plate. Trim and flute edges. Chill. Wrap remaining dough; chill or freeze for another use. For filling, sprinkle crumbled bacon into the chilled pie crust. In a bowl, beat eggs, cream, salt and nutmeg. Stir in cheese. Pour into crust. Bake at 425° for 15 minutes. Reduce temperature to 325°; continue to bake for 30-40 minutes or until a knife inserted near the center comes out clean. Let stand 10 minutes before cutting. **Yield:** 6 servings.

Tomato Quiche

"I first tried this recipe at a family gathering and loved it!" reports Heidi Anne Quinn of West Kingston, Rhode Island. *"This has become my most-requested dish."*

- **1 cup chopped onion**
- **2 tablespoons butter *or* margarine**
- **4 large tomatoes, peeled, chopped, seeded and drained**
- **1 teaspoon salt**
- **1/4 teaspoon pepper**
- **1/4 teaspoon dried thyme**
- **2 cups (8 ounces) shredded Monterey Jack cheese, *divided***
- **1 unbaked pastry shell (10 inches)**

4 eggs
1-1/2 cups light cream

In a skillet, saute onion in butter until tender. Add tomatoes, salt, pepper and thyme. Cook over medium-high heat until liquid is almost evaporated, about 10-15 minutes. Remove from heat. Sprinkle 1 cup cheese into bottom of pie shell. Cover with tomato mixture; sprinkle with remaining cheese. In a mixing bowl, beat eggs until foamy. Stir in cream; mix well. Pour into pie shell. Bake at 425° for 10 minutes. Reduce heat to 325°; bake 40 minutes more or until top begins to brown and a knife inserted near the center comes out clean. Let stand 10 minutes before cutting. **Yield:** 6-8 servings.

Russian Krendl

"While dining with a Russian immigrant family, I jumped at the chance to add this wonderful bread they served to my recipe collection," reports Ann Sodman of Evans, Colorado.

FILLING:
1 cup apple juice
2/3 cup finely chopped dried apple
1/3 cup chopped prunes
1/3 cup finely chopped dried apricots
2 tablespoons butter *or* margarine
2 tablespoons sugar
1 large apple, peeled and chopped
BREAD:
1 package (1/4 ounce) active dry yeast
5 tablespoons sugar, *divided*
3/4 cup warm light cream *or* milk (110° to 115°)
1/4 cup butter *or* margarine, softened
1-1/2 teaspoons vanilla extract
1/2 teaspoon salt
2 egg yolks
2-3/4 to 3-1/4 cups all-purpose flour
Melted butter *or* margarine
1/2 teaspoon ground cinnamon
Confectioners' sugar

In a saucepan, combine filling ingredients. Simmer, stirring occasionally, for 30 minutes or until fruit is tender and mixture has jam-like consistency. Cool to room temperature. In a large mixing bowl, dissolve yeast and 3 tablespoons sugar in cream or milk. Add butter, vanilla, salt, egg yolks and 1-1/2 cups of the flour; beat until smooth. Add enough remaining flour to form a soft dough. Turn onto a floured surface; knead until smooth and elastic, about 6-8 minutes. Place in a greased bowl, turning once to grease top. Cover and let rise until doubled, about 1 hour. Punch dough down. Roll into a 32-in. x

10-in. rectangle. Brush with melted butter. Combine cinnamon and remaining sugar; sprinkle over butter. Spread filling to within 1 in. of edges. Roll up from one of the long sides; pinch seams and ends to seal. Place on a greased baking sheet; form into a pretzel shape. Cover and let rise until nearly doubled, about 30 minutes. Bake at 350° for 45 minutes or until golden brown. Cool on a wire rack. Dust with confectioners' sugar. **Yield:** 1 coffee cake.

Cinnamon Coffee Cake

(PICTURED ON THIS PAGE)

"I love the excellent texture of this old-fashioned, streusel-topped coffee cake. Always a crowd-pleaser, its pleasing vanilla flavor enriched by sour cream is delicious," shares Eleanor Harris of Cape Coral, Florida.

1 cup butter *or* margarine, softened
2-3/4 cups sugar, *divided*
2 teaspoons vanilla extract
4 eggs
3 cups all-purpose flour
2 teaspoons baking powder
1 teaspoon baking soda
1 teaspoon salt
2 cups (16 ounces) sour cream
1/2 cup chopped walnuts
2 tablespoons ground cinnamon

In a large mixing bowl, cream butter and 2 cups sugar until fluffy. Add vanilla.

Add eggs, one at a time, beating well after each addition. Combine flour, baking powder, soda and salt; add alternately with sour cream, beating just enough after each addition to keep batter smooth. Spoon 1/3 of batter into a greased 10-in. tube pan. Combine nuts, cinnamon and remaining sugar; sprinkle 1/3 over batter in pan. Repeat layers two more times. Bake at 350° for 70 minutes or until cake tests done. Cool for 10 minutes. Remove from pan to a wire rack to cool completely. **Yield:** 16-20 servings.

Easy Light Pancakes

Ernest Foster of Climax, New York states, "Our house is often filled with our kids' friends, who always seem to be hungry, so there are seldom leftovers when I make these pancakes!"

1 cup all-purpose flour
2 tablespoons sugar
2 tablespoons baking powder
1/2 teaspoon salt
1 cup milk
2 tablespoons vegetable oil
1 teaspoon vanilla extract

In a large bowl, combine flour, sugar, baking powder and salt. In another bowl, combine milk, oil and vanilla; add to dry ingredients and stir just until moistened. Preheat a lightly greased griddle or skillet. Pour batter by 1/4 cupfuls onto griddle; cook until light brown. Turn and cook other side. Serve immediately with syrup or topping of choice. **Yield:** 8 pancakes.

A COFFEE BREAK WITH CAKE. Pictured above: Cinnamon Coffee Cake (recipe on this page).

INDEX